Loose

Mark

Twain

on the

Loose

A Comic Writer and the American Self

BRUCE MICHELSON

UNIVERSITY OF MASSACHUSETTS PRESS   *Amherst*

Copyright © 1995 by
The University of Massachusetts Press
All rights reserved
Printed in the United States of America
LC 94-37579
ISBN 0-87023-966-x (cloth); 967-8 (pbk.)
Designed by Mary Mendell
Set in New Baskerville
Printed and bound by Thomson-Shore, Inc.
Library of Congress Cataloging-in-Publication Data
Michelson, Bruce, 1948–
Mark Twain on the loose : a comic writer and the American
self / Bruce Michelson.
p.   cm.
Includes bibliographical references and index.
ISBN 0–87023–966–x. — ISBN 0–87023–967–8 (pbk.)
1. Twain, Mark, 1835–1910 — Knowledge — America.
2. National characteristics, American, in literature.
3. Humorous stories, American — History and criticism.
4. Group identity in literature.   5. Comic, The, in
literature.   6. Self in literature.   I. Title.
PS1342.A54M53 1995
818'.409–dc20   94-37579CIP
British Library Cataloguing in Publication data
are available.

For June and Helen

Contents

Acknowledgments

This book owes much to the informed, compassionate company in the University of Illinois English department. My colleagues Nina Baym, Frank Hodgins, Robert Dale Parker, and Don Florence have read and improved many pages; Richard Wheeler, Michael Bérubé, Janet Lyon, Jim Hurt, Richard Powers, and Zohreh Sullivan have tried to school me in an art they know, of blending fresh thoughts with gentle humanity and good sense. At the university library, Bill Brockman and Josephine Kibbee have been patient and skillful detectives, as has Will Goodwin at the Harry Ransom Humanities Research Center at the University of Texas at Austin. At the Buffalo and Erie County Library, Joanna Woyshner was a valuable guide in a prowl through crucial archives. The Mark Twain Circle has been a blessing, and two of its stars, Victor A. Doyno and Jeffrey Steinbrink, have robbed time from their own work to wade through long stretches of this book and make them stronger. A mentor and old friend, Harold Simonson, provided a sharp eye and much moral support. Craig Fischer, a young scholar with breathtaking knowledge of American cultures high and otherwise, has helped greatly in preparing the text. In different form, portions of Chapters 2 and 3 have appeared in the *Dutch Quarterly Review* and the *New England Quarterly,* and I am grateful for permission to expand and redevelop them here. The three smart, fierce people I keep house with, Theresa, Hope, and Sarah Michelson, provide the joy and the wisdom by which anything worth doing gets done.

Chapter 1

Mark Twain and the Escape from Sense

Bigger than life, allover white, and caught this time in molded paper, Mark Twain gazes soulfully through the glass front of a pizzeria named for him in a New Orleans suburb. Facing east, he has a lordly view of the afternoon commuter traffic parading from town. Unhappy drivers can squeeze compassion from his look: all-occasion sympathy from everybody's old friend. Because Mark Twain's connections to pizza remain doubtful, this particular effigy of him might amuse novices on this parkway. But it cannot astound. Even in high times of cultural illiteracy, most Americans over the age of twelve seem to know and like the face, the name, and their connectability to all sorts of national mischief.[1] Sweetly, the Face peers down from billboards for banks, hotels, restaurants, and whole towns; in popular magazines it hawks powerboats, bourbon, and pricey excursions. Eighty years dead, Mark Twain regularly turns up as a vigorous and sympathetic character in novels by somebody else, and does guest appearances in Hollywood fantasies, sometimes about starships and space-time adventure. In fact no other American writer is drafted so often into other people's dreams and far-fetched tales. He is acted, cartooned, cast in bronze and "Claymated"; Hawthorne, Melville, Dickinson, Scott Fitzgerald, and the press-courting Hemingway combined have never held the national spotlight so well. And if the Face has reigned through most of this century, then the Name stays a cultural mantra. In the newspapers, Mark Twain holds on as a most-favored quotable pundit on politics, society, theology, morals, and the weather; if his own actual words will not quite suffice, then other smart words are thought up and credited to him. He remains a father not only of our opinions but also of our language: the latest edition of the *Oxford English Dictionary* cites Mark Twain more than eighteen hundred times.[2] And of course he stays synonymous with big rivers, steamboats, and American mythology. At one of the planet's two most-mobbed theme parks, a *Mark Twain* stern-wheeler, armatured to an underwater track, cruises around a man-made and fully accoutred Tom Sawyer's Island; at the busiest park on the other coast, we can prowl all over a Tom Sawyer's Island exactly the same — and in a big pavilion nearby, a real-looking, real-sounding Mark Twain robot, with snow-white synthetic hair and supple, wrinkly, life-mocking plastic hide, works seven days and nights per week as our national Emcee. Several times an hour, teamed with an automated and equally jolly Ben Franklin, this scarily reliable and consistent Mark Twain presents "America" to hordes of visitors — Americans home-grown, most of them — at the world's one and only perpetual world's fair.

As literary icons and old cultural practices come under close and sometimes hostile scrutiny, some artifacts can be counted on to survive the roughest treatment. One extremely hard-to-get-rid-of presence has to be this "Mark Twain" — not only as name, face, commodity, artist, long shelf of books, and many-sided legend, but also as the robust and internationalized practice of discussing all such things,[3] of describing him, stabilizing him, catching him in print, on film-stock, in motorized plastic or stiff molded paper. For in retelling and constantly reinventing what Mark Twain was and is and means to this culture, we would implicitly say what this natural or enforced centrality might say about *us*.[4] Brilliant work has been done to discover in "Mark Twain" a meaning, an identity, and to chart high-serious themes running more or less steadily through the words, the biography, and the myth.

Even so, our various and often ingenious ways of reading Mark Twain can cause something crucial to be missed. Is it possible that this "self" that Mark Twain seems to exemplify in American culture, this literary-mythological identity with such stubborn appeal, defines itself by how it refuses and evades, rather than by how and what it affirms? Is it possible that from these evasions, ultimately and perhaps inevitably failed in their own right, come qualities that "identify" the work and the persona so strongly in individual texts, in the canon altogether, and perhaps in the life itself as yet another of these cherished Mark Twain narratives, incessantly and ubiquitously retold? The story has been admirably and repeatedly laid out, of a Missouri writer named Samuel Clemens evolving into one nameable and bounded thing or another: into Mark Twain the social philosopher, the dead-earnest satirist and moralist, the American prophet, the maestro of literary forms, the unlucky bourgeois materialist, shade-tree metaphysician, lonely man-child, and champion of realism, or modernism, or some other aesthetic or intellectual formulation.[5] Well-made biographical works keep coming out, and thanks to tides of such scholarship, we have many plausible theories to choose from regarding whom or what Mark Twain signifies — as many as we have for anyone else who has written English in the past two centuries.[6] Through such efforts, Mark Twain as a historical figure and cultural presence grows steadier in view, and more complex. Yet inevitably, and sadly, he grows more domestic as well.

As the critics and historians talk on, the loss is always to wildness. Delving to the affirmation, the grand serious theme, the noble design that lurks (or ought to, as Mark Twain's wisest readers have usually assumed) in the depths of a text or its creator, commentary risks degrading whatever must be dug *through* — and in the case of Mark Twain the violated surfaces include his uncontainable humor, rambunctious barbarism, spontaneity, changefulness, insouciance, and anarchy. Much of what we have learned and surmised about Samuel Clemens and Mark Twain is part of the legacy now, part of the amalgamated cultural artifact that Clemens and his pen name and his work have fused into. There is no sane way back to simpler myths or simpler interpretive practice. Yet if too much reason or sanity hobbles response to this "Mark Twain," then perhaps a bit of salutary madness can be recovered. I mean not to thwart this dialogue, but rather to help keep it pleasurably open, unsettled, and attuned to the fundamental experience of reading Mark Twain: a reading at once more innocent and complex, and not entirely ordained by old or newish habits of the academic mind.

I have heresies to suggest about Mark Twain as personage, as text, and as myth: that all of these Mark Twains — whether we labor to differentiate them or not — might be more broadly and absolutely heretical than commentary about them has usually granted. Yet such an anti-reading of Mark Twain, marking his delight in disorder rather than his putative quests for form and thematic coherence, will harmonize quite well with other readings, even some strongly thematic ones (except, perhaps, for a very few that resist lively pluralism themselves, or the refreshment of this culture's dialogue with itself). For Mark Twain as literary artist, body of work, not-quite-knowable man, and cultural legend, we *are* inasmuch as we refuse to be anything for sure. The self, to Mark Twain, remained *the* question, a question he attacked from so many directions, in texts that now seem to exemplify such questioning as a trait of the American identity. After decades of informed argument about Mark Twain's concealed organizing principles, it still seems possible that his most exciting narratives exemplify no formal strategy as yet defined or conceived by published criticism. Temples will not crash down on us if as readers we pay more respect to this penchant for anarchy in Mark Twain's comic art.

This rebellion against soul-confining consistency forms an eminently consistent quality in Mark Twain's works and public life. From his early days as a newspaperman and sketch-writer, his writings assault not only the intellectual processes and cadences of the much-maligned American middle class,[7] but also the self's acceptance of social station, ideology, or mental habit of any kind *as* a self. We read bright flashes of impatience with suspended disbelief, with prescribed literary forms, and with reverence toward conventionalized art, including imaginative literature. If Mark Twain began his career by evading identity as defined by the material culture and American economic and social practice, then more extravagant refusals came after: of the self as defined and bounded by literature, or history, or religion, or cultural practice of every sort. His war against convention widened toward the absolute — not just against sentimental and romantic tropes, but even against seriousness of literary intention, continuity, pretensions of transcendence and doctrinal *refusal* of transcendence, all as betrayals of the essential experience and the essential human being — whatever those mysterious things might be.

The threat, in other words, grew to be whatever seemed rigid and regulating to mind and identity: any confining orthodoxy, whether political, religious, aesthetic, imaginative, or even biological. To try to define or *con*fine Mark Twain ideologically is therefore a risky business, for the range and reflexivity of his own work can easily outrun — or overthrow — discourse about economic and political configurations of the self. Throughout his adult life, Mark Twain was keenly aware of the demands of culture, the psychological pressures of race, social class, and intellectual climate upon identity. Many of his most provocative works, even into his final years, are deeply engaged with such questions. That engagement was often stressful, and certainly untidy;

consistency, even in the cause of resistance, must lead only deeper into paradox. Escape from every kind of social pressure, escape from "seriousness" and conventional moral systems — these formed part of a larger quest, sensible or not, and sources of an anxiety that energized Mark Twain's writing and carried him in so many directions, as artist, entrepreneur, public and private citizen, and intellectual adventurer. So there it is: to resist consistencies means to face, sooner or later, the lethal consistency of one's own resistance, the ironic mind-trap of rebellion against all prisons of the mind. To cherish the self, in other words, as the whatever-it-is that must escape every stable form and refuse definition, to affirm freedom and identity in such uncompromising terms, leads straight into mazes of irony. To know and feel these complications is to understand better some of Mark Twain's artistic failures, yet also some of the triumphs. But the pleasure of recognizing Mark Twain's wilder possibilities lies beyond such measuring. It lies in seeing these works as liberated, at least provisionally, from certain deep-rooted habits of interpretation, and as stranger and more thrillingly disruptive to the complacent self and the world as "known."

What good in that? For one thing, we achieve an art more dangerous, yet also more enduringly important to an unstable American cultural scene. For another, we recover a little of the special experience of reading Mark Twain: those instants of anarchic delight, shock, recognition, *détournement*[8] that vanish in what a poet[9] calls our tapestries of afterthought, the habitual and perhaps instinctual domestication of moments that if left intellectually untended, could knock everything into hazard. This outrageousness matters: it distinguishes Mark Twain's imagination, and it may contribute in surprising and profound ways to his stature in American cultural life. Rediscovering this side of his work means reading some familiar texts from unusual perspectives, and looking also into some marginalized works, to understand psychological and intellectual conflicts running through them: how they go astray, and how they sharpen understanding of Mark Twain as both an artist and an emblem for an ongoing American crisis.

The self then, not as a formulation, but as a problem, as a mystery to be fiercely defended and never resolved.[10] At the moment, however, the word "self" figures in several different typologies, and simply uttering the term here might suggest, for example, an a priori political and materialist circumscription of identity.[11] Although I have learned from the New Historicist ferment, and although this study benefits from recent cultural-materialist readings of Mark Twain's works, I hold that Mark Twain's own investigation of "self" probed deeper in some ways, and encountered more paradox, than such approaches to him have as yet discerned. For Mark Twain the self was a traumatic dilemma, and if its various dimensions cannot be kept separate in a tour of works that engage that dilemma, so much the better. Mark Twain's was not a categorizing mind. It was a mind that resisted the delusion of categories, as constructs that dissect to do murder. And if the self was always the enigma, then to posit or borrow definitions for it at the outset would be counterproductive. To read Mark Twain afresh, some glossaries have to be parked at the trailhead; and here and there a familiar term has to be reproblematized, and reconnected to its own origins and its paradoxes.

"Realism" is a case in point. There have been strong arguments lately against counting Mark Twain as an American realist of any true sort, much less one of the ringleaders in the mode; Twain's fiction simply does not respect Howellsian doctrines. Michael Davitt Bell seems right about the evidence of *Huckleberry Finn,* that what Mark Twain shares with Howells, James, and other writers grouped retroactively into an American "realist" school was at most an inclination, a vague wish to achieve truth or break through to it; and that Mark Twain was not thereby restrained from trying anything he liked.[12] It seems, moreover, that even conventional realist practice of the late nineteenth century encompassed not only opposite strategies, but also two opposed assumptions about truth and its representation. By the evidence, realism is and was understood as the depiction of life and truth by strategies Howells endorsed and even employed (sometimes, anyway) in his own fiction, meticulous portraiture in written words. But realism was and is also the achievement, if not strictly the "representation," of a species of truth by strategies of surprise and disruption, challenging cultural self-delusion and narrative convention — including, at times, even bylaws of Howellsian realism. In Mark Twain's work some "realities" do indeed seem proffered as photographically there; the narrative aims the camera, as Hank Morgan at one point wishes he could, and things are recorded as they appear, with details of a river sunrise or a gritty Nevada street set down just right, and highlighting differences between such things as they are and the musty lies of romance and sentimentality.

But what if that "real world," in other direct or imagined encounters, is seen to be saturated with delusion, pretense, fantasy? The task of the realist in such straits may call not for box-cameras, but rather for dynamite: disorienting and even violent breakthroughs into the concealed truth about human experience. And if such breakthroughs require strange pyrotechnics — dream-selves, fantasies of time-travel, or "whoppers" embedded in supposedly factual travel narratives and personal histories — so be it. For Mark Twain recognized few if any all-weather rules, except perhaps that the literary act eventually arrives at something spiritually, logically, or psychologically true.[13] As far back as Coleridge, opposed practices of this sort have coexisted with regard to the relationship of imaginative literature and truth. We can take our choice, regarding this fundamental paradox in the matter of art as mimetic representation. My premise is that Mark Twain did *not* choose.[14] Nor does he seem to have cared whether posterity would count him as an orthodox realist or not.

After sixty years of academic formulations about realism, simplicity takes work to restore. The task is trickier in defining, or rather *de-*defining humor, though that task is much more important here than loosening Mark Twain's narrative practice from other people's rules about realistic fiction. There is a long tradition of locating dignified motives in Mark Twain's humor, of finding affirmations in it, or at least a point and a limit to the joke or the moment of ridicule. Thus the instant of bedlam, in which pretenses, social systems, and other values are blown up, transforms into the artifact of satire, in which substitute values are seen as implicitly endorsed.[15] Granting that in some instances Mark Twain's humor may be constructive and even solemn of purpose, or that respectable moral principles might be affirmed in some of his most outrageous-looking material, we need to keep open questions about when and how that happens — in the instant, as it were, of the comic outbreak, or rather in retrospect — and note the consequences if those two experiences, the all-disrupting moment of laughter, and the world restored an indeterminate moment after, are thought of as distinct.[16] As in the astrophysics of the Big Bang, the instant when the universe both blew up and began, an exploding universe of laughter might look immensely different, depending on what nanosecond you choose for a glimpse. Something almost comprehensible at one instant may fill the skies with chaos and possibility at the next. If American readers customarily elevate and transform humor into satire, or see humor as creating order amid the process of disruption, then that interpretive habit may reflect an honorable will to make world-wrecking experience understandable — but also perhaps a will to *contain*. In Mark Twain's humor, what must often be contained is potentially absolute fluidity, a danger of setting everything afire. We might bear in mind that four years before Henri Bergson published his landmark work on the process and cultural intentions of laughter, his erstwhile student Alfred Jarry jolted the Paris literary scene with *Ubu Roi*, which seemed to wage all-out war on Bergson's and everyone else's culture of process and intentions; and that throughout Bergson's life a species of laughter flourished that intended an overthrow of purpose, of logic, of a civilization rooted in such mad sanity.[17] Anarchism, nihilism, dadaism, lettrism . . . regardless of how such movements crossbreed or rearrange themselves in our tidied retrospects, and whether or not their great moment came in the Paris Commune of 1871, or in the Decadent Nineties, or in 1916 with the Cabaret Voltaire, or in 1952 with Guy Debord's durably outrageous *Hurlements en faveur de Sade*,[18] or in 1968 with *les jours de Mai* on the barricaded Left Bank and the dizzy "happenings" in midtown Manhattan, or in some shock-year still to come, such quakes along the fault lines of the Western consciousness were in full rumble through most of Mark Twain's career. In other works, Bergson lamented that the Western style of intellect is comfortable only when engaged with fixed realities, and that it reduces dynamic experience to static structures; but war had long since broken out against structures, stasis, the intellect, and even the Bergsonian critical mind.

Mark Twain traveled, read hungrily, and wrote furiously in the midst of a cultural and intellectual upheaval, yet discussions of his work, and especially of his humor, often treat him as essentially immune to such turmoil. Without recasting Mark Twain as of a mind with Wilde, Jarry, Kropotkin, or Rosa Luxemburg, some questions might nonetheless be asked. Is there a chance that Mark Twain's humor, no matter what else it supposedly does, at times subverts the practice of *expecting* subversions and underlying themes, subverts consistencies that literary critics and mainstream American culture seem to affirm? Boundaries to a Mark Twain joke may sometimes be where *we* want to set them. In Mark Twain's life, in his letters, in his published volumes and the manuscripts he left behind, I have found very little cause for such readerly scruples — and ample cause to read his work as much more attuned to the cultural upsets he knew firsthand.

A working definition then, heavily pruned, almost primordial: humor as a subversion of seriousness. It may have no other inherent patterns or effects than that, and indeed no cultural obligations at all, as "obligations" belong to that serious world that always comes groping after the loose leash of humor, seeking to regain dominion and train the comic outbreak into some better (meaning serious) intention. Post-Bergsonian definitions of humor often flinch at possibilities inherent in such a simple premise.[19] The anarchy of humor is conceded to spread, yet only so far—meaning only out to the comfort limits of a given set of readers. But what we might want from Mark Twain as a moralist and a humanist may not match potentialities in his comedy.

A nondefinition like this conflicts with some commentary about Mark Twain as Dean of American humorists, and it leads into mirror-halls like those entered when we problematize definitions of realism. James M. Cox helpfully divides Mark Twain's humor into four general categories of discourse: the hoax, the travel letter, the political burlesque, and the invective.[20] Such a division promotes a powerful reading, yet also a domestication; in Mark Twain's writing, these various motives, if motives they can even be called, will not keep separate, and turmoil generated by their interaction is no mere side effect of the humor. It is the humor in its essence. With complete liberty to expand or contract, humor can rise or widen like a released genie—to tell a story, or burst beyond the social milieu and invade the psychological, even the epistemological. It can challenge habits of the psyche and any assumption an American self might be founded on. Or it may do absolutely nothing of the sort. This power to spread to such horizons is sometimes thought of as a consequence Mark Twain understood only later in his career, the result of deep and value-corroding intellection.[21] Such a narrative makes sense, yet only up to a point. For though theology and metaphysics become more central as literary themes in Mark Twain's final decade, these disruptions clatter from the beginning of his career, when Mark Twain's unrestricted war against seriousness was just getting under way.

maps

Time for illustrations. To begin with an early and peculiar item—literally an "illustration"—does stack the deck, for in the trove of Mark Twain's humor this whatever-it-is could work as a backdrop for a stage

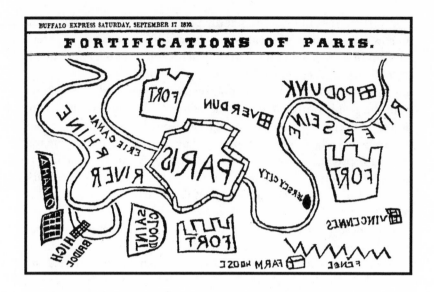

at the Cabaret Voltaire, or a good cover page for the *international situationniste*, the magazine which briefly rocked the Left Bank about fifty years after Hugo Ball had given up dressing as Metal-Man and shouting gibberish at the Cabaret audience. But this Mark Twain artifact first appeared in a respectable American newspaper, on the second page, and in the middle of a foreign war. Not much commentary has been written about it,[22] perhaps because the joke is as much visual as it is verbal, and perhaps because, according to those Bergsonian categories and rules of satire that have grown almost instinctive among college-trained readers, it seems to have a limited, reassuring point. But with such doctrines and expectations suspended, the curiouser this thing becomes. Beneath the map, the newspaper printed some "Official Commendations," running down the newspaper's front page:

It is the only map of the kind I ever saw.

U. S. GRANT

It places the situation in an entirely new light.

BISMARCK

I cannot look upon it without shedding tears.

BRIGHAM YOUNG

It is very nice large print.

NAPOLEON

My wife was for years afflicted with freckles, and though everything was done for her relief that could be done, all was in vain.
But, sir, since her first glance at your map, they have entirely left
her. She has nothing but convulsions now.

J. SMITH

If I had had this map, I could have got out of Metz without any
trouble.

BAZAINE

I have seen a great many maps in my time, but none that this one
reminds me of.

TROCHU

It is but fair to say that in some respects it is a truly remarkable
map.

W. T. SHERMAN

I said to my son Frederick William, "If you could only make a
map like that, I would be perfectly willing to see you die — even
anxious."

WILLIAM III

People in the offices of the Buffalo *Express*, which Mark Twain was
editing at the time and partly owned, remembered his delight as he
carved his "Map of Paris,"[23] while to general surprise Bismarck's armies were plowing toward the French capital to topple the Second Empire — and as it turned out, trigger the complete shattering of one
great city's vaunted cool. The map and the testimonials self-evidently
burlesque the reportage under way in American newspapers like the
Express itself, coverage replete with busy maps of terrain that most
American readers would never visit and knew nothing about, and of a
conflict whose meaning in the United States seemed trivial, especially
so soon after the American Civil War, in whose outcome these papers
and readers had shared such an enormous stake. Therefore the joke-
as-interpreted has to do with overblown treatment of foreign news,
with journalistic delight in violence, with the ritualized worship of
Paris as a cultural holy place, with armchair generaling by report-
ers and ordinary citizens, and perhaps above all with Yankee obtuseness about world geography. End of story — unless the joke corrodes
through the barriers and engulfs a good deal more: news, fact, truth,
and the very act of interpretation.

Readers who know of Mark Twain's earlier days on the unpredictable Virginia City *Enterprise* may see this map as deriding again the public mind-habit of taking newspaper items as truth, of basing ideas of Paris, modern war, current events, or anything else on the words one reads in the press. Published as deadpan news articles, famous sketches from Mark Twain's Nevada gold-rush days jolt relationships among the reader, the text, and the truth: they seem to delight in confusion, and mock any construction of reality out of published reports. Here was the Wild West, and here in the wilderness was the beacon of the *Enterprise*—except that the newspaper lied, sometimes deliberately, sometimes not, and sometimes even told the truth, and did none of these things predictably. Likewise, Twain originally published this "Map" under the headline FORTIFICATIONS OF PARIS, on a page of news. The counterfeit testimonials cite real people in the news, and there are terse additional comments even from this uncertainly real perpetrator who calls himself Mark Twain. A slip-sliding away may begin here, away from bounded, domestic satire and into *détournement* of "reality" as we contrive it, including the shabby material we contrive it from. But gaze longer at this map, with its contrails of endorsements and explanations, and more comes unstuck, with or without any prior knowledge, on our part, of Mark Twain as a credentialed un-reporter. Everything represented here grows suspect: maps, *any* maps, as plausible guides to geological, historical, or cultural reality; forts (we see three on this map, labeled with brilliant, idiotic instructiveness, "TЯOꟻ") as sane defense against the real dangers to culture or life; the reality of France as a world power, or Napoleon III as a statesman and strategist. The counterfeit remarks from the great and the momentarily notorious include one from General Bazaine, who had lately bungled a crucial campaign in eastern France; and we also read words attributed to Grant, Sherman, Napoleon III, and Bismarck. These "quotations" burlesque conventional politeness about outrageous incompetence, emphasizing the contribution that high position and its required courtesies make to the promulgation of big lies. But again the satire, or rather the satiric surfaces of the humor, seem to burn toward broader heresies, toward escape from civility, even from sense. On these pages eminent names may become for a moment only that, *names,* fabrications of ink, alphabets, and our own complacent or automated imaginations. We too could make up things for these "people" to say because in a sense we make *them* up, contrive Napoleons and General Grants out of lithographs, grainy photos, and word-woven accounts of wonders they supposedly worked and how important they supposedly are. For an instant, General Grant, Napoleon III, Bismarck, and the rest of these celebrities can seem as absurd as the map, especially as presences in our own minds, subjects for the serious attention of millions of people who really have nothing to do with them, but whose mental energies are everyday preposterously *detourned* by "news," "history," and stampedes of fashion. For a moment, in other words, anarchic freedom *from* the press, from the grip of public culture, stirs in this peculiar artifact, recalling perhaps Thoreau's refusal not only of news bulletins but of the warped culture that assigns them value. What need of newspapers? After the first far-off, meaningless catastrophe is printed up and inflicted on the mind, perhaps there is no other.

Yet Mark Twain's map-joke can outrun even this attempt to encompass it. The map appears backward, the surface gag being about the incompetence of this Mark Twain person as instant, self-styled mapmaker who does not know the first rule of the craft, that you must engrave the mirror image of what you want to show on the page. Beneath that surface, language itself shimmers with a possibility of its own absurdity, for there are currents here pulling into those depths. To look hard at this map — as we are supposed to look raptly at all maps of the World Situation, and as we must be patient to decode this backward thing — is to be drawn into whirlpools of decoding. Puzzles like "ЯИUDOꟼ" and "YTIƆYƎꙄЯƎႱ" first have to be turned around in the mind. Then they have to be understood, or dis-understood, as American places grossly misplaced in the Paris suburbs. And then perhaps comes an inkling: forward or backward, these names may really signify nothing, on this chart or on any other. From certain perspectives, including some nurtured by this map, "ТЯОꟻ" and "Fort" amount to the same nonsense, blots on a piece of paper, to which by necessity or habit we apply imagination and concoct absurd ideas about military strategy. American schools make an industry of teaching unhappy children to "find" Parises and Podunks on charts on the wall; being educated American-style means "knowing" (or having forgotten) where such places are — which means knowing where to mark them on pieces of paper, an inch or so from other blots and squiggles and relentlessly mysterious names. When it comes to knowing these places truly, Paris and Podunk, spelled eastward or the other way, may amount to zero, like "Blago bung!" — which dadaist Hugo Ball said was the substance of cultural discourse, or the "Ou-buom!" in the depths of E. M. Forster's Marabar caves, nihilistic noise that could drown out a whole meaningful English universe.

But there can be no stopping there. Especially not there. For a *doctrine* of absurdism presents only another doctrine, another trap of stabilized idiocy. From such traps Mark Twain's humor usually shies away, as it seems to here, because it *is* humor and not political tract. A glimpse into such abysses can momentarily thrill, but we can have no fun falling into them and staying lost. Maps, names, words, knowing — in the "Map of Paris" funhouse these things become for a flash preposterous, dizzying. Then the dislocated world can stop wobbling, and if we like we can proceed to read, credulously or skeptically, the rest of the daily papers, including perhaps "real" maps on other pages, and talk glibly again about people we have never seen and violence among strangers in unknowable places. This is comedy, not a manifesto about life's inescapable delusions; and one can never be quite sure about "serious" intentions, satire, intention-ridiculing absurdities in this — well, what is it? Counterfeit news report? Pastiche? Black hole in the midst of the journalistic universe? Anyhow, this pleasuring disturbance down where one perhaps assumed (and may freely, absurdly, and necessarily go on assuming) is the bedrock of truth.

petrified men

To stay with rock, and counterfeit journalism, dizzying contemplations, and the mysteries of identity: readers of Mark Twain's sketches may see harmonies between "Map of Paris" and a newspaper oddity that helped bring Mark Twain his first national audience. This sketch, also a counterfeit news story, appeared in the *Enterprise* somewhere around 4 October 1862. It seems fitting that the exact date of the hoax has stayed as unsure as its implications; we can come close, but never be certain:

> A petrified man was found some time ago in the mountains south of Gravelly Ford. Every limb and feature of the stony mummy was perfect, not even excepting the left leg, which has evidently been a wooden one during the lifetime of the owner — which lifetime, by the way, came to a close about a century ago, in the opinion of

the savan who has examined the defunct. The body was in a sitting posture, and leaning against a huge mass of croppings; the attitude was pensive, the right thumb resting against the side of the nose; the left thumb partially supported the chin, the fore-finger pressing the inner corner of the left eye and drawing it partly open; the right eye was closed, and the fingers of the right hand spread apart. This strange freak of nature created a profound sensation in the vicinity. . . .[24]

Notes to a definitive text of this undefinable joke offer several motives behind it: ridicule of a local bureaucrat named Sewall, to whom Mark Twain assigns the inquest into this jeering hunk of stone; and laughter at other petrifaction reports accepted by a gullible American public. Printed without such stabilizing helps and explanations, however, the piece can still delight readers who know nothing at all of this Mr. Sewall or the pseudoanthropology of bygone years. But why? A man profoundly coalesced, quite literally "stuck" as a self, thumbs his nose and winks at us. It matters that this first Mark Twain character to reach a national audience is made of stone, stuck in both a ridiculing *and* a ridiculous position, embarrassing himself and insulting everyone who gapes at him. As such, and as a burlesque of something, the Petrified Man hoax seems to escape Bergson's stipulation that rigidity is an essence of the comic[25] for there is complexity and vertigo here, a stony shape in the midst of a supremely unstable context; and delightful confusion about who finally is *more* stuck. The stone man? The commingled real and fictitious fools who marvel at him and cannot understand his gesture? The credulous journalist, both real *and* fictitious, who writes this "event" as a serious news item? The editors who reprinted the story in their own papers without reading it carefully? And what of ourselves, who might let our eyes roll halfway down a newsprint page before knowing that we have been "sold," given the culturally founded faith that ink and newsprint are the stuff of fact and truth? Parallels, then, to the satire that can be discovered or contrived for "Map of Paris" — yet like the map, the stone-man story makes a feint into riskier dimensions. The thumb against the stone man's nose might be read as being against Mark Twain's nose too, if contemporary readers of this anonymous "news" report could even have guessed that there was such a creature or a construct as a Mark Twain, a convicted "humorist" to whom one might assign blame for both the joke and the gesture, and thereby stabilize their meaning. But in 1862 most of America knew of nobody named Mark Twain, and "Petrified Man" spread eastward under nobody's byline. In the anonymity of the piece lay much of its power, though that may be eclipsed now by what the world knows, or *thinks* it knows, about this Mark Twain, and by the way such knowledge conditions reader response. Like "Map of Paris," the humor of "Petrified Man," or some portion of that humor, seems to involve public naiveté about news and newspapers; yet an edge of it pricks naiveté of broader sorts. The Petrified Man has no name, no time, neither tribe nor race. And if he bequeaths us only a thumbed nose and a wink, which are really from another unknown somebody whose name, even when the world found it out, was really no name at all, this stone man might also be ourselves. Does he gaze back at the modern reader as from a mirror, embodying the static and too-palpable self that each man or woman either is or shall become, unless luck and heroic "shiftiness" can save us? Is Petrified Man winking his possibility as a paragon of American, Judeo-Christian, material *and* materialist selfhood? He is a "made man," in every sense of the phrase, having made his mark, cheated death, spoken his mind to the world, left a legacy like nobody else's, and been made *up*. From another perspective, however, even death for him is no escape (and paradoxically it is his gesture of ridicule, of everything he surveys that catches him, fixes him) just as roles like "phunny phellow," and "Wild Humorist of the Pacific Slope" endangered the public, literary, and even private self of another nobody who, when he did "sign" his other nose-thumbings, tried hiding and flaunting himself as Quintus Curtius Snodgrass, Epaminondas Adrastus Blab, and Mark Twain.

But then again, this item was originally *un*signed, and the blank spot where a byline ought to be was part of the hoax. In fact it is the part that subverts the above reading, or *any* reading, and momentarily the compulsive practice of figuring out what anything means. The wink is everlasting. It is the same response to whatever we do, any application of reason or interpretive skill, including a reasoned interpretation that interpretation is impossible and that authors of texts are imaginative and linguistic constructs. To wonder what it all means is to be Mr. Sewall with his idiotic-scientific hypotheses; but to turn away is to be winked at behind our back, as somebody who "missed it."

With no one, in the autumn of 1862, to take credit for the joke or referee such decodings, this piece seems to play by rules that Jacob Brackman laid out in his crucial essay on the "put-on," that renegade sort of humor that has as its target the whole idea of targets, perpetrators, and moral ground rules for artistic expression. Come-on, fake-out, and cop-out — those are the three phases of the put-on. The victim is lured in by some plausible overture to curiosity, passions, common sense, goodwill (Victor Doyno, one of our eminent Mark Twain scholars, calls this "schmuck bait"); any such ordinary vice or virtue will do. The second phase, the fake-out, is the confounding of those expectations; and the third, the cop-out, is the vanishing of the perpetrator, the refusal to explain, or accept responsibility, or sometimes even to call an end to the deceit.[26] Beyond that pathology, there is nothing stable about put-ons, except paradoxical descriptions and explanations after the fact, usually by somebody else, who *needs to know* whether the signed Brillo box is or isn't a joke at his or her own expense, or whether the eight-hour fixed-camera film of the Empire State Building is or isn't a nose-thumbing at the supposedly hip art patrons who sit through it. Put-ons can seem to satirize satire, for their one essential intention might be the disruption of intentionality; they are a kind of antimatter for all convention and earnestness, including any assumed earnestness in conventional jokes. According to this Washoe dispatch, the good citizens had it in mind to blast their stone man off his perch and give him a good Christian burial. But because the "just and proper" Mr. Sewell determines that doing so would in this case be a sacrilege, the stone man stays put, and the leer goes on forever.[27]

Some resemblance, then, between two early Mark Twain sketches, conspiratorially selected. In each, a radical questioning of the grounds of culture, common sense, and identity; in each, possible satire of any mind that would entertain questions like these. Two sketches out of hundreds of texts: nonetheless, if readings of this kind can turn up outrageous intentions and anti-intentions for small early works, we can ask whether Mark Twain knew the dimensions of what he was doing here, unleashing jokes that seem to rise like uncontainable vapor, even if such outbreaks were only occasional. With so much known about Mark Twain and Samuel Clemens, and so much interpretive work done to link the human being and the persona to specific texts, this matter of intentionality cannot be evaded. It seems fair and even necessary to ask, in other words, whether such anarchic humor connects to Mark Twain's unconscious self, or perhaps to some element of the irrational he never fully comprehended.

The answer would depend, of course, on the joke or sketch in question. Yet in any such instant of laughter, might the gleeful disruption not only precede, but also eclipse — perhaps even permanently — the wider implications of the joke, even for the jokester, and even when that jokester is Mark Twain? With vast documentation available about Mark Twain's life and the motions of his mind, one might suppose that the psychological clockwork behind each famous comic moment could be plausibly mapped. But that job seems impossible, and not merely because he was clever at making maps and lists of motives look preposterous. In the notebooks, the autobiography, the letters, the testimony of Mark Twain's friends, there is surprisingly little to document these great comic moments, to account for their reach, or their possible violence against cultural and psychological order. Even awash in details of the life, readers can puzzle long over the humor, where it came from, what it means, and whether it turns its fire on us for *asking* what it means, or who the man who wrote it really was.

Yankee ceremonies

One joke-enigma that still bothers Mark Twain critics is the notorious Whittier Birthday Speech of December 1877,[28] which Mark Twain regarded ambivalently in subsequent years. He acknowledged it as his biggest platform disaster, a "hideous mistake," an affront to three great Americans, Emerson, Longfellow, and Holmes, who were all in attendance; but also as "the best speech I have ever contrived," about which he saw his purpose as "clean" and his "conscience clear."[29] Interestingly, most modern commentaries about this speech and its intentions ignore Mark Twain's own final statement about it, in which he muses on the changefulness and hidden places in his own mind:

> . . . I have examined that speech a couple of times since, and have changed my notion about it — changed it entirely. I find it gross, coarse — well, I needn't go on with particulars. I didn't like any part of it, from the beginning to the end. I found it always offensive and detestable. How do I account for this change of view? I don't know. I can't account for it. I am the person concerned. If I could put myself outside of myself and examine it from the point of view of a person not personally concerned in it, then no doubt I could analyze it and explain to my satisfaction the change which has taken place. As it is, I am merely moved by instinct. My instinct said, formerly, that it was an innocent speech, and funny. The

same instinct, sitting cold and judicial, as a court of last resort, has reversed that verdict. I expect this latest verdict to remain.[30]

Lore about this supposedly awful night implies that a dazed Longfellow, a deadpan Holmes, and a senile, unresponsive Emerson cast a pall over the crowd, which took its emotional cue from these elders and the mortified Howells, missed the point and spirit of the burlesque, and sensed insult to the great men. Some recent commentary reassures us that no, the evening did not go quite so badly for Mark Twain, and that at least a few people in the room did catch on and laugh. Though we can believe that a roomful of smart people could miss a broad joke, it is worth wondering if in fact they *did* somehow get it, catching reverberations that Mark Twain at the head table may not have consciously recognized himself, either then or in his fulsome apologies afterward. To each of the three kings he later humbled himself as a "heedless savage," assuring them that any offense in the speech was not "premeditated." It is a beguiling thought that Mark Twain might have guessed right about what had happened, that his words that night had a touch of savagery to them, intentional or otherwise, that some of his listeners had picked up.

To recap: a celebration of Whittier's eightieth birthday at the Hotel Brunswick in Boston had brought out the Brahmins in force, including Longfellow, Emerson, Holmes, and some younger literati: at the tables were Howells, Phillips Brooks, Edward Everett Hale, James T. Fields, Charles Dudley Warner, and others who embodied polite literary practice at that time. After dinner, Mark Twain stood and told a story of the gold-rush days of 1864, and of his visit to a miner in the Sierra foothills. When Mark Twain drops his *nom de guerre* on his host, the "dejected" simple man begins a story of how his hospitality has been abused by three visitors, Emerson, Longfellow, and Holmes — the gag being that these hard-drinking ruffians are clumsy frauds who could dupe no one except each other, and this isolated fool of a storyteller:

> "They were pretty how-come-you-so by now, and they begun to blow. Emerson says, 'The bulliest thing I ever wrote was "Barbara Frietchie." ' Says Longfellow, 'It don't begin with my "Biglow Papers." ' Says Holmes, 'My "Thanatopsis" lays over 'em both.' They mighty near ended in a fight. Then they wished they had some more company — and Mr. Emerson pointed at me and says:
>   Is yonder squalid peasant all

> That this proud nursery could breed?
> "He was a-whetting his bowie on his boot — so I let it pass."[31]

A foil for the Whittier Birthday speech, and in several ways a companion piece to it, is Mark Twain's "Plymouth Rock" address in Philadelphia, to the New England Society's first Annual Dinner on 22 December 1881, almost exactly four years after his alleged disaster with the Bostonians. The context was similar: on a birthday not of one New England poet but of New England itself, with men of pedigree, cherished traditions, and a liability to stodginess gathered in a ceremonial hall, Mark Twain was to rise after a feast and be amusing about sacred subjects. What he did here may shed light on this question of intentions, conscious and no, in the Whittier monologue. One of Mark Twain's livelier banquet performances, the Philadelphia speech is kin to the Emerson–Holmes–Longfellow burlesque, but on this second try Mark Twain gets the tone right. Both speeches play the American game of "kidding," a game that goes well, without misunderstanding and recriminations, when the discourse floats gracefully at an evident remove from seriousness. If a kidder brings up actual failings of the listener, then exaggeration can possibly save the joke, and sometimes the kidder's neck. But if one lampoons oneself in the process, as a curmudgeon or a raving fool, then the main event becomes the farce of one's own bad judgment and misplaced passions, rather than any seam of truth running through the attack. In "Plymouth Rock and the Pilgrims," Mark Twain's rant — kidding, on the face of it — echoes the Whittier Birthday speech, and suggests what might be a sharp, concealed edge in the earlier joke. Mark Twain opens the "Plymouth Rock" address with objections to the whole ceremony:

> I rise to protest. I have kept still for years, but really I think there is no sufficient justification for this sort of thing. What do you want to celebrate these people for? — those ancestors of yours of 1620 — the *Mayflower* tribe, I mean. What do you want to celebrate *them* for? Your pardon; the gentleman at my left assures me that you are not celebrating the Pilgrims themselves, but the landing of the Pilgrims at Plymouth Rock on the 22d of December. So you are celebrating their landing. Why, the other pretext was thin enough, but this is thinner than ever; the other was tissue, tinfoil, fish bladder, but this is gold leaf.
>
> Celebrating their landing! What was there remarkable about it,

I would like to know? What can you be thinking of? Why, those Pilgrims had been at sea three or four months. It was the very middle of winter; it was cold as death off Cape Cod, there. Why shouldn't they come ashore? If they hadn't landed there would be some reason for celebrating the fact. It would have been a case of monumental leatherheadedness which the world would not willingly let die. If it had been *you*, gentlemen, you probably wouldn't have landed, but you have no shadow of right to be celebrating, in your ancestors, gifts which they did not exercise, but only transmitted.[32]

So much for flattering the Pilgrims. Hereafter Mark Twain calls them "a hard lot" three times in about ten minutes of talk, and with flourish and not-quite-outrageous exaggeration he invokes them as Indian-skinners, slavers, and champion hypocrites. At the very end come twists that Mark Twain had neglected to add to the Whittier speech, a farewell to his own "stuff and nonsense," an unmistakable salute to New England's founders, and an affirmation of himself as a proud Connecticut Yankee as well as an unregenerate Missouri "border ruffian." Because there is no cop-out, there is no put-on, no satire left drifting in moral limbo. Shortly before the close, however, Mark Twain launches a diatribe that urges the negation of the Society, of these meetings, the New England legacy, and the burdensome American past. This mock Jeremiad (which might not be entirely mock) runs through two hefty paragraphs; here is the latter and hotter one:

Yes, hear your true friend — your only true friend — list to his voice. Disband these societies, hotbeds of vice, of moral decay — perpetuators of ancestral superstition. Here on this board I see water, I see milk, I see the wild and deadly lemonade. These are but steps upon the downward path. Next we shall see tea, then chocolate, then coffee — hotel coffee. A few more years — all too few, I fear — mark my words, we shall have cider! Gentlemen, pause ere it be too late. You are on the broad road which leads to dissipation, physical ruin, moral decay, gory crime and the gallows! I beseech you, I implore you, in the name of your anxious friends, in the name of your suffering families, in the name of your impending widows and orphans, stop ere it be too late. Disband these New England societies, renounce these soul-blistering saturnalia, cease from varnishing the rusty reputations of your long-vanished ancestors — the super-high-moral old ironclads of

Cape Cod, the pious buccaneers of Plymouth Rock — go home, and try to learn to behave! (784–85)

Sharp edges here are blunted by the way the speech closes, and by the clever tactics that precede it. From the opening lines, Mark Twain's trick of stopping to take correction and advice from "the gentleman on my left" bolsters connection with the group and subverts his own authority to chide. By the middle of the speech he is boasting a ludicrous all-American, all-New-England pedigree, telling whoppers of his descent from American Indians, Quaker martyrs, Roger Williams, and an African slave. By such devices venom is drained away . . . mostly. If uncomfortable truth remains — that there is something monstrous about these Pilgrim fathers and about free, supposedly democratic people worshiping their memory — then that truth strikes only as a twinge, a bit of spice in a confectionery address.

Readily one can see structural differences between "Plymouth Rock" and the Whittier speech, differences that take these works in different directions. Using a frame-tale strategy, the Whittier speech will *not* allow Mark Twain to play the wise fool, seem as ridiculous as whatever he ridicules, and keep the satire in that plasmic state between seriousness and harmless fun. One problem with the Whittier speech involves a layering of voices: the Mark Twain of time present, the Mark Twain of fifteen years earlier, a nameless backcountry hermit-miner, then Longfellow, Emerson, and Holmes, who prove to be bad counterfeits of these luminaries — and then back out through each layer again. In such a maze, who said what, in what context and with what measure of sobriety and authority, may be only half-remembered in a speech at a ceremony, especially a ceremony after dinner and wine. Critics at their ease may savor such complexity in a printed text, but in oral discourse the price for this degree of intricacy can be high. Mark Twain denies himself his own voice through most of the Whittier address; he uses other voices to muffle a Mark Twain persona that, were it sufficiently there, might combat the mistaking of this ostensibly-harmless comedy, as an insult to sacred New England relics.

Nonetheless, strategic blunders in the Whittier speech only partly account for its troubles. Failed or not, the joke does have to do with something, and comparison to the Plymouth Rock address may bring unstable and perhaps unconscious motives into light. Like "Plymouth Rock," the Whittier speech has a touch of blasphemy in its heart, about Brahmins and the sobriety of Boston-made, Morocco-bound, highly serious American literature, and more broadly about consequences of fame, of human beings transmogrified into partially alive institutions, philosophical, poetic, and also comic. If Mark Twain's tale of a miner's tale is ostensibly about the failure of three backwoods con men to masquerade as literary giants, to fool anyone but *this* fool, and to escape from their own dismal personalities, then this joke has a tricky undertow. Perhaps the unamused Brahmins in the hall weren't entirely wrong, as the sketch may bump a sad truth about elders in the American cultural church. Were the honored guests at this dinner actually petrified men? Emerson, Longfellow, Holmes, Whittier — by 1877, each of these writers had by design or default become a national monument, quarried from carloads of words and shaped by decades of public reverence. If frontier ruffians do badly at impersonating Emerson, Longfellow, and Holmes, and know nothing more about these great men than scattered and misattributed lines, then implications glitter: perhaps there are no persons here to impersonate. As cultural and psychological beings these people may already be gravestones with undecipherable epitaphs. Their verses may be quoted in far-off Nevada goldfields, but all is garbled; theme and context are forgotten, and beyond or behind those garbled words — nothing? As household gods of literary America, have these people failed to show, and perhaps to retain within themselves, any flicker of spontaneity, a capacity to play, talk, and act as plausible human beings? The unorthodox flattery in Mark Twain's speech seems to imply how much better these eminences are than the scoundrels who try to counterfeit them; the discomfiting truth embedded, perhaps not by conscious intention, but by some anxiety deeper in Mark Twain's own mind, is that to be so eminent is to be less free, less human. A frontier ruffian can enact the Great Emerson, if badly; but great, finished Emerson cannot dream of returning the compliment, cannot escape "Emerson," an identity as ponderous as the boulder that would soon stand over his Concord tomb.

Instead of the all-in-fun disclaimer that closes the Plymouth Rock address, restoring some measure of certainty about Mark Twain's intentions and easing the sting of any truth uncovered, the Whittier speech ends in a Marabar Cave:

> I said to the miner, "Why, my dear sir, *these* were not the gracious singers to whom we and the world pay loving reverence and homage; these were imposters."

The miner investigated me with a calm eye for a while, then said he, "Ah — imposters, were they? — are *you?*" I did not pursue the subject; and since then I haven't traveled on my *nom de plume* enough to hurt. Such is the reminiscence I was moved to contribute, Mr. Chairman. In my enthusiasm I may have exaggerated the details a little, but you will easily forgive me that fault, since I believe it is the first time I have ever deflected from perpendicular fact on an occasion like this. (699)

Mark Twain dodges the miner's question because no answer is possible. To be truly Mark Twain is to be nobody for real, for to be Mark Twain truly is to affirm above all a privilege of imposture, of falsification of historical and cultural fact, of personal history, of everything conventionally associated with identity; and to affirm as well a right *not* to exercise such privileges, not to be trapped by self-defining fakery. The miner's wise-fool question is the punchline of the Whittier speech, and a vortex into which it implodes. Although flesh and blood at the front of this uncomfortable dining room, Mark Twain is nonetheless a fiction; so is the man who asks him this identity question, and so were the men who came to the cabin — doubly so, being men who never existed except in a fable, impersonating other men who supposedly do have life beyond the spoken word and the printed text. Yet the vortex of the story draws them in as well, these Great Americans, these three names that everyone knows *as* names, as books, as strings of public-domain quotations: these men who may have sacrificed some basic power to be. If Emerson, Holmes, and Longfellow are petrified men, then petrification threatens everyone in that Boston hall, including one fame-laden outsider, come from the Wild West to try to make them laugh.

Did the Whittier address wreck, then, because it rattles with anxiety about selfhood, anxiety that paradoxically went far to *define* Mark Twain as a self, and make him a resonant American identity? Should it even be said that the address *is* a failure, either in its first hour or now in retrospect? The depth and duration of Mark Twain's resistance to definition, whether artistic, political, psychological, or spiritual, is more interesting than debate about whether a skirmish in his campaign went well or not. Inferences and inquiries regarding Mark Twain's ideas about identity, and how they may impact upon the canon, require a look at a much broader landscape.

We know that among these Boston intellectuals, Mark Twain opened this ungainly question about the consequences to the self of its own intellectual life, the power of philosophies and formulations to freeze people into monuments. This was a question that grew for Mark Twain in the last twenty years of his life, and later chapters of this book will be concerned with that phase of his thinking. But if Mark Twain's troubles over the intellect compound later, his lively quarrels with the ground rules of identity, of culture, and of art, range back to the beginning, to sketches that struck anonymously, and sketches that put his *nom de guerre* into the American vocabulary.

frogs

"The Celebrated Jumping Frog," which Mark Twain also published as, among other things, "The Notorious Jumping Frog of Calaveras County," "Jim Smiley and His Jumping Frog," and "The Frog Jumping of the County of Calaveras" (for in both name and substance this tale stayed appropriately restless in the retelling), indeed grew so "celebrated" that for years after its first appearance, an untitled frog-picture on handbills was advertisement enough for a Mark Twain stage show. Yet one can read long in the commentary without learning quite why the American public found this story so transcendently funny, such a frog-leap beyond Southwest humor of its own time. A pause over that mystery might help us turn as well to other Mark Twain works with renewed openness to their possibilities. This frog leads us into those narratives that helped make Twain a star, and that continue to be known around the world, no matter how hard it has been to describe the magic by which this particular sketch worked as comedy. If the secret lies in this tale's being just a little crazier and more deeply chaotic than we have wanted to believe, then that might be a secret worth remembering when Mark Twain's major works come into view.

Setting the frog in historical context is respectable, the "context" always being the humor of the Old Southwest. Without questioning Mark Twain's debt to that legacy, or our debt to scholars who have examined its workings, one can wonder about the tendency to romanticize Southwestern humor, to downplay its violence, its racism, its sexism, and its thematic instability. The best anthology of the mode seems wary about those problems,[33] and Kenneth Lynn's landmark study (still the best analytical book on this material) also presents patterns of sedate intentions that are seen as continuing through Mark Twain's best writing, not just in sketches but in the ambitious works that came years after. Lynn emphasizes continuity: the humor of the Southwest gains form, energy, and appeal thanks to the rise of Whig politics and the Jacksonian revolution; the comic tales sound rough fanfares for the common man, celebrate borderland cultures, and ease the terrors and dislocations inherent in such life.[34] Mark Twain, Josh Billings, Thomas Bangs Thorpe, Petroleum V. Nasby, and others were therefore comrades questing for a democratic literature and a true American vernacular, and Mark Twain owes much to the work of these others.

But Mark Twain was extraordinary as a Southwest humorist, and not just for his gifts in reconciling rustic dialects with readability, or for catching hilarious behavior and character in short narratives. If others pioneered and even perfected the Southwestern tale, it was Mark Twain who perfected the Southwestern *meta*-tale, the story of a story. He ventured to the frontiers of frontier humor early in his career. Frame-tale stories proliferate among Southwest humorists — but not frame-tale stories about being confounded by stories and storytellers, about stories not even getting told, tales and tellers derailing ordinary business, normal thinking, and basic assumptions about identity and real life. When a pratfall is taken by the tale itself, we leave rutted trails of conventional Wild West humor and plunge into Mark Twain's bewildering and trackless landscape. "The Celebrated Jumping Frog" is the best known of these breakouts, but there are others of note in the opening years of the career. "A Touching Story of George Washington's Boyhood" never comes close to talking about George Washington; it goes round and round about aggravations of living near people who fancy themselves musicians. The suspense and the running gag of the sketch involve waiting for this counterfeit news article to start being what the title says it is. "A Medieval Romance" spends three thousand humid words maneuvering cliché lovers into "hopeless, helpless peril." Then it drops them with a shrug:

> The truth is, I have got my hero (or heroine) into such a particularly close place that I do not see how I am ever going to get him (or her) out of it again — and therefore I will wash my hands of the whole business and leave that person to get out the best way that offers — or else stay there. I thought it was going to be easy

enough to straighten out that little difficulty, but it looks different, now.[35]

In "George Washington's Boyhood" the reader is "sold" if he or she simply expects that an account will come around to its subject; "Medieval Romance" cons us into assuming that a published story that begins by emulating overwrought sentimental romance will arrive at some kind of ending, sentimental or not. In other words, a reader is "sold" in trusting to common sense — or rather in assuming that common sense extends to the cultural practice of writing and reading. The subversion is not of some particular modes of discourse, but of discourse itself. Mark Twain plays with the rarely questioned expectations that beginnings lead to endings, and that titles and texts have obligations to one another, and that sentences on a printed page will have discernible intentions other than laughter at intentionality. If egalitarian or realist ethics rattle in such tales as these, rejecting sentimentality and calling for stories of new times and new heroes, then such ethics coexist here with their own negation, with profound suspicion about all these nets of words earnestly published by nobody at nobody else. The reading experience grows complex and exciting; such tales delight, rather than wag an admonitory finger in a reader's face.

"Interpreting" a Mark Twain sketch, therefore, can amount to reading only half a sketch, unless possibilities are allowed that if the sketch be about anything it might also be about the idiocies of interpretation. The co-presence of contrary themes, of sense and refusal of sense, may be part of the comedy. It is worth testing such a premise on "The Celebrated Jumping Frog," an international sensation in its time, and still perhaps the most famous light work in canonical American literature. But when "Jumping Frog" strikes students as less than side-splitting, when they wonder at its popularity in the late autumn of 1865, they seem unsatisfied by the standard explanations. Granted that the tale may have offered a flash of relief after four years of Civil War gloom. Granted too that "Jumping Frog" reflects patterns of the Southwest comic tradition and has *trompeur-trompé* archetypes in the foreground, of hustler Jim Smiley being hustled himself, and of a self-important narrator unwittingly revealing his own foolishness. The problem is that either line of talk about this story flattens it, for to categorize the tale either way, historically or aesthetically, reduces many possible dimensions to one surface or two. That is bad luck, especially if this tale could be about our own wrongful assumptions that knowing where we are, historically, aesthetically, or otherwise, means really knowing what in blazes is going on.

We can escape for a moment parameters of modern context-thinking and reawaken this story's possibilities. The trickster-tricked tale of Jim Smiley and Dan'l Webster is not the only situation farce in "Jumping Frog," but one of several, nested within each other like matrioshka dolls. Dubious in several dimensions, a character named Jim Smiley is swindled not once but twice: one story-within-the-story is of his hind-leg-clamping bulldog losing a fight to a dog with no hind legs, which makes the frame-tale narrator the butt (again, only perhaps) of not one but two put-ons and possibly more. Drunk, or stupid, or pointlessly crafty, the unfathomably deadpan Simon Wheeler has blockaded him in a bar and "reeled off this monotonous narrative" about a stranger he does not care about, and who may be Wheeler's fantasy or even a way for Wheeler to tell about himself. As a mistake or a practical joke, the friend back East has sent the frame-tale narrator to Angel's Camp, California, looking for one Leonidas W. Smiley, which has set this narrator in Wheeler's grasp. "I have a lurking suspicion," says this narrator, "that your Leonidas W. Smiley is a myth — that you never knew such a personage, and that you only conjectured that if I asked old Wheeler about him it would remind him of his infamous *Jim* Smiley, and he would go to work to bore me nearly to death with some infernal reminiscence of him as long and tedious as it should be useless to me."[36] At the end of the frog-jumping, Jim Smiley at least knows he has been swindled; the frame-tale narrator stays perfectly uncertain about his own experience, for these are (perhaps, always perhaps!) blue-ribbon put-ons, with exquisite fake-outs and cop-outs. In what dimension (history, dream, drunken hallucination, satire, whatever) was there a frog, a bull-pup dog, an asthmatic horse, or even a stranger? In what dimension is or was there a Jim Smiley, a Simon Wheeler, and a teller about them all? Who is it that believes in whom or dreams them up?

A moment ago I tried a nesting-doll analogy to catch this arrangement of stories within stories, each inner tale being as suspect as the tale that contains it. But that is just another gesture at *catching;* and part of the fun of this story of a story of a frog is its power to do whirls in the air and outleap its catchers. Arrangements, if they are here, are here to break down. The bulldog story and the asthmatic horse story do not frame or contain the story of the frog Dan'l Webster. They keep it company, certifying its uncertainty, its plausibility in a context that they make more implausible. If they mess up a tidy pattern of tale-within-tale, patterns are not the point.

Yet we cannot be sure even of interpretive chaos. For that certainty would give a species of dominion over this text, a key to these possibly compounded possible-put-ons, or at least an honorable escape. If there are tales within tales in "Jumping Frog," and tales next to other tales, then those patterns and anti-patterns can collide and produce whatever comforting or comfortless Great Disorder they will. Earlier, I mentioned the Big Bang theory of the universe as an analogy for a theory of humor, because it allows for vast possibilities. Let me go back to universes and big theories for a moment, to suggest that in a collision of models and thought-systems, a comic work can achieve liberation from everybody, including the model-happy interpreter. The great physicist Stephen Hawking retells the old story of an astronomer faced with a stolid English woman persuaded that the universe rides on an enormous turtle; when she was asked what this turtle stands on, she replied, "You're very clever, young man, very clever. But it's turtles all the way down!"[37] Preposterous and consoling at once, the idea puts literally everything into perspective. That perspective is mysterious and absurd — and perhaps no more unimaginable than the General Theory that Hawking has spent his imperiled life trying to get right.

If tales-within-tales do not quite work as a General Theory for "Jumping Frog," then is it frogs all the way down? Such a pattern may be here if patterns we must have, either to nullify still other patterns or bolster an illusion that this text can be stabilized and fully understood. A clue beckons in one of the story's most famous lines, Simon Wheeler's moment of actual praise for the thinking of this lunatic Jim Smiley: "Smiley said all a frog wanted was education, and he could do 'most anything — and I believe him" (174). In a never-land where one such frog has become Daniel Webster, and a deceased bulldog has been Andrew Jackson, Wheeler's real or put-on conviction about the limitless powers of education can trigger some wondering. Jim Smiley may be an educated frog, having "never done nothing for three months but set in his back yard and learn that frog to jump," and succeeding at teaching a frog to do better what frogs already know much better than men. As Wheeler portrays him, Jim Smiley thinks froggy thoughts. The only thing on the creature's mind and coming out of his mouth is bet-talk, and if there are whiffs of the amphibian in Wheeler's representation of Smiley before he is actually heard, then he sounds just as peculiar in his own words:

> "Maybe you understand frogs, and maybe you don't understand 'em; maybe you've had experience, and maybe you ain't only a amature, as it were. Anyways, I've got *my* opinion, and I'll resk forty dollars that he can outjump any frog in Calaveras County." (175)

Though this may be a comically right representation of a back-country drawl and dialect, it might also suggest the voice and mentality of something not entirely evolved from the swamp, something that understands frogs too well and human talk and thinking not quite well enough. A moment later, leaving the precious Dan'l Webster in the stranger's care, Smiley proves completely foolish about the betting he is obsessed with. As for the stranger, Mark Twain gives him the narrative's only repeated line, a line that whispers the craziness or frogginess of everybody in the region:

> "The feller took the box again, and took another long, particular look, and give it back to Smiley and says, very deliberate, 'Well — I don't see no points about that frog that's any better'n any other frog.' " (175)

So Jim Smiley may not be the only perfect frog-nut or frog-man in the county. Someone else — or perhaps everyone else — may have spent too much time in the mud, understanding the "points" of frogs as if they were thoroughbred horses. In other words, Smiley may not be crazier than the norm, and the stranger's egging remark to him (thoroughly stupid, for as yet the stranger has no idea how to beat this frog, not even as Smiley leaves Dan'l Webster in his charge) fits the local *Gestalt*. But when Smiley heads for the swamp, the stranger has time to ponder, and the narrative does another whirl, jolting expectations that the story's teller, Simon Wheeler, is a fully certifiable human being:

> "So he set there a good while thinking and thinking to hisself, and then he got the frog out and prized his mouth open and took a teaspoon and filled him full of quail-shot — filled him pretty near up to his chin — and set him on the floor." (175–176)

Now who saw this? Wheeler narrates as if *he* did — but if he did, why did he not warn Jim Smiley that Dan'l Webster had been sabotaged? There is no hint that Wheeler is in league with the stranger or bears Smiley any grudge; the hint, rather, is that Wheeler has sat and watched it all, like a man without discernible motives, just as he has no discernible motive for sitting and telling what might have become the never-ending story, had not the frame-tale narrator slipped away.

So the stranger is a fool for taking such a bet; Smiley is a fool for trusting his prized frog to the stranger he bets with; and "glassy-eyed, his voice never varying," Simon Wheeler is either a master put-on artist or — well, what? A man like these others, maybe an alcoholic, maybe a madman, maybe an educated frog? Whether or not he is froggy himself, the frame-tale narrator evidently does not know whom he has listened to, what he has heard, why the teller did the telling, or why or even *if* he has been sent to hear all this. Jim Smiley's frog problems seem a small farce, compared to the plight of his listener, this as-yet and perhaps-forever mysterious Mark Twain, who represents himself here as a trapped audience and a clueless storyteller at the same time.

But score-keeping of any kind only reenacts the earnestness that got this narrator into trouble in the first place. Worse, it evades reckoning with the master put-on of "Jumping Frog," the biggest nesting-doll of the lot, involving ourselves as readers of this text, within a world in which everyone's "reality" is called into question. If the narrator is not sure about either of these Smileys, the frog, the stranger, the contest, or anything else he hears from Simon Wheeler, and is not sure even about Wheeler, and fails (apparently) to see a shred of humor in what Wheeler tells him, then where are *we,* if not likewise in an absurd predicament, hearing a deadpan narrator telling a tale about another deadpan narrator telling a suspect tale? The frame-tale narrative (the outermost one) does not domesticate the Wild West story of Wheeler the storyteller, or insert Jim Smiley as a gentle amusement into the real world of an Eastern American audience. The frame-tale conspires with Wheeler's account to mock such "realities." If the narrator wonders what he is doing, in hearing and then retelling this evidently pointless tale, then the reader's situation is even odder, precisely because it is taken up voluntarily.

But no matter. These different interpretive pathways lead to the same predicament, the same funhouse where interpretive habits are confounded. A frog loses a contest because he is filled up with quail shot and "planted solid as a church." A nobody named Jim Smiley loses because he thinks this prize frog will stay the same when a man's back is turned for a few minutes, and that a frog weighs what it weighs;

his dog loses because he is a complete, four-legged dog, with one dogged way of fighting, not half-a-dog like the dog that defeats him. The narrator has come looking for a somebody, not realizing that in the Angel's Camps of the world, one "Smiley," one name or grinning, vacuous face, may be the same as another. The frog loses because he is "settled"; a narrator loses because in a place he cannot comprehend he hears a tale of idiotic obsessions, a tale he is not "shifty" enough to laugh at, not seeing that from some mysterious perspective ministers of the Gospel and frog-trainers may be alike. *To become, to be "settled," is to lose.* The stone man of Nevada thumbs his nose again; the stone men of New England stare at nothing in that Boston banquet hall and listen to their epitaph. If "The Jumping Frog" tale has "themes," they may concern the virtues of emptiness, lightness, the evasion of routine, sobriety, normalcy, including normal discourse with purpose, and some equality among the individuals involved. To be alive and lucky in Angel's Camp is to "understand frogs," empty ones that can leap quick and far, as you must be able to yourself. Bad luck is not only immobility, being stuck at the jumpline with a crop full of bird-shot, or cornered in the back of a saloon by a glassy-eyed stranger with a dadaist monologue fifty years early. Mark Twain's comic West is a world where the self that is founded on psychological consistency, logic, decipherable speech and behavior, on faith, on education even loosely based in values of a too-civilized world, is a self jammed full of quail-shot, a self that cannot move.

"The Celebrated Jumping Frog," then, as Lettrist manifesto *avant la lettre?* Of course not; this is humor, subversion of seriousness, a plunge away from meaning and only a quick visit to the abyss. In light of that, is not any reading, any serious floor we think we see at the bottom, only another "meaning," another culture-inflected delusion to be vandalized on an escape-run into the dark? If "stop making sense!" is a theme of "Jumping Frog," a source of its naughty pleasure for readers then and after, then even to say so is to scheme to make sense of it. Mark Twain knew that the compulsion to be sensible cannot be cured: human beings are too much like the blue jays of Jim Baker's yarn in *A Tramp Abroad,* a yarn that of all Mark Twain's sketches seems a perfect companion piece to the story of the frog (perfect, that is, to people compelled to think in terms of themes and symmetries). Dan'l Webster is undone because somebody has filled him up; Jim Baker's exasperated blue jay, described by Baker as human in his devious ways and dismal ethics, is laughed at by fellow birds because like them he is driven to fill things up, to keep putting acorns into holes even if the empty space on the other side of the hole is vast as a house. Human beings abhor vacuum, both in signification and in the self; they cannot leave empty things alone, though filling and meddling are mischief.

What are we to do, then, when we come across a "NOTICE" placed at the beginning of a long story that Mark Twain published about twenty years after?

> Persons attempting to find a motive in this narrative will be prosecuted; persons attempting to find a moral in it will be banished; persons attempting to find a plot in it will be shot.

Meaning what? That readers must not give way to human nature and look for meaning in *Adventures of Huckleberry Finn?* That there are no meanings to be found? That the book that follows is about the futility of motives, morals, and plots—which would make it very much "about" something after all? When readers debate signification, or lack of it, in the Blue Jay Yarn or "The Jumping Frog" or "Map of Paris," the stakes are low, as these are small works that, individually at least, play no great role in a search for Mark Twain's literary motives and morals. But the stakes are much higher, obviously, when the work in question is *Huckleberry Finn.* But reading Mark Twain's longer narratives in this spirit does not mean plunging into interpretive nihilism, nor contriving that chaos blaze up everywhere in works that have seemed measured, bounded, and more or less sober to wise readers. Granted that criticism always remains a culturally inflected practice, and that if American culture wants the Mark Twain we seem to have constructed out of the work and the life, then America is certainly entitled to him. If we want morals, plots, and handsome methods in *Huckleberry Finn,* then we can have them by the bale, thanks to Eliot, DeVoto, Trilling, Fiedler, Leo Marx, and scores of sharp-minded critics coming after, and thanks above all to an established practice of finding such themes and structures in countless classrooms and reading corners where *Huckleberry Finn* is perpetually reopened.

Even so, all-encompassing refusals in Mark Twain's voice (passions that could rise *against* form, theme, and conventional notions of self) broaden, compound, complicate, and liberate the experience of these works, fostering their life, and making them seem the more worthy of so much modern rereading. Scott Fitzgerald had it right (as he was cracking up) that a "first-rate" modern intelligence means a mind in which ideas can coexist with their own negation;[38] with that as a cue, one of my hopes is to come closer to Mark Twain's modernity, or at least to his perennial freshness, and his appeal to a public all over this paradox-ridden world.

A systematic reading of Mark Twain's art as systematically against system would be ludicrous. If Mark Twain celebrates change and open-ended becoming, if he suspects or even fears the static, the culturally prescribed, then each ambitious work may be its own creative adventure, faithful perhaps to no principle save liberty (which is to say, faithful only to values within itself). To entertain page by page, moment by moment, on whatever intellectual level he pleased (or on several at once if he pleased); to enact spontaneous, honest response to the world as found — perhaps these are the only genuine constants in Mark Twain's art, and the only motives we have to assume to begin reading. Superb biographies of the man make much of his internal conflict, growth, learning. Heretical or otherwise, textual commentary has every reason to follow suit. Shifts of attention in this book are meant to suggest realms of trouble into which Mark Twain's heresies could take him, how he experimented, as an artist, in such predicaments, and what lessons he may have learned, here and there, about the consequences of his rebellion.

From *The Innocents Abroad* through *Following the Equator,* Mark Twain's travel books, both domestic and international, tell of quirks and absurdities in Europe, the Wild West, the Great River heartland, and the Orient; yet they also tell of perilous self-renewal, the achievement of empowering suspicion about all cultures, including whatever culture one calls home — and of momentary escape from the doom of culture-inflicted identity. Growth and change can flourish within these books and among them, and even the lesser travel narratives hold surprises as inquiries into selfhood. Looked at in this way, the travel books present an altered background for reading Mark Twain's novels, shorter tales, and other imaginative writings; as direct encounters with worldly experience, the travel books suggest Mark Twain's radical and changeful critique of culture, of conventions of identity, common sense, and culturally obedient narrative. Looking afresh at the fiction that followed *Life on the Mississippi,* fiction about the river country of Mark Twain's boyhood, involves an assumption that may not please everybody: a letting-go of restrictions upheld for most of the twentieth century, having to do with where we should stop reading certain very good narratives, and which scenes and characters to skirt like homeless folk in the city park, and which of Mark Twain's bad books to keep out of mind when one talks about finer ones. Mark Twain's best novels are not spoiled by such licentiousness. Instead they can seem richer, more complex and honest as moral inquiry, and better.

As for Mark Twain's problematic realism, that subject opens nicely when we turn to his longer forays into domains of romance and again commit a misdemeanor of looking at light work and better novels as kin. In setting, in substance, *The Prince and the Pauper* is more like *A Connecticut Yankee* than is any other text Mark Twain published, and *The Prince and the Pauper* can suggest much about Hank Morgan and his portentous, troublesome story. A return to *Christian Science* and *Joan of Arc,* two generally sidestepped later works, opens up other perspectives, useful in understanding artistic and psychological effects of Mark Twain's quarrel with identity and stability, as his culture enforced such values. The family crises and financial woes of his last twenty years play a part in the myth, as soul-testing disasters in the narrative we construct of Mark Twain as an American Job. Dismissing none of that record, downplaying neither the personal losses nor the pain, one can nonetheless regret that another line of thinking about Mark Twain's last phase has been obscured by so much attention to family tragedy and to his writings as symptoms of that distress. For Mark Twain had an intellect as well as a heart. Some heightened regard for that intellect as a significant, if not a discrete side of this writer, can deepen understanding of his late works, allow them to show better that cultural significance that millions of American readers — again, often ahead of the critics — evidently understand to be there.

The 1890s brought to America a tide of intellectual formulations, totalizing "isms" like no other onslaught in the history of the West. Biology, physics, geology, politics, psychology, the arts and letters, the cosmos — in a period of about fifteen years almost every side of human experience underwent radical redefinition, and Mark Twain was in the thick of it. Whether or not he fully understood any of these new idea-systems or their implications does not matter. What matters is Mark Twain's special predicament, his vulnerability as this radically remade world swept over him. As a longtime heretic on the problems

of identity, questioning the persistence of mind in old tracks and habits and the thoughtless refusal of the new, strange, relentless, world-
altering truth, Mark Twain was open to prostration by new heresies
that came tapping at his door. Social constructionist readings of late
work seek to describe Mark Twain as an ideology-constricted bourgeois Victorian, caught in social pathologies of his time with regard to
gender, money, and race. Though there may be value in such thinking
about him, the Mark Twain it depicts is but part of the knowable
man — or the documentable myth — and a smaller fragment of Mark
Twain as literary experience. There is also the self-aware and embat-
tled intellect, an ideology-laden artist struggling to understand the
workings of his own mind, and to accommodate — imaginatively, psychologically, morally — astonishing new definitions of self and world.
These were years in which Mark Twain paid for his refusals and his
enforced uncertainty. Even so, the catastrophe that supposedly befell
him as an imaginative writer has been fleshed out into a dramatic final
act, in part to serve a cultural need for the narrative of Mark Twain's
career to close in some kind of great discovery or catharsis. The practice has been to attend closely to certain late works, or particular drafts
of rewritten but unpublished tales, and pass by others, works that Mark
Twain actually saw fit to publish in those same years. My sense is that
Mark Twain achieved at least provisional resolution of his intellectual
crisis — provisional as all solutions had to be for a man who resisted
absolutes — and that a broader review of late writings may make that
clear. But once more, whether or not Mark Twain resolved such dilemmas to his own or anyone else's satisfaction is a question of limited
interest, and one more opinion about all that is of no consequence:
To try to "settle" such matters about Mark Twain, to limit the experience of reading him, amounts in his special case to an act of cultural
vandalism.

No other American author has been turned to so often by our culture to represent so many sides of the putative national character. It is
possible, therefore, that understanding not what Mark Twain "was" or
finally "became," but rather what he *resisted* becoming, will help us
know why it is that Mark Twain represents so much to a much-changed
world, why he has not become another Petrified Man, another too-
stable icon in halls of fame, theme parks, and pizza parlors; and why he
means such diverse things to an enormous audience that adores him
beyond the prescriptions of English faculties. Are Americans known

better, and more surely united, by what they do not want and do not like than by what they affirm? Are evasion, escapism, and psychological turmoil still the identifying Yankee traits that Tocqueville and D. H. Lawrence have said they were?[39] Those are mysteries for demographers and political theorists. The relevant questions for Mark Twain readers have to do with the poignancy of his continuing presence in our cultural life, and how that presence is informed by the depth and courage of his insurrections.

Chapter 2

Fool's Paradise

In the three years between the American debut of *The Innocents Abroad* and the first authorized British edition in 1872, there was considerable action in the Europe that Mark Twain had written about, changes that might lure any other travel author back to the desk for revisions, to keep the facts reasonably factual and prevent a forthcoming edition from looking obsolete and foolish. Months before Mark Twain's "Author's English Edition" of *The Innocents Abroad* went to the London presses, his France, the leading state on the Continent, and a nation preeminent in fashion, culture, and might, had collapsed in an eight-week war. Its emperor, disgraced, had fled the country; and in the lovely streets of its capital city, the supposed jewel of Western civilization, there had been holocaust. The "Fortifications of Paris" joke was published in the *Express* on 17 September 1870, two days before Bismarck's armies began their siege. With no organized French force left to resist, a quick, comic, and bloodless ending to Gallic militarism was a reasonable forecast from Buffalo. No one there could have foreseen that Gambetta would keep the hard Prussians at bay with a pick-up force of farmers and townsfolk, or retake Amiens and Orleans, or cover Paris until an armistice was argued into shape the following January. No American dreamed that when spring came a Commune would burst into life in those cafés, silk shops and "gay and enlivening" boulevards of Mark Twain's "magnificent Paris," a Commune threatening a more radical overthrow of French politics, culture, and identity than the Revolution of 1789: an end to private property, the class system, religion, fashion, the national memory, and those ponderous, tourist-attracting public icons. Notre Dame barely escaped burning by a Communard mob; the archbishop of the city was taken hostage by the new government (if it could be called that) and subsequently shot; on one festive morning the Vendôme Column was toppled with hawsers onto a heap of manure; the Louvre and the other palaces were closed up amid cries for trashing the paintings and busts in their galleries and heaving all traditional values into the Seine. Hastily revived and rearmed with help from the triumphant Bismarck, the Armée de France moved in to crush the Communards, and the street fighting raged day and night for a week. The Tuileries Palace and other public buildings were burned to the ground, and the body count in the city surpassed the toll for the uprisings of 1820, 1830, and 1848 combined. When Mark Twain's "patient and conscientious revision" (as his new preface page called it) of *The Innocents Abroad* was ready for the London bookshops in the next year, there were fresh graves at Père Lachaise Cemetery, where Mark Twain had been so whimsical about Abelard and Héloïse, and where the Commune had tried to make a last stand. Herded against the southeast wall of the graveyard and shot, 147 were buried in a ditch very near where they fell. But that was nothing: the Parisian dead at the barricades and in the streets ran to between twenty and thirty-six thousand — when a world comes unglued, nobody keeps an official score.

With his Paris exploded, Mark Twain did amend the text of his travel book (or whatever it was) for British readers, but only in trivial ways.[1] From the Paris chapters he expunged a sentimental passage about seeing Napoleon III at a public ceremony with the sultan of Turkey, and about how this Louis Napoleon had returned from obscurity and shame to become "Emperor of France!" and so much grander than the Ottoman strutting at his side. But nothing else of consequence was altered. Not a word was added about the catastrophic war, the fall of France, the mayhem in Paris, the crushing of *la belle vie* that Mark Twain had admired, or the shocking frailty of this capital that *The Innocents Abroad* presents as unshakably established and serene. Even the following passage, made outrageously wrong by the events of 1871, kept its 1869 state, lauding the new boulevards of Baron Haussmann and the emperor, and declaring the Parisian street uprising to be a thing of the past:

> But they will build no more barricades; they will break no more
> soldiers' heads with paving-stones. Louis Napoleon has taken care

of all that. He is annihilating the crooked streets, and building in their stead noble boulevards as straight as an arrow—avenues which a cannon ball could traverse from end to end without meeting an obstruction more irresistible than the flesh and bones of men—boulevards whose stately edifices will never afford refuges and plotting-places for starving, discontented revolution-breeders. . . . The mobs used to riot here, but they must seek another rallying-place in the future. And this ingenious Napoleon paves the streets of his great cities with a smooth, compact composition of asphaltum and sand. No more barricades of flagstones—no more assaulting his Majesty's troops with cobbles. I cannot feel friendly toward my quondam fellow American, Napoleon III, especially at this time, when in my fancy I see his credulous victim, Maximilian, lying stark and stiff in Mexico, . . . but I do admire his nerve, his calm self-reliance, his shrewd good sense.[2]

In the first American editions, well before the Franco-Prussian trouble started, Mark Twain glossed "at this time" as "July, 1867." Nothing was deleted or added to this passage for the first Routledge and Sons British edition; in years after, even the hyperbole about mighty Napoleon III was restored.[3] Perhaps it isn't surprising that Mark Twain did not fuss with his observations once they were in book-form somewhere, though facts had changed utterly and his impressions and shirt-sleeve prophecies had proved dead wrong. But from what perspective *aren't* we surprised? How does Mark Twain get away with this? Because he was notoriously sloppy about putting some of his volumes together, readers attracted to this side of the myth or the man, the "jackleg" genius, can find comforting signs of the anti-artist they favor; Mark Twain as "phunny phellow"—to his 1870s audience and to many readers now—provides license of another sort, because blunders of a traveling clown may be translated as more clowning. Yet it seems clear that the Mark Twain who narrates here isn't a clown all the time, or even most of the time, in *The Innocents Abroad.* Because the voice we hear is complex, and because the text does roll for long stretches very like a straightforward travel account, this question will not go away; nor do the mistakes and gross misvaluations seem to matter, though they might be grounds to damn a travel book by almost anyone else.

The Innocents Abroad, after all, professes to tell reasonably-up-to-date truth about Europe, to report and respond to things as they are. Mark

Twain seems clear (up to a point) about this intention at the outset, that this is "a record of a pleasure trip," that the key idea is "to suggest to the reader how *he* would be likely to see Europe and the East if he looked at them with his own eyes."[4] And, indeed, most of the published commentary on *The Innocents Abroad* concerns Mark Twain's tactics in fulfilling that promise.[5] Nonetheless, though much of value has been said about what travel signified to Samuel Clemens on some personal level,[6] that still might be a different matter from what Mark Twain intended a travel *narrative* to be, and one need not press hard on these opening lines for paradoxes to seep into view. This ordinary or archetypal American who designs to react in our stead, think and feel as our delegate to the Old World—who *is* this person? This fine-sounding declaration of democratic purpose may finesse mysteries about the relationship of travelers to the experience of travel, and dodge the problem that some adventures might not merely refresh but re-*create* an American tourist, or even one of these American "pilgrims." Proxies who would play at being "us," and enact the biases of people whom they think they represent, not only risk locking a narrative within dreary limits, but also risk failure of another sort: failure to respect the basic covenants inherent in being a traveler.

Accounts that did such mischief were common in the bookshops when Mark Twain set out on the *Quaker City,* which is why *The Innocents Abroad* seems in comparison the most heterodox Anglo-American document in the genre since Sterne's *A Sentimental Journey.*[7] "My giant goes with me wherever I go," sighs the great (and possibly petrified) Emerson, and because of that he writes off travel—for everybody—as a "fool's paradise."[8] If "Self Reliance" doesn't bother proving the point, then the travel writings of Fiske, Todd, Albert Dean Richardson, Bayard Taylor, and the much-ridiculed William C. Prime can give some evidence. If Emerson's "giants" signify the culture-based habits of the mind, narrow ranges of psychological response to the new and strange, then giants do indeed trail these popular writers wherever they go. What seems to be lacking in their work, and what energizes and sets apart Mark Twain's own travel writings from *The Innocents Abroad* onward, is a dimension of agon, of psychological unsettledness, a self not only moving *through* new cultural experience, but being challenged *as* a self: enticed, humbled, amused, or surprised into recognition, and now and then into change, sometimes fleeting, but sometimes profound.

From that perspective, *The Innocents Abroad* does not give the lie to Emerson's sweeping judgment. Mark Twain's book seems rather to broaden and complicate it. If travel is misery for Emerson and a paradise only for fools, then perhaps it is so because Emerson will not countenance one possible virtue of foolery. I mean the fool's power to escape, at least provisionally, from all those culture-inflected yesterday-selves that, as Emerson himself declares a few lines before in the same essay, a free and courageous human being should have no qualms about casting away. So if Mark Twain did next to nothing with his text when France sank and Paris blew up, he made no grave error in leaving his impressions and forecasts pretty much as they were. For Mark Twain's Paris is a time as much as a place, a moment in the adventures of a self that in this book turns out to be *also* a moment, an unconstricted then-and-there identity whose nurture, presentation, and conservation are what *The Innocents Abroad* is essentially about. The survival of such primordial, precultural freedom, under the compounded pressure of strange new worlds and implanted American habits, constitutes the plot (as well as much of the appeal) of Mark Twain's first big-book success.

Along with exploring that possibility here, I suggest truth in it with regard to all of Mark Twain's published travel narratives. A conservation of this spontaneity and basic wildness, and an evasion of the "giants," meaning all-too-coalesced identities of homebred and foreign sorts alike, bring these later works to life and keep them interesting, as something other than fossilized geography lessons, or as cluebooks for readers who want above all to penetrate to a "real" Mark Twain. There is a forty-year range of material to consider, and excursions carried out in an array of public identities. On the *Quaker City* voyage Mark Twain is presented as an undistinguished come-along with an affluent, pedigreed group, a nobody in the back row of the tour, moving through the cathedrals and museums and looking for chances to wander off and get into unscheduled trouble. In *A Tramp Abroad* the galleries, great cities, and pilgrimage sites are supplanted with wild landscapes, and the Mark Twain offered here is a self-styled robust Victorian trekker who does not really mean to dirty his boots with trekking anywhere. Wilderness and rugged byways, however, do set the scene, in Germany, Switzerland, France, and in some imaginative detours back to the American West. In *Life on the Mississippi* we have at least two Mark Twains to encounter: the naive cub pilot, and the narrator as a great and possibly too-finished personage coming home. The Mark Twain who narrates and wanders in *Following the Equator* can make no escape from his own achieved public self, for his fame and his advanced years require a "progress" in the royal sense, with retinues, obsequious functionaries, and eminent hosts obstructing the way. The impression this Mark Twain constructs of himself, in this last and most undervalued travel work, is nicely caught in one of the illustrations from the first edition, of an elderly "made man" strolling along with a train of porters and baggage handlers coming up respectfully behind him—and what they seem to carry are the accumulated *impedimenta* (the Latin term for baggage seems especially right here) of life and selfhood, of notorious success and failure: Mark Twain as humorist, author, social philosopher, international public identity, and now world-champion bankrupt.[9]

The proportions of the conflict do change, therefore, along with the odds against escaping the giants. But basic dynamics in these travel books remain much the same, whether the Mark Twain in question faces multitudes of worshipers, scatterings of locals who have never heard his name, or no one at all. In these narratives the lonely Alps and American empty spaces are never quite empty, for there are always histories and myths and expected behaviors to delight in and contend with. Whether the setting is Paris, Jerusalem, Bombay, Virginia City, New Orleans, or a two-man camp at Lake Tahoe, new venues pose both opportunity and danger to the self: opportunity to try on new masks, new mentalities, costumes, ways of being—and danger that such masquerades or holidays from identity will slip out of control and ramify. Early and late, what is afoot, when these books are at their best, is perilous renewal. These are narratives of escape from the confines of identity. They celebrate adventures into other possible selves, and they rejoice in neither being killed in the act nor caught overlong in any make-believe, cultural praxis, or ideology as threatening to psychological freedom as any self left behind. Other well-known travel writers of Mark Twain's lifetime—even Trollope, Dickens, and Oscar Wilde—rarely enact such exhilarating jeopardy.

excursions, subversions, evasions

The opening pages of *The Innocents Abroad* suggest the conflict straightaway. The much-remembered opening line calls the voyage a "pleasure trip;" the flyer for the *Quaker City* cruise, reprinted as the bulk of the opening chapter, describes a ceremonial pilgrimage to religious and cultural holy ground. By the end of the chapter, however, it seems clear that our delegate's intention is to go along and subvert the psychological and social constrictions of that flyer, and of his fellow voyagers too if necessary. What this Mark Twain will have to do, to be "tourist" rather than pilgrim, and one of the "boys" rather than a pious, ossified grown-up personage, is a mystery at the start.[10] His own Père Lachaise rebellion, against the sentimental, dead-serious legend of Héloïse and Abelard, is his first sustained imaginative break from the *Quaker City* crowd — which is to say from both conventional Yankee and European pilgriming — and a sign of how free he will let his fantasies run, to break the hold of both mausoleumed Europe and his own home experience. Thereafter, in Italy, in Greece, in the Ottoman Empire, this narrator's guerrilla war against stasis of mood and mind, self-loss in the sober business of pilgrimage, is everywhere in full swing.

Roughing It, the second travel book, indicates early, and with considerable wit, that the warfare this time will be total, and also that there are odd consequences to winning. Several opening skirmishes in this war are clustered in the first four chapters, as the stage coach from St. Joseph lurches west toward the front range of the Rocky Mountains. The adventure has not really begun, but the enemy has been met, and a big part of it is the English language. The coach is stacked to bursting with mail from the East: "There was a great pile of it strapped on top of the stage, and both the four and hind boots were full. We had twenty-seven hundred pounds of it aboard, the driver said — 'a little for Brigham, and Carson, and 'Frisco, but the heft of it for the Injuns, which is powerful troublesome 'thout they get plenty of truck to read.' "[11] Translation: all this chatter from the East ought to be dumped in the wilderness and forgotten — and so it eventually is, yet not before the weight of so much transhipped language breaks the suspension system of the coach and strands the passengers. But the young Missourian has several more lessons to learn about English discourse as a hazard in this new place. One woman traveler in the coach has been eerily quiet, and when our narrator finally gets a conversation going, he rues the effort:

"What did I understand you to say, madam?"
"You BET!"

Then she cheered up, and faced around and said:

"Danged if I didn't begin to think you fellers was deef and dumb. I did, b'gosh. Here I've sot, and sot, and sot, a-bust'n muskeeters and wondering what was ailin' ye. Fust I thot you was deef and dumb, then I thot you was sick or crazy, or suthin', and then by and by I begin to reckon you was a passel of sickly fools. . . ."

The Sphynx was a Sphynx no more! The fountains of her great deep were broken up, and she rained the nine parts of speech forty days and forty nights, metaphorically speaking, and buried us under a desolating deluge of trivial gossip that left not a crag or pinnacle of rejoinder projecting above the tossing waste of dislocated grammar and decomposed pronunciation! (48–49)

Yet "located" grammar and composed composition menace as well. Along with the ton of word-baggage, an Unabridged Dictionary travels west, the ultimate arbiter and stabilizer of meanings, spellings, and usage. Riding with this thing is dangerous business:

Every time we avalanched from one end of the stage to the other, the Unabridged Dictionary would come too; and every time it came it damaged somebody. One trip it "barked" the Secretary's elbow; the next trip it hurt me in the stomach, and the third it tilted Bemis's nose up till he could look down his nostrils — he said. The pistols and coin soon settled to the bottom, but the pipes, pipe-stems, tobacco and canteens clattered and floundered after the Dictionary every time it made an assault on us, and aided and abetted the book by spilling tobacco in our eyes, and water down our backs. (58)

In a symbol-reading of *Roughing It,* sport can be had with this cluster of episodes.[12] If going westward in the right psychological trim means being ready for anything (which includes being ready for *nothing*) then the rules of discourse itself must go out the window, the too-stable civilized world's authoritative spellings, definitions, and constrictions on words and speech and the identities we concoct from them all. Liberation achieved then, by casting out one Emersonian giant, provided one can thereafter keep talking, make some kind of sense, and not let words themselves become a tormenting anarchy, a pestilential, "decomposed" composition.

In the Wild West of *Roughing It,* liberation from confinements of cultural identity seems easier than in the lands of *The Innocents Abroad*. In the Nevada Territory, breathtaking freedom and self-renewal can be had almost for the asking; the problem, as this liberated Mark Twain realizes at the start of a later chapter, is "What to do next?" *The Innocents Abroad* and *Roughing It* make interesting opposites in broader ways: the earlier book is about keeping free, psychologically and culturally, under the pressure of Continental history, artifact, and lore, free from all the architectural, artistic, and literary bric-a-brac that threatens not merely to encumber but overwhelm and petrify any American self that too worshipfully comes calling. The implicit danger of traveling to Europe reverently is twofold: one can be prostrated or grotesquely Europeanized by the experience, but to resist overmuch is to be too confirmed as a Yankee barbarian, the "American Vandal" whom Mark Twain thought of naming in the title of the book.[13] Either route leads to trouble; the psychological and literary magic prevail only by succumbing neither to reverence nor to barbarism. In *Roughing It* the necessary magic could be called Life After the Unabridged Dictionary. The trick lies in sustaining some sort of identity on abridged and overhauled principles, or perhaps on no principle at all, except ripeness to change everything, down to the deepest roots of selfhood, should new experience confound old cultural habits, or common sense, or any premise on which identity is elsewhere defined. In both of these books, however, special pleasures of Mark Twain's narrative involve his representation of complex, American-style ambivalence about what we now ambivalently call "Western Civ.," meaning officially sanctioned culture, Great Books, manners, art, public solemnities, and established values. It seems wrong to read such ambivalence as no more than vulgarian resentment of the unknown or the refined, for Mark Twain's accounts offer something much more interesting: a many-sided uncertainty about how a grand style and grand formulations have to do with our being ourselves.

To raid Emerson once more: one urgency in both *The Innocents Abroad* and *Roughing It* is to escape carrying ruins to ruins, to shed old confinements of mind *before* engaging with mind-traps and soul-seductions in new places. It has been argued that a strategy in *The Innocents Abroad* is to invent and enact the American tourist, and not be the pilgrim that Mark Twain's traveling contemporaries frequently became; to maintain a free, improvisatory, playful dialogue with the shrines of the Old

World, avoiding the called-for and stifling reverence as much as possible.[14] In making that case, it has also been said that achieving such absolute freedom means moving from voice to voice in narrative, putting on masks and dropping them again, trying on for size moral stances and rhetorical strategies, yet spotlighting always this business of trying on, of make-believe, of masquerades not merely to keep Old Europe at a safe distance, but also to make it a stage, a vast, musty dressing room to raid for moods, perceptions, and demeanors. Mark Twain's crucial decision to do away with Mr. Brown, the fictitious gruff sidekick whom Mark Twain had leaned on heavily in the Sandwich Island letters and some of the *Quaker City* correspondence to the *Alta*, was a move in the same direction. It was a move toward narrative freedom — and possibly narrative chaos. Brown's drearily consistent personality may have offered comfort to a young writer, a way to foist contrarian views on a somebody-else, and speak with one voice and personality himself while indulging in contradictions and huge changes of mind.[15] Yet there could be no such comfort without confinement; Brown had to go if Mark Twain were to represent, and as a narrative presence *risk,* engagement between a consummately settled antique culture and a supremely unsettled American self.

whistling in the graveyard

A general premise, then, about *The Innocents Abroad:* this agon between a free-floating identity and the psychological and cultural pressure of the Old World is played out page by page in this long narrative; if in one place Mark Twain escapes seduction or demanded reverence, in others he seems to succumb, yet then bounce back to that condition of readiness, neither reverent nor heretical, neither indifferent nor abjectly enthusiastic, in which he functions so well as our proxy. A generalization like that has value only if it adds resonance to major and favorite motifs in this book, or clarifies what happens thematically and stylistically when this self-styled American traveler finds himself in a tight place, as a transformer of this pilgrimage and a teller of its story. But the thought does have such heartening ramifications.

For the tourist and the narrator, plenty of difficult moments come up along the way eastward, and rising tension over the course of the book is generated by the itinerary itself, as laid out in the first chapter, and by a sequence of spirited evasions of both seriousness and cynicism. The *Quaker City* was on a wavering, fitfully hedonistic pilgrimage, but a pilgrimage it was nonetheless. One hundred and fifty Christian Americans were on their way to one contemplation that threatened to shut down the imaginative free play of any American tourist, and also perhaps the very act of verbal representation.

We can join this tour at two of its jokes, one of which comes fairly early, the other quite late. The two most famous comic sequences in the book, widely quoted and cartooned in Mark Twain's lifetime and after, have complex connections to each other and to this essential conflict between high-cultural experience and the self that refuses to keep still. The "Is he dead?" running gag in the Italy chapters became a Mark Twain trademark, so thoroughly that he reports being teased with it in exotic places when he toured the world thirty years after.[16] At the risk of spoiling the laughter with explication, it is worth pausing to think about the strategy here and, cautiously, about the meaning, for "meaning" is one of those stifling cultural habits that Mark Twain and his companion "Boys" of the *Quaker City* are sated with and out to overthrow. Europe and its pompous guides want reverence for whatever they point out; after retaliating with gape-mouthed idiocy, the Boys light on the perfect way to exasperate them:

> We use it always, when we can think of nothing else to say. After they have exhausted their enthusiasm pointing out to us and praising the beauties of some ancient bronze image or broken-legged statue, we look at it stupidly and in silence for five, ten, fifteen minutes — as long as we can hold out, in fact — and then ask:
>
> "Is — is he dead?"
>
> That conquers the serenest of them. (232–33)

The gambit is the classic backwoods strategy of playing stupid, of frustrating the learned, intrusive outsider and thereby protecting the self and the invaded community (and concealing in the process the depths of one's own ignorance). Ferguson the Guide, no matter what nationality he might be in any episode, cannot "make out," as Henry James would say, these Americans whom he is paid to herd around, cannot tell whether anything he has to say will register with them or inspire the wonder he requires from them. As a continuing joke, "Is he dead?" fits the patterns of Brackman's put-on: erasure of identity for the sake of confounding or ridiculing someone else — which is ridicule, not satire, because no recourse, no alternative conduct or point of view, is hinted in the game of "guying the guides."

But is that really the case? Could there be some echo in "Is he dead?" when the question is spoken aloud, over a " 'Gyptian mummy," a bust of "The Great Christopher Columbo," or only in the mind before the ravaged corpse of a monk in a Capuchin ossuary? Perhaps several harmonics can be heard, and a kind of wisdom inherent in the all-weather response of these self-styled Yankee fools. If Simon Wheeler intends, possibly, to teach his nameless, schedule-happy visitor lessons about time, or about getting mired in business, in Eastern-style expectations, or in meanings and identities, then this "Is he dead?" motif might have something to it as well, an implication if not a full-blown meaning. For instance, this sanctified relic before us, on the pedestal or in the glass coffin: Is it in fact "dead" as a cultural artifact, imaginatively unenterable, and of no consequence for the living, especially for these Americans with their own culture to accumulate, yet also keep at a safe imaginative distance? Does the inane question suggest that ancient or otherwise, the dead and the ruins of Europe or anywhere else *never* have valid claim on the mind of the living? Huck Finn stops caring about the Moses story because he "don't take no stock in dead people," a judgment that at the opening of Huck's own tale seems absurdly brusque, and yet sensible and promising, a hint that the story that Huck himself will tell shall escape from the sacred, burdensome literary past. The Boys of *The Quaker City* are Huck's American cousins, and eventually they will have a nephew named Ezra Pound. Always launched at the bewildered Fergusons, the consummately inane "Is he dead?" question might be darkly wise, and from more perspectives than one. Out beyond the inert facts, measurements, remembered dates and calculations of centuries lapsed, this bust, this wrapped dead thing or piece of parchment is only dubiously alive, as a signifier, even to Ferguson himself as a living European. Battered books and a few gross of broken statues: Do they matter truly to these Continental Fergusons, and to the European identity except as a way to make money by astounding the Yankee tourists? What "stock" *should* a living culture take in its own dead people? And to try wringing the question all the way out: Is *Ferguson* dead? Is there a human being present at all before these bored tourists, a personality capable of feeling or spontaneity, capable of being something more than a walking Baedeker, always offering the conventional relic and the culturally correct response? Ferguson's frustration, his anguish, may not be unkindly afflicted. One inference is that these deadpan jokes do him a favor, in a backhanded way. They may redeem *this* day, this tour, from the grey routine of all others, air and confirm whatever spontaneous emotions he actually has down within, humanizing him and the programmed experience of the guided visit.

A grandiose finish to a speculation — if only the speculation could finish there! Tidy as it might be to stop a chain reaction of implications at this point, it can whirl onward. Europe's questionable dead are a much heavier presence in *The Innocents Abroad* than this recurring joke in the galleries of Italy; if "Is he dead?" highlights some unsettled business between the old culture and these pilgrims to it, then the problem seems to show up almost everywhere in the narrative. The ghosts that haunt Europe's galleries and crypts are not simply of its antique dead. Intellectual and cultural ghosts of other sorts squeak and gibber in the streets of Venice, Rome, Paris, and the agon of travel requires that they be kept at a distance, lest these pilgrims and tourists fall too much into their thrall.

Very much alive and at the peak of his cultural influence in the 1860s and 1870s, John Ruskin had become one such wraith to reckon with. Our narrator seems to have as much imaginative trouble with diluted and popularized Ruskinism on his rambles through Venice and Rome as this Mark Twain does with morgue corpses, mummies, grinning skulls, or "dead and dried up monks."[17] But the core of the trouble is much the same: a trouble with somber, mind-fixing contemplations, the closing-in of the ever-shadowing giant. *The Stones of Venice* and Ruskin's other great essays of a quarter-century previous, essays that had been crucial in restoring respect for the art and spirituality of the High Middle Ages, had also reenergized the Grand Tour and the conservation of crumbling cathedrals, and spawned an industry of Fergusonian art-history pundits. The passionate insights of a younger Ruskin spoiled into guidebook dogma, and dictated what was to be seen and *not* seen when "doing" an antique city. In Ruskin's brilliance, Pater, Millais, Morris, Henry Adams, and Proust may have had been nurtured, but the pop-cultural effect was ritualized obliviousness to three hundred years of Renaissance craftsmanship, an art and architecture that to an American laity seemed livelier, better executed, more accessible imaginatively, and in much better condition:

It seems to me that whenever I glory to think that for once I have discovered an ancient painting that is beautiful and worthy of all praise, the pleasure it gives me is an infallible proof that it is *not* a beautiful picture and not in any wise worthy of commendation. This very thing has occurred more times than I can mention in Venice. In every single instance the guide has crushed out my swelling enthusiasm with the remark:

"It is nothing — it is of the *Renaissance*."

I did not know what in the mischief the Renaissance was, and so always I had to simply say:

"Ah! so it is — I had not observed it before."

I could not bear to be ignorant before a cultivated negro, the offspring of a South Carolina slave. But it occurred too often for even my self-complacency, did that exasperating "It is nothing — it is of the *Renaissance*." I said at last:

"*Who* is this Renaissance? Where did he come from? Who gave him permission to cram the Republic with his execrable daubs?"

We learned, then, that Renaissance was not a man; that *renaissance* was a term used to signify what was at best but an imperfect rejuvenation of art. The guide said that after Titian's time and the time of the other great names we had grown so familiar with, high art declined; then it partially rose again — an inferior sort of painters sprang up, and these shabby pictures were the work of their hands. Then I said, in my heat, that I "wished to goodness high art had declined five hundred years sooner." (189)

Walter Pater's one-man renaissance of the Renaissance for Anglo-American readers — a revival that turned loose yet more culture-ghosts for the true nonpilgrim to fend off — had not begun to sway its public when Mark Twain came to Rome,[18] but Michelangelo, or rather Michelangelism, had no need of Ruskin or Pater. If Mark Twain's Rome, Florence, Pisa, and other towns are portrayed at times as haunted mansions, then Michelangelo is the chief haunter, raised to that status by ghastly conventions of gaping and worshiping:

But I do not want Michel Angelo for breakfast — for luncheon — for dinner — for tea — for supper — for between meals. I like a change, occasionally. In Genoa, he designed every thing; in Milan he or his pupils designed every thing; he designed the Lake of Como; in Padua, Verona, Venice, Bologna, who did we ever hear of, from guides, but Michel Angelo? In Florence, he painted every thing, designed every thing, nearly, and what he did not design he used to sit on a favorite stone and look at, and they showed us the stone. . . . But here — here it is frightful. He designed St. Peter's; he designed the Pope; he designed the Pantheon, the uniform of the Pope's soldiers, the Tiber, the Vatican, the Coliseum, the Capitol, the Tarpeian Rock, the Barberini Palace, St, John Lateran, the Campagna, the Appian Way, the Seven Hills, the Baths of Caracalla, the Claudian Aqueduct, the Cloaca Maxima — the eternal bore designed the Eternal City, and unless all men and books do lie, he painted every thing in it! Dan said the other day to the guide, "Enough, enough, enough! Say no more! Lump the whole thing! say that the Creator made Italy from designs by Michel Angelo!"

I never felt so fervently thankful, so soothed, so tranquil, so filled with a blessed peace, as I did yesterday when I learned that Michel Angelo was dead. (227–28)

The culminating joke in this passage is not only multiedged but delightfully destabilizing. Our narrator's ignorance, funny for its dimensions, is also funny as a source of vertigo, as "real" grand-scale ignorance revealed behind that *feigned* preposterous ignorance that Mark Twain and the Boys have used to gull the guides. But the tremor of this "discovery," that Michelangelo is dead, registers at farther removes, because as a discovery it cannot be "real." Or can it? Can our narrator have possibly *not* known, as an English-speaking adult writing a travel account, that Michelangelo is long since dead and gone? Is it possible that this "representative" of ours has believed for a moment, or has heard from some Italian Simon Wheeler, that Michelangelo designed Lake Como, the Tiber, and the Coliseum? Or is this free-floating joke not only profoundly ridiculous but also in a sense profound: that this special case that the Old World would make of Michelangelo, as a human being dead yet *not* gone, is fundamentally another lie, and that for all the paint and stone he laid upon the face of Italy, Michelangelo, or rather this cult of Michelangelism, is most wisely comprehended as something finished indeed, dead as any other Old World artifact held up for veneration? The narrator, the guide, the official line on Michelangelo, and the true makers and origins of all these places, are all plunged into question, and along with them the killing idea that one name or word explains or stabilizes anything, that nothing in Michelangelo's legacy can be faced without wordless reverence, and that spontaneous, untutored aesthetic experience must always be humbled.

If there were cause to tally the ghosts and the dead in *The Innocents Abroad,* this could be a beginning, but only that; and the hunt would stretch onward through other travel books Mark Twain completed. Even if we discount cultural ghosts, Walter Scottism, Byronism, and Ruskinism, all of which seem to block the way of the *Quaker City* adventurers, this narrative fixation about the real dead, about corpses, morgues, charnel houses, funeral practices — the more macabre the better — rattles loud in *Life on the Mississippi* and *Following the Equator* as well, and sounds in both *Roughing It* and the later chapters of *A Tramp Abroad.* Historicist explanations are easy to reach for: Victorian morbidity, leftover romantic sensationalism, bourgeois self-gratifications in a time-out to contemplate Yorick's skull, the genteel graveyard-love that Mark Twain satirized early and late in his career, but that, as a full-blown citizen of his time, he could indulge in wholeheartedly. If none of these diagnoses seems quite right, more interesting possibilities turn up when a few patterns are skeptically observed. For instance, the unburied, moldering dead are usually offered as an exotic experience. To see them and smell their pollution one has to go overseas, up into high mountains or down into caverns, downriver to the alien world of New Orleans, or into digressive tales-within-a-tale. Implications suggest themselves, that expand and perhaps validate this theme glimpsed in *The Innocents Abroad:* cultures that will not put dead folk hygienically away cannot be trusted in their valuation of other old things — old paintings, statues, religions, furniture, folk practices, philosophy. In other words, this cult of the dead that Mark Twain delights in finding in Roman Catholic shrines in France, Italy, and the Holy Land, lets him cast empowering American Protestant suspicion on everything else he must contemplate, as possible symptoms of the same cultural perversity.

So far so good, yet thematic consistency of that sort does nothing to explain the surprise, freshness, and strangeness of the humor that often crops up on these excursions, running counter to Mark Twain's impulse, as traveler and writer, *not* to become something stuck in viewpoints and themes. If there is ghoulish voyeurism in some of these episodes, then what are the dynamics of ghoulishness? Summary judgments about what the dead signify in Mark Twain's travel accounts have to wait awhile. First we need to look at the special role which these graveside and corpse-side ruminations play in *The Innocents Abroad.* They both intensify and evade the conflict that announces itself in the book's opening chapter. And they embed suspense within the comedy and serendipity of the book's first half.

The conflict, the reckoning, is announced and underscored in the first three sentences of the first chapter:

> For months the great Pleasure Excursion to Europe and the Holy Land was chatted about in the newspapers every where in America, and discussed at countless firesides. It was a novelty in the way of Excursions — its like had not been thought of before, and it compelled that interest which attractive novelties always command. It was to be a picnic on a gigantic scale. (17)

The Holy Land as "pleasure excursion," as "novelty" and as picnic on a grand scale: Kafka in "The Metamorphosis" does not give away his conflict and his own narrative dilemma more quickly. Kafka's problem is what to do for an encore, once he has turned his protagonist into a giant insect in the story's first sentence. Mark Twain's problem is how to make a "picnic," a pleasure-*book,* out of a voyage that bends always toward the gravest of graves in Western cultural experience. If the giant cannot catch Mark Twain at the Paris Morgue, at Père Lachaise Cemetery, or at the bier of "dead Borromeo," it waits for him at journey's end. William C. Prime, the sentimental and notorious "Grimes" whom Mark Twain ridicules so frequently in the last quarter of *The Innocents Abroad,* knew perfectly well where every such trip by an English-speaking Christian writer had to arrive. Here is the opening half-sentence of his *Tent Life in the Holy Land:*

> To see the sun go down beyond the Sepulchre and rise over the mountain of the Ascension, to bare my forehead to the cold dews of Gethsemane, and lave my dim eyes in the waters of Siloam, to sleep in the company of the infinite host above the oaks of Mamre . . .[19]

Because the Church of the Holy Sepulchre is the omega point of dead-serious Christian traveling, and the uncontestable dominion of pilgrims, a countdown is ticking in *The Innocents Abroad* as Mark Twain, "the Boys," and "the pilgrims" scramble up lovely hillsides, wander plazas, and look at other tombs or into withered faces of the undivine dead. For though these European excursions have pleasures and scares of their own, they are also a kind of warm-up, for narrator and for reader alike: rhetorical and psychological practice-sessions for a traumatic and inevitable main event. Jerusalem's empty tomb is out there to the east as a catastrophe — for Mark Twain as humorist, as a putative Yankee Christian, as a word-created identity, and as an evasion of identity.

Not only will confrontation with Christianity's holiest places defy comedy of any stripe; it will force a crisis between the humorist-barbarian and his own spirituality, a discourse in which his reverence and his wild irreverence, swinging in and out of the narrative up to the Palestine chapters, must parlay and reconcile, and the anarchic free spirit must either be abjured, disgraced, or enigmatically merged with the pious Christian. If buoyant skepticism is paradoxically both resistance to the Old World culture *and* a species of imaginative access into it, then the ultimate skeptical question, lurking in every visited morgue, cemetery, ossuary, royal tomb, or saint's reliquary, is not "Is he dead?" but rather something like "Shall these bones live?" Is the controlling faith of the Old World and the New founded on truth, and is the culture, as an extension of the faith, alive somehow, in its bric-a-brac of veneration? Or is everything, whether cluttered or no, only one vast empty crypt?

For the self-conscious tourist or the comic narrative, such a question is not to be faced for the first time in the caverns of the supreme shrine. There are special reasons, therefore, why *The Innocents Abroad* whistles and elegizes through so many graveyards before the *Quaker City* travelers come to the Near East. Aside from putting the narrator through rhetorical and imaginative calisthenics before the big event, this sequence may give Mark Twain a firmer right to profess exhaustion or numbness in Jerusalem, as he eventually does just when circumstances seem to call for immense response. If the Holy Sepulchre is the last in a succession of tombs, or to borrow from Bryant, is one more spot in the vast sepulchre and brotherhood of death, then the effect is not to trivialize either Jerusalem or its Tomb, but rather to rob them of their menace to this "record of a pleasure trip." A larger context has been laid: the mystery of Jesus' resurrection is subsumed into mysteries more vast, the mortality and consequence of every human life. Even so, if exhaustion is Mark Twain's best hope, and perhaps his only recourse, when he reaches the Holy Land, then that exhaustion has to be earned, and the saturation of earlier chapters with tombside contemplations does much to wear out that rhetorical mode.

All of which would make Mark Twain out as a cagey stylist maneuvering around a subject he has to talk about but very much wants to avoid. Such a professional gambit, though repeatedly in evidence here, need not obstruct more compassionate reading, or at least a speculation that Mark Twain's unshakable interest in graves and the dead, which takes an unexpected and wonderful turn in the midst of the Church of the Holy Sepulcher, and in the slough of his Holy Land weariness, comes from some deeper layer of the man than the cool professional satirist. If these are stylistic warm-ups, tactics to buffer or defuse an approaching and potentially explosive reckoning, then they may also rise from a born skeptic's doubt about doubt, an anxiety that all belief systems might be founded upon the dead and gone, that the self and the culture face unmanageable dangers if such doubts are given full voice.

The cadenza on Père Lachaise Cemetery and its ornate new tomb for Héloïse and Abelard is a case in point, a commentary in which burlesque fuses with exhilaration, and perhaps with a dram of fear. Exhumed after six hundred years and carted to Père Lachaise to be the main attraction and validation of the new city graveyard, Héloïse and Abelard had buttressed centuries of French and English sentimental poetry and fiction, as Arthur and Guinevere supported a Victorian industry of English chivalric romance. And so a swipe at the myth of these medieval lovers is a blow at a literary practice of considerable scale and consequence, and an emotional habit or indulgence that involved English poet laureates and American back-country schoolrooms. But there are darker implications to Mark Twain's burlesque, and he gives them an uneasy sideward glance as he begins:

> But among the thousands and thousands of tombs in Père la Chaise, there is one that no man, no woman, no youth of either sex, ever passes by without stopping to examine. Every visitor has a sort of indistinct idea of the history of its dead, and comprehends that homage is due there, but not one in twenty thousand clearly remembers the story of that tomb and its romantic occupants. This is the grave of Abelard and Heloise — *a grave which has been more revered, more widely known, more written and sung about and*

> *wept over, for seven hundred years, than any other in Christendom, save only that of the Saviour.* All visitors linger pensively about it; all young people capture and carry away keepsakes and mementos of it; all Parisian youths and maidens who are disappointed in love come there to bail out when they are full of tears; yea, many stricken lovers make pilgrimages to this shrine from distant provinces to weep and wail and "grit" their teeth over their heavy sorrows, and to purchase the sympathies of the chastened spirits of that tomb with offerings of immortelles and budding flowers. (112, emphasis added)

This is a Holy Sepulchre of love, the heart of the cemetery, an altar around which the greats of modern French culture are laid out in rank and row. If the tomb of these two love-legends is a cenotaph to a lie, if Peter Abelard, whose name signifies to the pilgrim mind an ideal blending of passion, intellect, Christian piety, and self-sacrifice, was in truth a deceitful, philandering cleric who very much needed gelding, then the whole landscape hereabouts is shivered, for a moment, as a place to venerate or even regard: this sacred cultural shrine, and Paris, and the other glories of France, and centuries of sentimental literature, and perhaps reverence and sentiment itself.

But these are only tremors. Nothing is really cast down and nothing is set up in its place, because just here the satire takes its unexpected and delicious turn, justifying the pages this narrator has spent grumbling at the Héloïse–Abelard myth and its variance from historical fact. The narrative seems coiled to strike at Victorian sentimentality, but doesn't. Instead, the text makes a show of conserving and even honoring sentiment by ludicrously diverting its course, "bailing out" Twain's tear-floods on people who, to his thinking, really deserve them:

> The historian says:
> "Ruffians, hired by Fulbert, fell upon Abelard by night, and inflicted upon him a terrible and nameless mutilation."
> I am seeking the last resting-place of those "ruffians." When I find it I shall shed some tears on it, and stack up some bouquets and immortelles and cart away from it some gravel whereby to remember that howsoever blotted by crime their lives may have been, these ruffians did one just deed, at any rate, albeit it was not warranted by the strict letter of the law. (115)

If this is the best joke in the episode, it is also in a sense no joke at all, because it suggests a psychological truth, and fulfills emotional and cultural needs that must "out" one way or another. If weeping for Abelard means grieving for a very bad sort, then visitors here, be they pilgrims or tourist "boys," must find somebody else to mourn, because doing so allows what they may really intend in coming to this place: to shed tears for themselves. If shrines prove false and saints or love-saints are not worth those tears, then all the more reason to wail. Our narrator mourns for these "ruffians" as one of their lot, having himself gelded the almost-sacred myth of Héloïse and Abelard, which, though it may have needed undoing, leaves an empty place in the mythology, an unsatisfiable desire, and a cause for mourning. There may be more afoot in this passage than ridicule for millions who grieve over genteel, sanctimonious lies. The satire whirls with a touch of celebration, and a touch of standard Victorian melancholy, about that unquenchable drive to worship and to grieve, a drive which may outlast any earthly subject we can find to revere.

Yet vertigo, not thematic contrivance, is the essence of this moment: in dislocation there is comedy, and also a measure of safety. Significations here are pollinated, yet not entirely ripe — which is perhaps for the best, at the *second* holiest spot in Christendom. Père Lachaise is a rehearsal for the main event, in which the narrator, at a tomb that cannot be questioned, enacts his funniest, most dizzying *détournement* of feelings mandated by his context and his culture, yet unleashed by his own *in*ability to feel on cultural demand.

The Tomb of Adam joke, which is only a few paragraphs long, is so famous as to be frequently lifted from *The Innocents Abroad* and published in collections. Contemporary illustrations of the moment — Mark Twain in a daze or bawling over a slab marked "Adam" in a stone floor — helped introduce the world to Mark Twain's public face and skillful outrageousness. His maneuvering had to be deft here: the weary tourist has finally come into the tightest of places. Through hundreds of pages, Mark Twain and the boys have gazed at bones, bodies, and occupied tombs, and made jokes or scoffed or merely moved on to the next exhibit. Now, however, he must look into the ultimate Empty Tomb, and believe, or contrive to do something that can stand in the place of an expression of fervent belief. I have suggested that *The Innocents Abroad*'s preliminary bouts with corpses and tombs have been practice for this event, and a process of inuring narrative and reader for its onset: cause has been offered for Mark Twain to sound exhausted and numb, "tombed-out," as it were, when he comes to the most important place in Christendom. The moment is buffered before and after with catatonic visits to a flood of other holy places. And as a sort of benediction to the Holy Land adventures, the narrative offers this bit of wisdom about the motions of the mind:

> We do not think, in the holy places; we think in bed, afterwards, when the glare, and the noise, and the confusion are gone, and in fancy we revisit alone, the solemn monuments of the past, and summon the phantom pageants of an age that has passed away. (482)

Nonetheless, a compounded and paradoxical suspense has risen by the time the narrator reaches the site of the Resurrection: a need to be funny, and a dire need to *feel*. Having spent fifty chapters developing the agon between the tourists and the pilgrims, and siding almost always with the tourists, he has to act as one or the other now, with the crisis upon him. The Père Lachaise troubles return like a storm: the holy places of the Holy Land may be ruined, as emotional, spiritual, and literary experiences, by tawdry ornament, sectarian rivalry, trumpery, greed, and the published hyperbole of other travelers;[20] yet comic or no, in Mark Twain's own narrative something has to be thought and felt about this place, and right *there*, not in bed afterward. With reason, the site of the Crucifixion, within the walls of the same Church, moves Mark Twain more than does the Tomb, because the place of such a catastrophe would be, he thinks, reliably remembered—and because this Mark Twain can at least believe in death. As he makes his tour to the Church's other "places," he does journeyman work as a reporter to a nineteenth-century Protestant audience, impugning the lore and bric-a-brac of the Catholic and Eastern rites, yet affirming his "absorbing interest" in what would matter most to readers at home:

> All about the apartment the gaudy trappings of the Greek Church offend the eye and keep the mind on the rack to remember that this is the Place of the Crucifixion—Golgotha—the Mount of Calvary. And the last thing he looks at is that which was also the first—the place where the true cross stood. That will chain him to the spot and compel him to look once more, and once again, after

he has satisfied all curiosity and lost all interest concerning the other matters pertaining to the locality. (457)

Yet as a preliminary, and almost as an aside to his long and moving passage on the site of the Crucifixion, Mark Twain says this too:

> When one enters the Church of the Holy Sepulchre, the Sepulchre itself is the first thing he desires to see, and really is almost the first thing he does see. The next thing he has a strong yearning to see is the spot where the Saviour was crucified. But this they exhibit last. It is the crowning glory of the place. One is grave and thoughtful when he stands in the little Tomb of the Saviour — he could not well be otherwise in such a place — but he has not the slightest possible belief that ever the Lord lay there, and so the interest he feels in the spot is very, very greatly marred by that reflection. He looks at the place where Mary stood, in another part of the church, and where John stood, and Mary Magdalen; where the mob derided the Lord; where the angel sat; where the crown of thorns was found, and the true cross; . . . he looks at all these places with interest, but with the same conviction he felt in the case of the Sepulchre, that there is nothing genuine about them and that they are imaginary holy places created by the monks. But the place of the Crucifixion affects him differently. (454–55)

Fair enough: if this subverts a holy of holies, the subversion is at least not an Abelarding. Furthermore, the moment is compensated or balanced, to some extent by all this about the emotional impact of Calvary. But compensation, balance, and politeness here are strategies for tactful truthtelling that have little to do with the fluidity and autonomy of self, which has been both the life and the agon of *The Innocents Abroad*. The peculiar suspense building in the episode is neither raised nor relieved by such gestures. And so for a flood of reasons the sane, cowed Mark Twain has a cadenza of madness in the middle of the episode, in the middle of the Church, a cadenza that answers and completes the "Is he dead?" question that rattles in the middle of the book. Mark Twain offers an all-out performance of the *detourned* grief that was dress-rehearsed at Père Lachaise, an indulgence of that need to laugh and lament, and momentary escape from both camps, the laughers and the lamenters, the tourists and the pilgrims. The passage is one that Mark Twain zealots know by heart:

The tomb of Adam! How touching it was, here in a land of strangers, far away from home, and friends, and all who cared for me,
thus to discover the grave of a blood relation. True, a distant one,
but still a relation. The unerring instinct of nature thrilled its
recognition. The fountain of my filial affection was stirred to its
profoundest depths, and I gave way to tumultuous emotion. I
leaned upon a pillar and burst into tears. I deem it no shame to
have wept over the grave of my poor dead relative. Let him who
would sneer at my emotion close this volume here, for he will find
little to his taste in my journeyings through Holy Land. Noble old
man — he did not live to see me — he did not live to see his child.
And I — I — alas, I did not live to see *him*. Weighed down by sorrow
and disappointment, he died before I was born — six thousand
brief summers before I was born. But let us try to bear it with
fortitude. (451–52)

The dislocations here are more interesting than as histrionics at a
grave next door to the one that matters. In his fervor Mark Twain
eradicates history, erases not just intervening ages but the direction
and ground rules of time itself. Mark Twain mourns Adam first as a
blood relation; a second later Adam is close family, and a half-second
after that he is Mark Twain's father. But then the line "I — I — alas, I did
not live to see *him*" turns the whole bogus and chaotic relationship
upside down, and Mark Twain becomes something like *Adam's* father.
The rebel outbreak here seems not merely against the mythology of
Genesis. As the longest-dead of all the dead people whom this expedi-
tion has been mounted to venerate, Adam signifies either the founda-
tion stone or the pinnacle (depending on Mark Twain's whim) of a
crushing accumulation of history, of tradition — and from an American Protestant perspective, the father of Original Sin, informing and
jeopardizing the soul of every human being yet alive. Mark Twain has
turned his Adam into the first of those lovable, mournable brother
ruffians, the perpetrator of the "terrible and nameless mutilation"
that Jesus Christ came to heal, the sin that both damned and freed the
human race. And this moment of lament, supercharged with comedy,
with poignancy, and with displaced or misplaced catharsis, stays exquisitely uncertain. Does our proxy weep foolishly or wisely? Selfishly,
or for us all? Does he weep indeed on the sacred spot, or only afterward in bed? Or does this moment constitute another of those (possi-

ble) put-ons, disrupting the covenants of written narrative and mythologies that loom over everyday American life, including a myth that
satire must be bounded, sensible, and clear?

a cure for the truth

Though *The Innocents Abroad* moves on to other adventures, the Tomb
of Adam moment is a culminating subversion in the book, when everything seems laughed and mourned into question, even the questioning of reverence and cultural authority. In *Roughing It* a moment that
parallels this one, at once culminating a process and discovering that
this process is absurd, comes in chapter 53, shortly before the quitting
place in one popular and respectable edition of the book (critics have
tended to dismiss most of the material after chapter 55).[21] The advice
seems reasonable, for the Old Ram story, which like the Tomb of
Adam has been endlessly reprinted as a comic *geste* in itself, climaxes
our narrator's education, and most of what follows Jim Blaine's story is
borrowed from Sandwich Island letters to the *Alta California*. Working
as a reporter-comedian for the Virginia City *Enterprise,* our narrator
remembers being rushed to the cabin of a miner who is, at that rare
and lucky moment, "tranquilly, serenely, symmetrically drunk" and in
prime shape to tell the ram story, which has mysteriously become a
Washoe legend. What this Mark Twain does not know, and what makes
him the dupe of the evening, is that the tale's fame lies in the fact that
it never gets told, that this is a narrative to end all narratives because it
defies logic, obeys no rules, goes everywhere except to its own conclusion — and that only a "sucker," in the insane world of the American
West, would be such a fool as to expect stories to have anything to do
with linearity, form, or common sense:

> The tears were running down the boys' cheeks — they were suffo-
> cating with suppressed laughter — and had been from the start,
> though I had never noticed it. I perceived that I was "sold." I
> learned then that Jim Blaine's peculiarity was that whenever he
> reached a certain stage of intoxication, no human power could
> keep him from setting out, with impressive unction, to tell about
> a wonderful adventure which he had once had with his grand-
> father's old ram — and the mention of the ram in the first sen-
> tence was as far as any man had ever heard him get, concerning it.

He always maundered off, interminably, from one thing to another, till his whiskey got the best of him and he fell asleep. What
the thing was that happened to him and his grandfather's old ram
is a dark mystery to this day, for nobody has ever yet found out.
(348–49)

The nonstory resonates wonderfully with the account of the trip
west in the stagecoach, lessons in the oppressiveness of eastern-style
words, definitions, and rules, but also in the dangers of discourse
without them. An absolute, unnerving freedom was yearned for so
early in this narrative, as the mail broke the thoroughbrace, the dictionary crashed down, and the "sociable heifer" chattered. And this
ram story is the ultimate lesson in how to achieve it. This is one of
those moments when the wonderland of *Roughing It* seems complete,
when even narrative itself is set apart and perfectly free (at least for as
long as this narrator can defend such anarchic freedom), liberated
from all need for continuity, for custom, logic, or the expectations of
even the most agreeable audience. Jim Blaine's story, if it can be called
that, is a joke on Mark Twain as a credulous listener, a joke on us as we
play a parallel role in reading this book, and a parody of the book
itself, this meandering, digressing, all-encompassing "story" that Mark
Twain has been spinning all the while.

Perhaps it should be taken for granted that the Mark Twain who sets
out for the West in *Roughing It,* as secretary to his older brother, is
actively looking for escape into free play and make-believe, quitting
workaday life and seeking adventures for the sheer thrill of having
them. The first paragraph makes that clear: the question is where this
idea of the West comes from, what happens to it in the pages that
follow, and what it does to give *Roughing It* vitality and forward drive, if
not a structure everyone can agree on:

I was young and ignorant, and I envied my brother. I coveted his
distinction and his financial splendor, but particularly and especially the long, strange journey he was going to make, and
the curious new world he was going to explore. He was going to
travel! I never had been away from home, and the word "travel"
had a seductive charm for me. Pretty soon he would be hundreds
and hundreds of miles away on the great plains and deserts, and
among the mountains of the Far West, and would see buffaloes
and Indians, and prairie dogs, and antelopes, and have all kinds
of adventures, and maybe get hanged or scalped, and have ever

such a fine time, and write home and tell us all about it, and be a
hero. (43)

It might be, therefore, that the agon of *Roughing It* originates in the
fantasies of the American audience Mark Twain sought to entertain,
for the initial mood and misconceptions of this young Mark Twain
create a kind of suspense, both for the young adventurer and for this
narrative. There are at least two Mark Twains here, a young traveler
and a reminiscing storyteller. The young man wants unadulterated
freedom, freedom especially from his former self, from conventions of
Eastern life, from the ground rules of life and death in any locale; the
narrator, in the exaggerations and apparent miscellaneousness of
these opening pages, seems to claim a similarly outrageous licence.
What will happen when the "real West" is encountered, when other
men and women are met on the roads and in the mining camps, when
"experience" in its mingled and disillusioning way brings euphoria to
an end, threatens the make-believe and the refusals of this traveler?
Rude awakenings abound in *Roughing It,* and the real West revealed in
its pages is a land of barrenness, banalities, costly mistakes; of mangy
coyotes that can somehow outrun your strongest hound; of dissolute,
apparently harmless Indians who suddenly shapeshift and kill unwary
travelers; of blank but dangerous wilderness, where bad water and
back-alley streams can rise in an instant into killing floods; where gold
and silver strikes can lure supposedly sane people into slaving for years
over worthless rubble. Real life, then, is its usual intractable self. Keeping freedom and make-believe alive in such a place — and a commen-
surate spirit at the center of a book about the West — requires extreme
measures. If the truth will not cooperate it must be forced. If sanity will
not suffice here then sanity must go out the window with the dictionary. Illusions and delusions must prevail as the order of the day, not
just for the young Mark Twain but for the population of the Nevada
Territory. In an early digression, Mark Twain summarizes the mentality that both his West and his narrative depend on: incongruous,
crazy playfulness as a stay against intolerable truth. An older and supposedly wiser author shakes his head over his younger self and a world
left behind — but there is another voice here too, nostalgic for insane
festivity:

> In a small way we were the same sort of simpletons as those who
> climb unnecessarily the perilous peaks of Mont Blanc or the Mat-
> terhorn, and derive no pleasure from it except the reflection that

it isn't a common experience. But once in a while one of these parties trips and comes darting down the long mountain-crags in a sitting posture, making the crusted snow smoke behind him, flitting from bench to bench, and from terrace to terrace, jarring the earth where he strikes, and still glancing and flitting on again, sticking an iceberg into himself now and then, and tearing his clothes, snatching at things to save himself, taking hold of trees and fetching them along with him, roots and all, starting little rocks now and then, then big boulders, then acres of ice and snow and patches of forest, gathering and still gathering as he goes, adding and still adding to his massed and sweeping grandeur as he nears a three-thousand-foot precipice, till at last he waves his hat magnificently and rides into eternity on the back of a raging and tossing avalanche!

This is all very fine, but let us not be carried away by excitement, but ask calmly, how does this person feel about it in his cooler moments next day, with six or seven thousand feet of snow and stuff on top of him? (84–85)

This is the mentality that characterizes the Mark Twain who comes to Nevada, and it also dominates the Nevada he finds. Arrival in Washoe County is arrival in the heart of a collective madness, where in the face of hardships all men are as mad as he. The economy of the Territory depends upon "assays" that preposterously exaggerate the value of mining claims, not just so miners can fool outsiders but so they can keep fooling themselves. Dreams, not gold dust and nuggets, are the currency of Washoe: "feet" in endlessly postponed mining bonanzas take the place of hard cash, and everyone anticipates getting rich on the furious trading of worthless promises. Daily existence is sustained by extravagant fictions, wild lies of gold and silver strikes touted in the newspapers, banks, and saloons. Mark Twain describes a nearby town called Unionville as even crazier than Virginia City, a place of institutionalized make-believe and self-delusion:

It was the strangest phase of life one can imagine. It was a beggars' revel. There was nothing doing in the district — no mining — no milling — no productive effort — no income — and not enough money in the entire camp to buy a corner lot in an Eastern village, hardly; and yet a stranger would have supposed he was walking among bloated millionaires. Prospecting parties swarmed out of

town with the first flush of dawn, and swarmed in again at nightfall laden with spoil — rocks. Nothing but rocks. Every man's pockets were full of them; the floor of his cabin was littered with them;
they were disposed in labeled rows on his shelves. (201–2)

Everything runs on a concerted refusal of truth, and nothing must
be allowed to break the spell and let the other world's values flood in.
As for catastrophes caused by this make-believe and daydreaming, not
even these can be allowed to matter. Soon after Mark Twain reaches
Washoe he goes off on a holiday with one John Kinney, on the pretext
of looking for gold around Lake Tahoe. After some listless prospecting, they stake claim to a wooded hillside along the shore, and give
themselves over to drifting in a boat and dreaming in the marvelous
landscape:

> There, the rocks on the bottom are sometimes grey, sometimes
> white. This gives the marvelous transparency of the water a fuller
> advantage than it has elsewhere on the lake. We usually pushed
> out a hundred yards or so from the shore, and then lay down on
> the thwarts, in the sun, and let the boat drift by the hour whither it
> would. We seldom talked. It interrupted the Sabbath stillness, and
> marred the dreams the luxurious rest and indolence brought.
> (168)

When this luxurious mood allows the campfire to get out of control
and set off a huge blaze on the hillside, Mark Twain and Kinney seek
refuge again on the lake, and watch as their lovely world goes up in
smoke. But in this passage, more striking than its dramatic irony is the
spirit in which Mark Twain takes the lesson — which is to say that he
doesn't take it at all. Like the doomed tourist on the avalanche, he
keeps up a holiday spirit against all sense and an overwhelming truth:
he enjoys the splendor of his disaster, and staring into the waters he
decides that the false image of the fire makes a better show than the
fire itself:

> Every feature of the spectacle was repeated in the glowing mir-
> ror of the lake! Both pictures were sublime, both were beautiful;
> but that in the lake had a bewildering richness about it that en-
> chanted the eye and held it with the stronger fascination.
>   We sat absorbed and motionless through four long hours.
> (170)

If a definable first segment of *Roughing It* resembles *The Innocents Abroad,* as a fun-seeker's passage into an alien culture, then the second part is this entry into a world defiantly suffused with fantasy and the refusal of rules, reason, stabilized identities, and recognition of things as they are. The climax of this second part is the famous "blind lead" episode, which is often read as a transforming experience for young Mark Twain and a turning point in the book;[22] but any transformations here, for the protagonist and the narrative alike, involve some remarkable flips and spins along the way. As a moment in the evolution of a fully and appropriately Western self, this euphoria of feeling rich matters at least as much as the subsequent rude awakening that the claim has been lost. The happy ten days signify that becoming a millionaire in the Wild West is not a matter of cash in the bank or gold in the ground. It is a matter of acting and *thinking* like a millionaire, with greed and obsession giving way, in a flash, to complacent ease. The richest joke in the episode is how quickly the mentality of vast wealth transforms this narrator and his partner Calvin Higbie, how ludicrously they forget about actually mining the gold, and drift off to other "business" as if the money were already in a vault, leaving magisterial notes to each other about getting the work started. And when nobody does the work and the lead is lost, the narrative takes another twist. Neither of the two men seems changed by the loss of their dream-millions; after a few days of mourning and recriminations, they get over the disaster as they would a passing case of the flu. The abyss of materialist identity has opened under Mark Twain's feet and threatened to swallow him up; paradoxically, however, becoming rich in a daydream has ruined the opportunity, forestalled fate, and left him poor but free, to try other "leads" for inventing or discovering an identity. Though Mark Twain and his partners in the "Monarch of the Mountains" (as they pretentiously name their strike) learn that the route to success is literally rockier then they had imagined, there is no pretending that a rude awakening cures this tenderfoot of delusions, or of a preference for never-lands over real ones.

What happens, rather, is that the Mark Twain of *Roughing It* is cured of notions like "reality" and "truth."

In a territory of childlike men, make-believe is not merely a sanctioned indulgence, but also a paying job in the public interest. The next phase of *Roughing It* is about Mark Twain becoming a guardian of those illusions that sustain the territory. The chapter after the blind-lead episode is called "What to do Next?" — a question Mark Twain answers by signing on as a reporter for the Virginia City *Enterprise*. True to how things go in Washoe, he wins the job not by reporting, not by demonstrating respect for facts and their accurate conveyance to a public, but by writing humorous letters as a way, he tells us, of amusing himself. In the Territory, reporting is the plausible telling of "stretchers"; a newspaper here is only as good as the lies it can make this world believe. The upside-down hierarchies of lies and fact are clear in the pep talk that editor Joe Goodman gives to his staff, and what follows when the new recruit sets out to live the creed:

> "Never say 'We learn' so-and-so, or 'It is reported,' or 'It is rumored,' or 'We understand' so-and-so, but go to headquarters and get the absolute facts, and then speak out and say 'It *is* so-and-so.' Otherwise, people will not put confidence in your news. Unassailable certainty is the thing that gives a newspaper the firmest and most valuable reputation." (268)

"I moralize well," says our narrator in paying homage to Goodman's values, "but I did not always practise well when I was a city editor." Actually he practices like a master. For life at the *Enterprise* soon makes clear what Joe Goodman actually means: settle not for pallid half-truths, but work them into full-blown, full-color dreams and lies. Nobody, not even on this newspaper, has any use for reality unless reality happens to match the dream-stuff that the world is made of. As a curator of public make-believe, Mark Twain's first venture is cautious, on a day when nothing is going on; and Goodman suggests that he try once more, with imagination in high gear:

> I canvassed the city again and found one wretched old hay truck dragging in from the country. But I made affluent use of it. I multiplied it by sixteen, brought it into town from sixteen different directions, made sixteen separate items out of it, and got up such another sweat about hay as Virginia City had never seen in the world before. (268)

He gets the hang of it, pumping up a barroom murder and inventing out of nothing "an Indian fight that to this day has no parallel in history." Joe Goodman hails his new recruit as a model journalist, as worthy as their veteran reporter Dan DeQuille — the paper's champion liar nicknamed "The Unreliable" and a master of practical jokes.

Everyone in the *Enterprise* newsroom is a prankster as well as a story-teller; practical joking seems to take as much professional time as con-cocting "news" for public good. Pranks highlight the Washoe chapters hereafter, and if the Old Ram experience proves to be Mark Twain's ultimate lesson in how much must be given up for membership in this crazy community and for preservation of the crazy freedom it affirms, then the community's strategy of practical jokes against outsiders and newcomers tells a similar story. It seems that the entire town of Carson City conspires in gulling a too-sane, too-rational, too-civilized outsider named General Buncombe. "Now the older citizens of a new Terri-tory," Mark Twain comments, "look upon the rest of the world with a calm, benevolent expression, as long as it keeps out of the way — when it gets in the way they snub it. Sometimes this latter takes the shape of a practical joke" (224). A lawyer and a sophisticated Easterner, this Buncombe is a perfect target for a frontier-styled overthrow. For in Washoe, what must be stopped before it spreads is systematic thinking, the menacing possibility that rules, precedents, syllogisms, cultural institutions and common sense from the outside world will conquer a land that flourishes upon their very absence. Like the ram story, the "Great Landslide Case," which undoes Buncombe, has a complex ef-fect. It brings townspeople together against an unbeliever. It shows this outsider that fundamental rules of real life have to be forgotten in this new place. And beyond surprising and amusing a reader, the "case" bolsters the narrative's resistance to "serious" interpretation, to serv-ing any purpose but moment-to-moment delight, and to entangle-ment in conventions like unity, progression, or even signification.

Buncombe is hired to argue the side of reason and solid American justice in a trumped-up, outrageous lawsuit: somebody's ranch has supposedly avalanched down on someone else's, and the question before the local court is which party owns whatever is left. Common sense and legal precedents are all on Buncombe's side — that a prop-erty buried by mud and rock is still a property rightfully owned — and so the crowning joke on Buncombe is the crushing of his impregnable argument by the presiding judge, who like nearly everyone else is in on the conspiracy:

> "Gentlemen, I have listened attentively to the evidence, and have perceived that the weight of it, the overwhelming weight of it, is in favor of the plaintiff Hyde. I have listened also to the remarks

of counsel, with high interest — and especially will I commend the masterly and irrefutable logic of the distinguished gentleman who represents the plaintiff. But gentlemen, let us beware how we allow mere human testimony, human ingenuity in argument and human ideas of equity, to influence us at a moment so solemn as this. Gentlemen, it ill becomes us, worms as we are, to meddle with the decrees of Heaven. It is plain to me that Heaven, in its inscrutable wisdom, has seen fit to move this defendant's ranch for a purpose. We are but creatures, and we must submit. If Heaven has chosen to favor the defendant Morgan in this marked and wonderful manner; and if Heaven, dissatisfied with the position of the Morgan ranch upon the mountain side, has chosen to remove it to a position more eligible and more advantageous for its owner, it ill becomes us, insects as we are, to question the legality of the act or inquire into the reasons that prompted it. No — Heaven created the ranches and it is Heaven's prerogative to reärrange them, to experiment with them, to shift them around at its pleasure. . . . And from this decision there is no appeal."
(227–28)

The real verdict, from which no appeal can be allowed, is that an avalanche of "masterly and irrefutable logic" is an intolerable danger to the Territory, that it is the prerogative not of Heaven but of Carson City to rearrange reason and common sense, experiment with them, and shift them around at its pleasure. This is an apex moment in a series that begins early in *Roughing It,* running through anecdotes about monstrous criminals riding high or brought low for all the wrong reasons, about Mormon assassins hunting a man for giving a child a tin whistle, about fortunes made or lost on preposterous technicalities. The wrongful idea about courts and justice in Mark Twain's Wild West is not that justice will and should prevail, but that justice, or any other logic-based, language-based institution in such a place, will not be so inherently mad as everything else here, in this world exquisitely and transiently beyond the reach of sense and civilization.

Appropriately, *Roughing It* is not a travel book, yet not a satire on a travel book either, for both of these forms are too much confined by *obligations* to form, to consistencies of tone and theme, to either logic and truth and real life, or to the peculiar logic and "seriousness" of satire. Yet *Roughing It* is by no means formless. To reject truth when truth is intractable, to delight in imagination and the sheer fun of make-believe, to side with the initiated against the ignorant spoilsport eastern multitudes, to stand fast against all attempts to wreck this make-believe free world with doses of fact and the real — these serve as informing values. Washoe, Virginia City, Carson City, and the Nevada Territory are not separate places but parts of one extended interlude, on the edge of a civilization of rule enforcers, reality instructors, and reliable journalists who are closing in already, an interlude as doomed as all such dream-places must be. The air of nostalgia that pervades *Roughing It* is nostalgia for a fleeting "time-out" from ordinary ways of living, ordinary patterns of identity and of framing a narrative. Sooner or later the young goldseeker and adventurer will have to settle down and earn a living. Sooner or later, Mark Twain the teller must make an end, falling prey to fatigue and to the end that fatigue spells for enchantment — or face up to the awkward truth that a sustained refusal of conventions eventually decays into a convention itself. Sooner or later, play becomes work. For a short time the job of reporting (i.e., storytelling) for the *Enterprise* is an honor, a job of Master of Revels; after a while, however, it must become a job like any other, and *having* to imagine can take all the fun out of it.

In the parallel world of his own narration, Mark Twain, after chapter 55, no longer amuses either himself or his readers with reminiscences of former identities. He falls instead into reporting about himself as a reporter, and differences begin to show in both what he relates and how he relates it. The benign critical neglect of the last third of *Roughing It* seems testament enough to its falling off, to the narrative's own loss of zest for the all-out fictive life. As the traveler wearies of this adventure, running out of money and exuberance, the form and controlling imagination of the book seem to exhaust themselves too, and *Roughing It* deteriorates toward hackwork, a padded travelogue that for hundreds of pages it had avoided becoming. To put it another way, this narrative has depended for energy and success on being an act of play in and of itself, taking full advantage of play's transient dominion over truth, consistency, and common sense. It depends on a Tom Sawyer license to raid the realms of fact without obligation to them, to move at whim in and out of the imagination, from raw reality to exuberant make-believe. This racing back and forth is essential to Mark Twain's creative freedom here, as well as to our pleasure, and the role that make-believe plays shows up as clearly in the movement *among* episodes, passages, voices, as it does in these moments themselves.

The pattern is there in a first spectacular example in the book, in the midst of the account of the stagecoach journey, even before the dictionary begins to fly. The narration has been busy with an apparently sober report of the virtues of sagebrush, a drab-enough subject. But the discourse suddenly veers into something more than mere digression to liven a page; what breaks out is an elaborate joke about the reliability of the voice we have been trusting, and of this "history" we have yet to hear. Sagebrush is forgotten, and every "fact" affirmed thus far — about sagebrush, jackass rabbits, mosquitoes, thoroughbraces, coaches, mule-trading — transmogrifies into something dubious, from a chaotic, delightful condition whirling between fiction and truth:

> Mules and donkeys and camels have appetites that anything will relieve temporarily, but nothing satisfy. In Syria, once, at the headwaters of the Jordan, a camel took charge of my overcoat while the tents were being pitched, and examined it with a critical eye, all over, with as much interest as if he had an idea of getting one made like it; . . . He put his foot on it, and lifted one of the sleeves out with his teeth, and chewed and chewed at it, gradually taking it in, and all the while opening and closing his eyes in a kind of religious ecstasy, . . . Next he tried the velvet collar, and smiled a smile of such contentment that it was plain to see that he regarded that as the daintiest thing about an overcoat. The tails went next, along with some percussion caps and cough candy, and some fig-paste from Constantinople. And then my newspaper correspondence dropped out, and he took a chance in that — manuscript letters written for the home papers. But he was treading on dangerous ground now. He began to come across solid wisdom in those documents that was rather weighty on his stomach; and occasionally he would take a joke that would shake him up till it loosened his teeth; it was getting to be perilous times with him, but he held his grip with good courage and hopefully, till at last he began to stumble on statements that not even a camel could swallow with impunity. He began to gag and gasp, and his eyes to stand out, and his forelegs to spread, and in about a quarter of a minute he fell over as stiff as a carpenter's work-bench, and

died a death of indescribable agony. I went and pulled the manuscript out of his mouth, and found that the sensitive creature had
choked to death on one of the mildest and gentlest statements of
fact that I ever laid before a trusting public. (55–56)

Immediately after, having painted himself as a champion unreliable
narrator, Mark Twain moves into his next "mild and gentle statement
of fact," which his supposedly trusting public is now apparently to
swallow:

I was about to say, when diverted from my subject, that occasionally one finds sage-brushes five or six feet high, and with a spread
of branch and foliage in proportion, but two or two and a half feet
is the usual height. (56)

This moment, a bizarre jump from one narrative stance into another, is a travel tip for touring the forty-odd chapters that follow,
about this Mark Twain's exploits in the American West. Some of *Roughing It* can be "swallowed," some cannot be, and there are no warnings
to spoil the fun, no easy ways to know whether God's truth, eastern-
style truth, or some camel-choking whopper lurks in the next chapter,
paragraph, or line. *Roughing It*—the first fifty chapters, anyway—is
one of Mark Twain's great escapes into places away from the real, and
from culturally grounded laws of selfhood and storytelling. This is
narrative as extravagant subversion.

ice and fire

Even so, a familiar, dubious reading habit has already turned up, in
such traveling through this traveler's subversion of habit and pattern.
I have been following the old practice of talking about these books up
to a traditional stopping point, of lifting out the interesting half or
two-thirds of *Innocents* and *Roughing It* and letting the rest of them
drift, as padding, as a falling-off in conviction and energy, and as a
disappearance of that anarchic evading of stable selfhood. In these
two works especially, I find that strategy hard to avoid, given that
in both cases, previously published travel letters were reworked into
chapters and long book-sections, sometimes with verve and conviction, but sometimes not. *A Tramp Abroad* cracks into two big pieces as
well, though perhaps not with such a quality difference between them.

Roughly the first half of *A Tramp* is about touring in towns and river valleys. The second half, high-altitude adventure in Switzerland and southeastern France, is embellished (or padded) with grisly tales of other people's mountaineering (tales that in some cases Mark Twain shamelessly pirated, right down to the illustrations,[23] from which only the incriminating signatures have been removed). There isn't much question that in the closing chapters of *A Tramp* Mark Twain plays to popular tastes for catastrophe, for gore, and for the sentimentality he satirizes elsewhere. In several ways he plays fast and loose with the ethics of making a book. Yet there is something eerie and consistent about these two halves of *A Tramp* when they are looked at as one narrative. Throughout, Mark Twain portrays himself as somehow over-the-hill when it comes to real adventuring, or real experimentation with identity and escape from old habits of mind. From the beginning, this narrator sounds trapped, by money, laziness and worldwide repute; and the voyage he describes is a life lived out of steamer trunks, in hotels and on café terraces, where any real work to be done, whether physical, psychological, or literary, gets done at the last minute and by someone else. In *A Tramp* Mark Twain seems to have turned from all-out cultural tourist and psychological escape artist into personage, and travel has turned into a "progress" in the Shakespearean sense, an encumbered, luxurious passage, disconnected from the landscape, the human world, and imaginative possibilities. The famous gags of the alpine chapters, about looking the wrong way and missing a spectacular sunrise, about ascending the Riffelberg with a preposterous retinue of guides, bearers, and servants, are fables about disconnection; not the discovery of better sights to see and worthier tombs to weep over, but the contemplation and achievement of nothing, as either adventure or point of view. Granted, this disconnection and ease create running jokes in the book, but they do far more. They contribute to its peculiar mixed mood of complacency and longing: a longing for passion, perhaps even for stupidity, but above all for rediscovery of that alien mind that risks, sacrifices, and perseveres in the confines of an unimaginative, too-domesticated self.

During Mark Twain's lifetime *A Tramp Abroad* was his biggest bestseller in the British Isles.[24] If tonal and thematic consistencies contributed to its success with a late Victorian English audience, then they also mark a coming of trouble for Mark Twain as the absolute traveler, voyaging among possibilities of response, of selfhood, yet following this time his baggage — trunks, suitcases, and public identity — from mountain to mountain, town to town. The pathos in *A Tramp Abroad*, the tristful tone that builds into something like Victorian morbidity by the time Mark Twain comes to the Matterhorn and Mont Blanc, has to do with the giants catching up. The culminating, belabored slapstick of setting off to the peaks with legions of help and tons of encumbrance speaks of that anxiety, as does the obsession in the Mont Blanc visit, not with mortal dangers of mountaineering, but rather with postmortem dangers of being buried yet *not* buried, and ultimately exhumed again by an immensity of malignant ice. The fixation is on freezing solid, being denied a true funeral, and what consolations there might be in decomposing back into perfect anonymity and the grand scheme of things — and then being coughed up again, into the light and the human world decades after, as one's own grotesque monument, a too-fresh disaster from another time:

> There is something weirdly pathetic about the picture of that white-haired veteran greeting with his loving hand-shake this friend who had been dead forty years. When these hands had met last, they were alike in the softness and freshness of youth; now, one was brown and wrinkled and horny with age, while the other was still as young and fair and blemishless as if those forty years had come and gone in a single moment, leaving no mark of their passage. Time had gone on, in the one case; it had stood still in the other. A man who has not seen a friend for a generation, keeps him in mind always as he saw him last, and is somehow surprised, and is also shocked, to see the aging change the years have wrought when he sees him again. Marie Couttet's experience, in finding his friend's hand unaltered from the image of it which he had carried in his memory for forty years, is an experience which stands alone in the history of man, perhaps.[25]

Mark Twain's preoccupation with such business seems to be other than Emmeline Grangerford necrophilia, especially when these moments are allowed to resonate with others in the canon. These frozen mountaineers are the ghastly consequences of that avalanche ride that Mark Twain describes with such zest, admiration, and ridicule in *Roughing It*'s alpine digression. The hiker's mad acceptance and defiance of mortality, of human powerlessness to resist nature and doom, of life itself as a headlong, helpless fall into oblivion — this is what such theatrics come to. The vanishing wayfarer waves his hat high in the air like a show-off bull-rider, refusing death and enormous interment; they arrive in an instant nonetheless, and the hard corpse that the glaciers eventually cast up makes a mockery of those few seconds of existential freedom. The outcome is always ice, a congealed human being, a horror and an offense to a living world.

Though Mark Twain's last travel book, *Following the Equator,* contemplates similar nightmares, it enacts resistance of another kind, and toys with hopes that are not imaginatively possible in the cold, conserving culture of Northern and alpine Europe. Not a narrative that waves its hat very much in moments of glee and broad comedy, *Following the Equator* is Mark Twain's most thorough nonfiction immersion in worlds of death, yet death here is contemplated as something fundamentally different from what it was in *A Tramp Abroad.* The result is not his best or strangest travel narrative; that distinction — strangeness — is best assigned to *Life on the Mississippi,* with which I shall close this chapter. But *Following the Equator* has much more to offer than a few amusing moments. With mingled dread and fascination, this last travel book gazes at what for Mark Twain were new possibilities of escape from identity, whether Western-style or absolute and universal among human beings. And that encounter, which unfolds chiefly in India, reverberates through some of the strange writings that came after.

The action of *Following the Equator* opens with a story about not being able to finish a story; thereafter the book spends many chapters contemplating what to break loose *from,* and how. Chapter 2 unfolds on shipboard, as Mark Twain, a Great Personage now, crosses the Pacific to lecture his way around the world and pay his notorious debts. As an entertainment he and a few shipmates — in one of the book's rare instances of direct discourse and substantive conversation — play a game of "the completing of non-complete stories." One player offers fifty dollars for a satisfactory ending to the yarn he presently spins, about a pious young suitor faced with giving up his lap robe to his beloved as an act of tenderness and chivalry, and thereby revealing to her, and to her suspicious mother, that he has lost his trousers in an elaborate highway accident. The conundrum is both moral *and* literary, for the challenge before the players has to do with good storytelling, and only indirectly with what virtuous real young men ought to do in such straits. But on both planes at once, Mark Twain passes judgment. The story, he decides, cannot be finished, because of *who* these people are:

> Of course none but a happy ending of the story would be accepted by the jury; the finish must find Brown in high credit with the ladies, his behavior without blemish, his modesty unwounded, his character for self-sacrifice maintained, the Old People rescued through him, their benefactor, all the party proud of him, happy in him, his praises on all their tongues.
>
> We tried to arrange this, but it was beset with persistent and irreconcilable difficulties. We saw that Brown's shyness would not allow him to give up the lap-robe. This would offend Mary and her mother; and it would surprise the other ladies, partly because this stinginess toward the suffering Old People would be out of character with Brown, and partly because he was a special Providence and could not properly act so. If asked to explain his conduct, his shyness would not allow him to tell the truth, and lack of invention and practice would find him incapable of contriving a lie that would wash. We worked at the troublesome problem until three in the morning.
>
> Meanwhile Mary was still reaching for the lap-robe. We gave it up, and decided to let her continue to reach. It is the reader's privilege to determine for himself how the thing came out.[26]

So this time it is character that confines, not circumstance. The trap that denies the young lovers happiness is the trap of their own social and moral training, the culturally inflected drives and inhibitions that define them and lock them up as individuals. Thus the trap of the Western world, the cage that Mark Twain subsequently tries to escape vicariously on the *Equator* journey, through unprecedented celebration of blood and fire. The Sandwich Islands this time around are glimpsed as a place of lush, hideous death, where death has been the penalty for every sort of crime, and disfiguring disease the penalty for "sins committed by their ancestors," where cholera has ravaged the population for decades, where lepers lose their physical integrity and seem to dissolve in paradisiacal surroundings.

Yet Hawaii is only glimpsed in *Following the Equator.* The obsession is with India, which dominates the second volume: not merely or broadly "India," but an India of incomprehensible faith, of violence, and especially of funeral rituals that enact passage into unimaginable liberation. Some historical accounts are paraphrased, plagiarized, and quoted wholesale from other writers, and the effect of these official-sounding reports is to reinforce the impression that the Mark Twain we have here is himself isolated and consecrated as never before. To call this narrative a morbid fascination is to stop too soon in thinking about this peculiar and very long stretch in this most peculiar book, which offers no lively traveling companions in the foreground, no repartee, no conspiracies to avoid guides or the ardors of fashionable big-budget journeys. Mark Twain seems very much an isolated celebrity in *Following the Equator,* dealing with baggage bearers and official greeters and local sycophants—yet never with friends, mentors, or even amiable strangers. This is Mark Twain's most official progress, the travel of a "finished man," all too dissatisfied with the completeness and limitation of his own temperament, his own ingrained habits of belief and cognition. Mark Twain's India is a long, yearning look into incomprehensible otherness, mysterious faith, appalling war, terrible and beautiful celebrations of mortality and its dark promise.[27]

The narrative centers of *Following the Equator*'s second half are the Thuggee atrocities of the early nineteenth century, the Great Mutiny of 1857, and the details of "Hindoo" devotional and funeral practices. Amid all that, there is little dialogue and situational humor. The fascination is much more with dying, murder, and especially with the disposal of human bodies—as signifying release from corporeality, liberation from form. There is a long chapter on the speedy reduction of dead Parsees to dry, clean, anonymous bones thrown into a well of oblivion at the Towers of Silence; there are long passages on the etiquette of suttee, and of bereaved women settling back easefully on a pyre to go literally up in smoke. There is much on the breaking of cremated skulls into powdery ash, and the pouring of these ashes not into the confinement of Western-style tombs, but into the holy river that sweeps all away, absorbing, cleansing, and obliterating outward limitation.

A death wish might be heard in these numerous pages, or more precisely a release wish, blended of course with plenty of horror at death, Western-style horror at this prospect of losing one's dignity, comfort, and identity. In Calcutta, Mark Twain takes his turn at retelling the Black Hole nightmare, and with considerable verve; his tale is of white Westerners like himself crushed and tormented into suffocating plasm. The long-since-finished Thuggee uprising is belabored as well, with accounts of unsuspecting wayfarers suddenly and expertly garrotted, and buried in unmarked cemeteries. In his heavily borrowed account of the Mutiny, Mark Twain favors tales of heroic and stoic folk of both races butchered ritually, or slaughtered in a haste of rebellion and conquest. Death breaks out everywhere in Mark Twain's India; that much is sure. But it is death in unexpected shapes and styles, and death that dissolves the self and its legacy, as death in Mark Twain's other writings rarely does. Yet visits to worlds so alien do not in themselves make for rich and complex meditation: Mark Twain's narrative *looks* at this wholly other world, yet cannot enter.

the crookedest river

Of all the travel books, the voyage into something both old and new, familiar *and* alien, happens but once, in *Life on the Mississippi*, which taken as a whole constitutes Mark Twain's most interesting engagement, in his nonfiction prose, with possibilities and perils related to his own identity. *Life on the Mississippi* is his sometimes brilliant campaign to get away from the giant once more, on a voyage that is also an uneasy return home.[28]

But where does the emphasis fall? On the first word of the title, or on the last? This is only a glib way of asking whether *Life on the Mississippi* is essentially about a river, or a human-created world on and along that river, or about "Life" itself, as something large and evasive, with "the Mississippi" as the stage on which this vexing business of life might be observed. *Life on the Mississippi*, if we consider the whole published text, is Mark Twain's only nonfiction volume, or at least his only nonnovel, about going back, to visit scenes and circumstances of a former life and former selves. That process of return, first imaginative, then in the flesh, calls into question much that *A Tramp Abroad* never chances: success, the past, the natural scene, art, fiction, historical narratives, the validity of guilt, the prospect of salvation, and of course identity. The seam that joins the book's two major parts is even more obvious and telling than in *Roughing It:* chapter 21, a single page that reports the achieving of the pilot's license, the coming of the Civil War and the end of the riverboat golden age, and adventures between those days and the present. Life *after* the pilot-house is sketched as a process of getting stuck, of becoming what he calls "an immovable fixture among the other rocks of New England."[29] A theme latent in

A Tramp opens quite dramatically here: American-style identity has closed in around Mark Twain, and identity of that sort is a menace.

Is this why *Life on the Mississippi* was so hard to write? By reliable accounts the book was a great labor, even though with his abundant recollections and his freshly completed five-week, five-thousand-mile journey, from St. Louis to New Orleans and north again to St. Paul, Mark Twain apparently had no end of material to write about. But apparently the intention was not simply to embed in a thick tome the "Old Times" reminiscences that he had written in 1874 for William Dean Howells and *The Atlantic Monthly.*[30] There are crises of other sorts in *Life on the Mississippi,* and they come clear if we attend to the drama of the book's entanglement, right from the year it was published, with "Mark Twain" as a cultural icon. At the core of *Life* (that is, the entire work as first released in 1883, and not merely the "Old Times" chapters it absorbed) is a drama of homecoming after long absence, returning as a stranger in a broad, dangerous sense of the term. For these once-familiar landscapes have not only changed and grown strange. They whisper a threat, that this mysterious thing that was Sam Clemens but that is now widely known as "Mark Twain," has altered beyond recognition — by others *and* by the self. Former enthusiasms and patterns of consciousness may have become unrecognizable, unenterable; encountering the boyhood world, or rather its ruins, might mean facing the horrendous truth that the self, or some essential part of it, the "one microscopic atom" of lost or too-deep-buried actuality that Hank Morgan yearns for in *Yankee,* has been swept away forever, like whole towns along this restless river.

Reasons, then, for reading *Life* as it was constructed, published and sold worldwide in Mark Twain's lifetime: nothing terrible happens if we read the text as featuring this return trip down and up the river twenty years after Mark Twain's pilot days were done. No unities or political subtexts have to be coerced in order to value such a book, as an episode in the re-creation and complication of "Mark Twain" as a presence on the American scene. The title, in other words, is an eerily good one, the most resonant that Mark Twain came up with for a long work, and perhaps better than he knew. For the "life" contemplated here is more than the social and economic scene from Minnesota to the Delta, before the Civil War and two decades after. It is also more than a personal past, rediscovered in ways that may have spurred the completion of *Huckleberry Finn.* The "life" contemplated is something more on the order of life itself, as a mystery on a scale unimagined in Mark Twain's other narratives about himself on the move. What the book seems to whisper is a profound moral and psychological vertigo, and much of the suspense in *Life* has to do with deepening uncertainty about who or what one is: whether young, ignorant wanderers or settled and finished adults have more integrity, are more themselves; and whether dry, solid Yankee ground or "the crookedest river in the world" is a better representation of life and the human condition.

Taking a cue from Mark Twain's elegiac voice, much has been said in our popular culture to lionize Mississippi riverboat pilots in their golden age twenty years before the Civil War, and to sing of the sovereignty and romance of that profession, as a trade closer to medieval romance—knighthood or perfect Tom Sawyer ecstasy than any other in Mark Twain's industrializing world.[31] Mark Twain's own nostalgia is of course tempered. There is strangeness in piloting as he recollects it, and in the dynamic yet coalesced self that piloting absolutely required, strangeness that made the work unlike any other travail he knew of before or since, including perhaps the travail of writing. In the "Old Times" material that became the first twenty chapters of *Life*, the Mississippi River has been presented as *change*, from bend to bend, tide to tide, week to week, and the glory, if not the joy, of a pilot's life lies in knowing a grand arcanum that is always in the process of becoming something else, always challenging and reconstructing the intellect, the memory, and the intuition. If Mark Twain was thoroughly on record by 1880 as hating purveyors of dusty antique wisdom — imperious tour guides, Old World priests, sorcerers, romancers, unimaginative teachers, repetitious bores — then piloting and newspaper work, the professions Mark Twain practiced in his younger days, were also on record as his recourse from that kind of oppression, as they offered power, respect, and a furnished mind, and all in the service of change, of attending to and comprehending realities altered or made new every morning. For a printer, a reporter, a pilot, and an author like Mark Twain, history, established fact, and precedent could provide only general guidance for the individual mind, charged with interpreting what is happening on this day and what might happen tomorrow. In each of these roles, knowing "what was" is power, but greater power lies in knowing when "what was" no longer matters, when circumstances and the self demand new narratives, new explanations. Much of the verve in the cub-pilot chapters has to do with young Sam finding out how much river he must learn, acquiring humility, and then learning to trust in what he knows. Much has been made of his elegy for his own lost innocence, the wonderworld of the river transformed, by study, into an array of appalling symptoms and scientific indications. But two chapters farther on there is a wonderful and generally overlooked hymn to life as mystery, and to the grown-up, educated, yet *intuitive* sensibility that can improvise and sixth-sense its way through danger:

> An embankment ten or fifteen feet high guards both banks of the Mississippi all the way down that lower end of the river, and this embankment is set back from the edge of the shore from ten to perhaps a hundred feet, according to circumstances; say thirty or forty feet, as a general thing. Fill that whole region with an impenetrable gloom of smoke from a hundred miles of burning bagasse piles, when the river is over the banks, and turn a steamboat loose along there at midnight and see how she will feel. And see how you will feel, too! You find yourself away out in the midst of a vague dim sea that is shoreless, that fades out and loses itself in the murky distances; for you cannot discern the thin rib of embankment, and you are always imagining you see a straggling tree when you don't. The plantations themselves are transformed by the smoke, and look like a part of the sea. All through your watch you are tortured with the exquisite misery of uncertainty. You hope you are keeping in the river, but you do not know. All that you are sure about is that you are likely to be within six feet of the bank *and* destruction, when you think you are a good half-mile from shore. And you are sure, also, that if you chance suddenly to fetch up against the embankment and topple your chimneys overboard, you will have the small comfort of knowing that it is about what you were expecting to do. One of the great Vicksburg packets darted out into a sugar plantation one night, at such a time, and had to stay there a week. But there was no novelty about it; it had been done before. (295)

No mental map of worldly experience can help an individual mind maneuver through such precincts, foreshadowing those supremely uncertain worldscapes, hypnagogic realms between the real and the dream that provide settings for Mark Twain's puzzling late tales. Memory can be trouble, if it rules too absolutely or takes too big a place in the identity. Even consciousness can be a threat to the survival of boats and human beings. Just after this hymn to mystery comes a tale of the right sort of man to steer through it, a Mr. X who navigates a crooked, treacherous piece of river at night while sleepwalking, and who earns this resonant praise from a fellow pilot:

> "You just ought to have seen him take this boat through Helena crossing. *I* never saw anything so gaudy before. And if he can do such gold-leaf, kid-glove, diamond-breastpin piloting when he is sound asleep, what *couldn't* he do if he was dead!" (298)

A memorable Mark Twain syllogism, absurd yet also dadaist-wise. If we are freer, wiser, and more in touch with truth when we are not awake, then we might be our supreme selves, supremely competent, when out of life and mind entirely. Introduced in chapter 13, Mr. Brown, who becomes the heavy of the cub-pilot chapters, seems to validate this crazy midnight exclamation, for Brown is memory's prisoner, besotted with wakeful and worldly experience. He has Jim Blaine's disease, and worse, because Blaine has to be drunk for the symptoms to take over. Unchecked, undifferentiated memory is what Brown has and *is*, along with a touch of Claggart's malice. What the man lacks are "two higher qualities . . . good and quick judgment and decision, and a cool, calm courage that no peril can shake" (309). Those are loose terms, of course, that nonetheless have edges as Mark Twain invokes them, coming as they do near the end of this account of a younger self learning that he *must* learn, master the facts of the river, achieve and pay the price for heightened wakefulness, and then learning the truth in George Bernard Shaw's epigram, that "the unconscious self is the real genius." Being a cub pilot comes to mean achieving balance between memory and improvisation, furious wakefulness and the liberation of sleep (even perhaps of death). The worldly "Rank and Dignity of Piloting" are only part of the pleasure that the constructed and settled Mark Twain wants to remember and reexperience in coming *back* to the river, which is the central drama of *Life on the Mississippi*.

Then why so much about death in the account of the return trip, which makes up fully two-thirds of the published book? One answer is that death has acquired a duality for Mark Twain that it has not had before in his nonfiction narratives, representing not only his predicament as a grown-up, dangerously complete American archetype, caught in a public self and a skein of his own words, but also a lost and mysteriously promised escape from all that, liberation into absolute, unimaginable freedom, and into discovery of true and transcendent identity. The return to the river is a surprising concentration upon stasis, considering how much has changed in Mark Twain's absence and continues to change before his eyes. These final two-thirds of the book also obsess upon death, not as existential fact, or terror, or threat to identity, but as both horrifying continuity and escape from it, an appalling yet comforting coming-to-rest, with reduction of the body to a pestilential monument, and of the world-burdened soul to an ephemeral caricature in the memories of the living.

On the pretext of telling yet another Jim Blaine–style tale whose essential gag would be its own lack of structure and conclusion, Mark Twain planned a chapter to be inserted just before the account of the Vicksburg siege, a tale about a Mr. Harvey's two-year balloon ride, carrying him into the everlasting company of fifty-four starved, dead, air-mummified adventurers who had ascended into that same perpetually still patch of high air:

> "Up there, matter attracts matter — and powerfully. As the years rolled on, one ragged balloon after another came along and bunched up with us — and all of them full of dead people in all possible stages of greenness and mildew, and all of them grinning and staring; sixteen balloons in all, fifty-four corpses and a lot of dried animals of one sort and another — hailed from various countries — all strangers; and also came other corpses that got joggled out by balloons colliding; and these joined the drunken priest — eleven of them, there were, and all fluttering with rags — and week in and week out, and night and day, they noiselessly and drunkenly balanced and sasshayed to each other, there in the empty air, and wagged their skinny arms, and grinned and leered, and the balloon-audience looked on, as if from opera boxes; and they, too, grinned and leered, and — excuse me just a moment, I will be back right away."[32]

End of story. As the inexplicably alive Mr. Harvey dashes from the riverboat, allegedly on business, the tale is left in just this condition, bobbing in the mind, without resolution. Mummies and balloons — this nightmare image might pass muster in a surrealist narrative half a century later; ten years on, Mark Twain belabored the idea again in *Tom Sawyer Abroad,* in which a great deal of space is given over to scenes of Tom and Huck crossing the Sahara in a hot-air balloon, and gaping at desiccated remains of murdered and battle-dead bedouins in the timeless sands beneath them. The stasis and horror of these two interludes, and their lack of plausible connection to the narratives in which they appear, do suggest some species of obsession, and the psychological symbolism is not difficult. Changeless death, death deprived even of the transformations and liberations of decay; and perfect lightness, floating on the pure oceans of air and sand: to borrow from Pascal, *qu'est-ce que l'homme entre les deux abîmes?* In Mark Twain's version, the two abysses are terrifyingly absolute freedom and perpetual confinement. Or to read a bit more cheerfully, the best condition of mankind is to be fluid like the great river. The alternatives are here together in these balloon dreams: too much of solid definition, physical being, and mortality; and too much of airy disconnection from solid, worldly life, a horrid exile "utterly cut off from the world." Chapter 35, which was to be the very next, uses that phrase to introduce a reverie on life under siege at Vicksburg — and here starvation matters little in Mark Twain's imaginings. Neither does the lack of basic comforts; the nightmare and the holiday of the siege, as Mark Twain recounts it, have to do with being caught in one small, grim, too-real place, and yet so experientially deprived as to be not in the world at all. The nightmare this time is not akin to Poe's, but something more like Dickinson's: the horror and appeal of a timeless state, with too much and too little in the way of certainty, danger, or form. The citizens of besieged Vicksburg are buried alive, and even time itself is mummified:

> Population, twenty-seven thousand soldiers and three thousand non-combatants; the city utterly cut off from the world — walled solidly in, the frontage by gunboats, the rear by soldiers and batteries; hence, no buying and selling with the outside; no passing to and fro; no God-speeding a parting guest, no welcoming a coming one; no printed acres of world-wide news to be read at breakfast, mornings — a tedious dull absence of such matter, instead; hence, also, no running to see steamboats smoking into view in the distance up or down, and ploughing toward the town — for none came, the river lay vacant and undisturbed; no rush and turmoil around the railway station, no struggling over bewildered swarms of passengers by noisy mobs of hackmen — all quiet there; . . .
>
>   . . . Could you, who did not experience it, come nearer to re-

producing it to the imagination of another non-participant than could a Vicksburger who *did* experience it? It seems impossible; and yet there are reasons why it might not really be. . . .

Years ago, I talked with a couple of the Vicksburg non-combatants — a man and his wife. Left to tell their story in their own way, those people told it without fire, almost without interest. . . .

"It got to be Sunday all the time. Seven Sundays in the week — to us, anyway. We had n't anything to do, and time hung heavy. Seven Sundays, and all of them broken up at one time or another, in the day or in the night, by a few hours of the awful storm of fire and thunder and iron." (443–45)

And so on through several more pages of balloon-ride hell as both spectacle, ordeal, and dreary routine, a life with intervals of real fire, yet almost without interest. The dreamed-up dead in *Life's* excised balloon story, and the real dead and the living dead of the Vicksburg siege are described with stress upon removal from the world as known, and on the epistemological problems of being alive. They float high in the still air, or wander catatonically in a ravaged landscape, or they are glimpsed in neat straight rows in a meticulously kept and timeless Federal cemetery. The mystery they tell Mark Twain is familiar enough; it is of loss: loss of voice, of animation, memory, presence, and consequence in the world, merged always with an ambiguous promise of peace and perfect escape from confines and consequences of selfhood. But the moldering dead that come after in *Life on the Mississippi,* the dead of New Orleans, the river feuds, subsequent digressive tales, and the unforgotten Hannibal of Mark Twain's youth — these other dead who crowd into the second half of the book have palpable consequences for the living. The truth they speak is about retribution, madness, and peril. After a slick "yarn" about a poker game, a cadenza on "The House Beautiful" bad taste of Southern parlors, and a quick look at Natchez and Baton Rouge, *Life* settles in for an extended visit to New Orleans — and at the start of the account there are two full chapters on above-ground graveyards and their contagion:

I will gradually drop this subject of graveyards. I have been trying all I could to get down to the sentimental part of it, but I cannot accomplish it. I think there is no genuinely sentimental part to it. It is all grotesque, ghastly, horrible. Graveyards may have been justifiable in the bygone ages, when nobody knew that for every

dead body put into the ground, to glut the earth and the plant-
roots and the air with disease-germs, five or fifty, or maybe a hundred, persons must die before their proper time; but they are
hardly justifiable now, when even the children know that a dead
saint enters upon a century-long career of assassination the moment the earth closes over his corpse. It is a grim sort of a thought.
The relics of St. Anne, up in Canada, have now, after nineteen
hundred years, gone to curing the sick by the dozen. But it is the
merest matter-of-course that these same relics, within a generation after St. Anne's death and burial, *made* several thousand people sick. Therefore these miracle-performances are simply compensation, nothing more. . . . A saint can never *quite* return the
principal, however; for his dead body *kills* people, whereas his
relics *heal* only — they never restore the dead to life. That part of
the account is always left unsettled. (477–78)

For considering "too curiously" and morbidly, Hamlet with Yorick's
skull cannot match Mark Twain on New Orleans. The subject here is
hygiene only in part, for the "disease and death" Mark Twain dwells on
here, as propagated by the dead upon the living, seems more than
biological. The meditation opened by Mr. Harvey's unfinished balloon
story veers in a new direction now. The mummified folk who keep
Harvey ghastly company, who caricature the living traveler and teach
something of fear and humility, are sobering, not menacing. But from
New Orleans onward in *Life on the Mississippi* the dead rise again —
from the tomb, from the muddy waters of the river, from the personal
or familial past or the depths of dream — and they rise transformed to
threaten and kill.

Why this duality in *Life*, between dead who keep their place, who gri-
mace and even gesture but do not endanger, and these other sorts who
do? Though it is tempting to concoct a progression in *Life*, it is unnec-
essary to do so. The dry and the polluting dead might be two sides of a
turmoil about the self and mortality, two answers to a question that
whirled in Mark Twain's mind throughout his career. Is there something dry, wholesome, and enduring in us, some bone of truth that
persists in decent, dignified, or at least innocuous ways after we die,
like the white, clean bones of the dead in *Roughing It*'s visit to ancient
Hawaiian battlegrounds? Or like the boiled-clean skeleton of Captain
Cook, cleansed in his death (or at least in Mark Twain's fantasy) not

only of corruptible flesh but of the corruptions of life, and made tasteful as a relic; Captain Cook cooked down to a tidy skeleton and a copper-clad, understated monument on a clean, deserted beach? Or is our legacy, our afterlife — physical, spiritual, cultural, literary — only noxious, an infection of other lives and minds?

New Orleans is only the beginning of this altered nightmare. The dead in the latter half of *Life* will not stay out of sight. The return to Hannibal encompasses a return to childhood guilt and nightmare, to private torments brought on by the drowning deaths of Lem Hackett and a German boy nicknamed Dutchy, and the death by fire, in the town jail, of a drunk to whom the boy Sam Clemens (or so a grown-up narrator tells us) passed the lucifer matches that killed him. There are more: chapter 53 tells of an unnamed woman who has died after thirty-six years in a madhouse; as a small boy, Sam has watched as a handful of girls sent the skittish creature into a convulsive fright from which she never recovered. One could make a case that the last thirty chapters of *Life* are essentially "Death on the Mississippi," given how the body count rises and the reminiscences and embedded yarns brim with murder, fatal violence and vendettas, cemeteries, drowned Indian maidens, duels, lynchings, people who drop stone-dead on duty in the wheelhouse or die drunk of "spontaneous combustion" in tanning vats. But the most protracted death tale in all of *Life* is a wild fable that gnaws at the boundaries between fact and fancy. It is about one corpse sitting up and talking about another corpse sitting up and talking, a double-frame tale in which the casualties are a now-old man, his young wife and child, two robbers, and finally an entire Arkansas town. The tally matters much less than the impact of this narrative upon *Life*, and readers who have seen the tale as padding, as Mark Twain reaching around for odd materials to fill out the book for the subscription trade, have not been able to accommodate Horst Kruse's discovery that the Ritter tale, as it has come to be called, was planned for *Life* from early on,[33] really from the opening weeks of Mark Twain's quest to make "Old Times" into a weighty book, and that he resisted advice by Osgood and others to cut the story out. In chapter 31 Mark Twain — which at this point in the narrative signifies, without irony, the storyteller rather than the social observer, or rather something between storyteller and teller of fact and truth — launches into a recollection of Munich at "the end of last year," and a dying German he had befriended for two months, as his "daily and sole intimate." Formerly a watchman in a Bavarian death-house (it is Mark Twain's interest in awful places that has brought them together), this Karl Ritter tells a story of his life in Napoleon, Arkansas, of the robbery and murder of his family by two German soldiers in the Union Army, and of eventually finding the one true killer by coincidence. The plot takes twists that Mark Twain the vaunted realist loved to pirate from nineteenth-century gothic and romantic fiction. To find the robbers and take revenge, Ritter has disguised himself as a fortune-teller in the nearby Union camp, collecting the thumbprints of dozens of clients before coming upon Franz Adler, whose print marks him as the killer; Kruger, the "gentler robber," has no thumb on his right hand. When Kruger is confronted he begs for mercy, offering instructions to a hidden treasure of ten thousand dollars back in Napoleon; Ritter stalks Franz Adler in the dark when Adler is on guard duty, and stabs him to death — or so he supposes. But when Adler is carted into the Munich dead-hall, years later, as an anonymous corpse, the murderer's faint movements ring the "dead-bell" that signifies stirrings of life. The story's wildest scene unfolds, with Adler, a "re-dying rascal," terrified to see himself already in the raiments and precincts of the tomb. Ritter is in turmoil, relishing a miraculous chance to torment this enemy in his last hour, but appalled to learn from Adler that he has executed the wrong man, poor, frightened Kruger, who had tried to save Ritter's wife and child, and who had taken Adler's place on guard duty on the night Ritter came for revenge.

So ultimately we have Ritter, as another man dying in anguish, passing to Mark Twain a scrap of paper telling where the treasure is hidden: in the rocks of an old chimney in the town of Napoleon, Arkansas. The Poe-like cleverness and opulent terrors of this tale only thinly overlay turbulence of other sorts. Compared to it, "The Fall of the House of Usher" and "The Cask of Amontillado" seem tidy, even consoling as gothic tales, for the "Thumb-print" story (as the chapter title calls it) and its denouements upon denouements — for it has several, and is not quite finished where my summary broke off — does not respect, as "Usher" and "Amontillado" do, the separateness of natural states, metaphysical planes, or even characters (including narrators) as either real or fictive. Hundreds of pages into what has seemed a plausible travel account, full of personal reminiscence, national history, riverboat technology, doses of geology, and lore easily identifiable *as* lore, Mark Twain eases into this recollection — a story of telling a story, that becomes a story of *hearing* a story—that slides into gothic romance, and then back into something that sounds like truth again, or that at least occupies realms where truth has reigned before. For the last denouement is this: back on the riverboat, in the midst of American "real life," Mark Twain and his two traveling companions plot to hunt up Kruger's treasure and keep it for themselves, instead of sending it back to Kruger's son in Germany, as the remorseful, dying Ritter had wished. But fate has a trick to play on these would-be pillagers, just as Kruger, Adler, and Ritter have all been tricked by fate. The town of Napoleon is gone, obliterated by the Arkansas River, which years before "tore it all to rags, and emptied it into the Mississippi!" (436). Among the listeners—and they exist in three dimensions: Mark Twain listening to the dying German, the "two friends" listening to Mark Twain's tale of the tale, and ourselves, unsure where we are and what we are hearing—compassion and noble sentiments erode into greed. And then the whole elaborately set stage is washed clean by natural catastrophe, erasing the drama, the question of its truth, and perhaps the whole point of the tale, unless the point of the story is that stories and twists of fate, false or true, ultimately have no point, no consequence, save as fuel for nihilistic irony. Thus the trickiest and most subversive tale in all the travel writings, and Mark Twain insisted on putting it into the heart of *Life on the Mississippi*.

Yet who or what, just now, is this Mark Twain?

In other words, does he narrate here as the grown-up former cub pilot, cured (or so he said earlier) of the illusions and fantasies of youth, guiding us downriver to show us how it was and is? Is he the inscrutable practical joker popping up here and there as in *Roughing It*, weaving "whoppers" seamlessly into factual accounts, and subverting distinctions between the real and the fabricated? Has he become another character in what has turned, for a while at least, into *Ritter's* narrative, a gothic romance so compelling and vertiginous as to transform this "Mark Twain" persona who tells it, or rather tells of its telling? As a plot device in a very different sort of narrative, Mark Twain seems to slip over an epistemological threshold to represent, suffer, and confess a last anagnorisis, in a drama that has had two or three climaxes already.

If Ritter's story is a romantic "stretcher," then what it stretches, ties in knots, and even breaks, is the coherence and authority of Mark Twain as narrator. One could say that behind these shifts from travelogue to tall tale and back again, there is something consistent, a voice of intoxicating reminiscence and the enchantment that comes of returning to loved country, a voice that allows fact and fiction to blend in *Life* as they do in *life*, when a mind returns to places where that mind once romped "like the mind of God," as Nick Carraway observes about American men in their youth. Fair enough. Yet death, not life and its celebration, is the music of the Ritter story, which climaxes in word of the death of a whole town — and in a classic put-on evasion. Was any of this possibly true? Napoleon, Arkansas, which might have been an actual place, has been erased from existence like a magic village in a romantic tale, and with it of course any proof of Ritter's story to Mark Twain and of Mark Twain's story to *us*. And having been supremely unreliable in narrating a tale by somebody else who was either supremely unreliable himself or never existed at all, a tale set in a town that was real once (possibly) and in a German chamber of horrors so awful that it could not be real (or could it?) Mark Twain rolls smoothly onward, without a rhetorical wink, to talk of geology, shifting river courses, and the legal and political status of Mississippi islands. There is a conflict here that has been seen before in Mark Twain's travel books, and that will turn up again in his major novels: romance suddenly unleashed, romance nurtured and flourishing in the midst of Mark Twain's best work, until the threat to truth or life beyond romance becomes too great, and with it some menacing confusion of worlds, of the real and the make-believe. Only then are fire and flood called down to drive romance away, so that the self might remain imaginatively and morally and psychologically free. Ascents and descents from fact to fiction have been met with before; yet the *development* of these two chapters seems more dramatically subversive of narrative, and of ontological, moral, and psychological convention than anything *The Innocents Abroad, Roughing It,* or *A Tramp Abroad* can offer.

The narrative, the narrator, life, death, the past, the present, every represented fact — all are now as certain and as suspect as the shifting surface of the river waters. The drowned boys, immolated drunks, and depraved spinsters of Hannibal, the subsequently "remembered" catastrophes of this Sam Clemens's youth (or perhaps we must say *Mark Twain's* youth now, the fiction-inflected "childhood" of a semi-fictitious human being) are recollections that in their unsureness affirm a dominion of the self *over* recollection, a Mark Twain, neither fictitious nor real, and made by his past, affirming and remaking that past in order to affirm and remake himself, not as private psyche or public persona, but in any and all dimensions at once.

An altered interpretive light casts backward through the book, even to young Sam's high adventures as a cub pilot. Biographers have been busy at such mysteries for most of this century, in part because *Life on the Mississippi* provides such treacherous guidance. Ritter's tale is one interlude among many that throw *Life on the Mississippi* off course, if this north-and-south, then-and-now, journey-reminiscence-anatomy could be said to have a course. The "crookedest river in the world," as Mark Twain calls the Mississippi on his opening page, is a universe constantly rearranging itself, and requiring, for human survival, a consciousness liberated from charts, old facts, conventions of discourse, and habits of mind. What is the death-grin absurdity of the Ritter tale, the death-grin derision that Mr. Harvey, either a consummate victim or consummate liar, says he endured for two years in the high-up doldrums of his balloon trip? It is all darkness, all around: mortality, the indifference of the spheres, the horror and absurdity of being confined, in belief, in social role, in discourse, in any life method or life design that inherently endangers some perfect, riverlike fluidity, some indwelling, fragile, yet inexplicable power to obliterate the towns, the landscape, and even history. In embracing and resisting that darkness, Mark Twain found power: as an artist, an American celebrity, and a frightfully free human being.

Chapter 3

The Quarrel with Romance

"You don't know about me . . ."

— the opening half of the opening line of the great work; and if mysteries glimmer straight away, then the rest of Huck's first proposition, and several that follow, can heat them up. To introduce himself, Huck hesitantly refers us back to *The Adventures of Tom Sawyer,* a fiction in whose pages a semifictional somebody-else called "Mr. Mark Twain" brought Huck to life as an ignorant, sweet-natured, weak-willed fool, sidekick to this younger boy who likes borrowing his identities from other fictions, yet who offers whatever psychological drama his own novel can be said to contain. So if it seems uncertain (to put it mildly) that reading *Tom Sawyer* means knowing much about the "Huck Finn" who does the telling now, it *is* certain that this Huck is not "telling" by himself, because one substrate joke of the first half-page of *Adventures of Huckleberry Finn* is that this almost-unknown boy, whom we could "know," or whose *name* we could know from a different book by this Mr. Mark Twain, who told the truth "mainly," is that Mr. Mark Twain not only makes Huck's lips and pencil move, but also flaunts himself as Huck's inventor and sustainer, by having Huck assert straight off that such bedrock epistemological facts about "his" book are not true.

If we want conundrums about fictitious narrators and semifictitious authors, or about the authority of printed words and the oddness of this cultural practice called "realistic fiction," then here they are for the gathering.[1] Three paragraphs on, this boy who does not exist passes judgment on stories about people who do not exist anymore, if ever they existed at all. When Huck decides that he "don't take no stock" in Moses or other dead people, implications can flare up, having to do with these consoling, validating, yet inherently absurd personal and social rituals of reading novels and "taking stock" in Huck himself or any other talkative illusion. *But so what?* Do a few fun-house complications turn *Huck Finn* into *Finnegans Wake* or a Left Bank *anti-roman?* Paradoxes dredged from the first pages of Huck's narrative (or rather Huck's best narrative, as there are others which Huck's admirers would rather ignore) hardly ripple the conversation about this book, an old conversation that has weathered much bigger disturbances. At a balmy academic conference in southern California, a prolific scholar pounds his rostrum with a flat hand, rages that *"Huckleberry Finn* is *the* most moral novel in the American canon!" and no one in the hall objects; this incantation has rung out in one key or another through seventy-odd years of good commentary.[2] It is gratifying to put such cases, fun to retell Huck's story, and the story of its making, and achieve a kind of dominion over them both, which is to say, dominion over a reading experience that has struck first, and overwhelmed. So we have generations of ingenious response to *Huckleberry Finn:* the need to dignify what we love may run deep in American academic culture, and this particular narrative is perennially dressed up in clean, starched clothing, this talk of solemn themes, moral crises, patterns, always patterns. Commentary on Huck has cherished patterns,[3] especially ones that assure that something momentous and orderly is at the core, and that implicitly reassure us readers about ourselves and our own supposed growth: that a ripening into adulthood means a firming and a bettering of the self, with hard-learned ethics set deep and sure. We may crave a story, in other words, that we are all actually getting someplace by becoming so self-defined.

Such structures and themes may also be inherently there for the seeing in *Huckleberry Finn,* mirroring whatever side of the American self might desire them. Yet the marvel of this book, or at least one of its marvels, is nonetheless that it has always escaped the purview and containment of moralist readings. There are powers in this novel that refuse not just moral growth, but any idea that such shape-taking amounts to maturity, to selfhood, or to some other devoutly-to-be-wished consummation. Part of the fun, in other words, is the way that our consummately moral *Huckleberry Finn* also insinuates that in growing up we may get nowhere, that not only are most of the so-called adults in Huck's world static or outright depraved, but that adulthood as conventionally defined, depraved or not, is a process of obsolescence and of losing, of the self's reduction into code, creed, habit, job, temperament, or worse. To sidestep the romantic anarchy of *Huckleberry Finn* is to enjoy only a part of the novel. And one inference to be drawn from the accumulated attempts to say what Huck is, as a character, a moral presence, an archetypal American, child, principle, or anything else, might be that critics are leery about considering what Huck is *not*. Doing so opens possibilities that from some perspective Huck and his tale might not be anything, or might be imaginative experiences we cannot intellectually domesticate. "Persons attempting to find a motive in this narrative will be prosecuted," warns a voice without a name, a something called "G. G.," which might signify General Grant or just Impersonal Authority; yet for generations critics have queued up to find motives and morals and plots. This industry thrives all over the world, and sometimes with results that can astonish Americans in the trade. Two weeks after my prolific colleague set his beachside listeners straight on the supreme moral authority of *Huckleberry Finn,* I received this thought in a letter from a former student, a Japanese teacher of English in Kyoto:

> Thinking of Mark Twain, I was surprised at Huck's running away when I first read *Huck Finn.* In a fixed, stable society, like that of Japan, running away meant a social death, leading to a physical death. In Chikamatsu's kabuki, it actually means suicide, which was highly praised as a practice in Japan before World War II. If he or she who runs away tries to live, he or she has to become a monk or a nun. Seen from the point of view of Japanese culture, Huck's flight is therefore understood differently, and it surprises: he lives in nature, and yet he returns to society. He must be a ghost!

Huckleberry Finn as kabuki: if following that premise heartens no more than reading *Huck* as PoMo French metafiction, a moment of patience with the idea does break ice. In the episode where Huck stages his murder and becomes a bit like a kabuki ghost, he does escape everything that has vexed him, everything: a father, adoptive parents in the form of the Widow Douglas and Miss Watson, the complications of the fortune that Huck and Tom have stumbled on in their adventure with Injun Joe, and Tom Sawyer himself with his book-borrowed fantasies and his tyranny over Huck's imaginative life. Much is cast off and left behind: society, family, money, and soon after, at least for a while, whiteness, meaning the political and psychological confinement of racial identity. Yet there is evasion to top that. As a character, as an imaginative, word-generated invention, Huck seems to escape *The Adventures of Tom Sawyer* in that moment of self-slaughter. Huck stops being, for a few precious days anyway, "Tom Sawyer's Comrade" and Pap Finn's son, and he may also begin here a protracted escape-struggle against the Mark Twain who made that other sort of Huck, as an idiot sidekick taking his cues from a child several years his junior.[4] In other words, Huckleberry Finn does die here as one sort of *literary* fabrication; and, as I mean to show, he keeps on dying, over and over, on his river journey, dies eventually even as Jim's companion, friend, and moral pupil. Therefore, in the paradoxical spins of *Huckleberry Finn*, Huck does become "Tom Sawyer's Comrade" once again, mirroring Tom's own succession of deaths in *Tom Sawyer,* and experiences a touch of Tom's exhilaration in perfect escape, in being ghost, living boy, plausible and outrageous imaginative construct all at the same moment: the best of being alive, and dead, and within and beyond the pale of both psychological and artistic possibility.

Patterns again. There may be no avoiding them, and really no reason to. Finding or inventing moralities and structures for *Huckleberry Finn* might be a cultural need that is best not trifled with — and by now it ought to be clear that as a stick-in-the-mud reader, I do prefer narratives to mean, and to engage with big-scale insanities that have something to do with being human. But if a great work outruns novel-ness, if it ultimately escapes not only the moralist but also the formalist reading, and if there are voices here that challenge not just the idea of moral growth, but also challenge stability and shape-taking as *literary* values, then the great work grows all the more suggestive as a cultural presence.[5] In other words, part of the pleasure of *Huckleberry Finn* — pleasure not fundamentally at odds with reading the novel as some species of moral and (one way or another) orderly text — has to do with how it keeps possibilities alive: for selfhood, for storytelling, for new relationships among teller, listener, and tale.

Therefore the premise of this chapter: neither the novel nor the American moral universe will fall apart if one tries out for a while the text's opening restrictions. We can safely think about Huck as "Tom Sawyer's Comrade" (which is what he was called on the title-page of the first edition) and consider what it means to take the book's warning label "seriously" — this warning against doing what we've been taught and looking for morals, plots, and motives. This Huck who is introduced — flaunted, really — as a literary construct at the very start of his namesake work, is also constructed in not one or two Mark Twain narratives but in six, four of which were published in Mark Twain's lifetime. Some of these others may be botches or shameless potboilers; but alas, there they are, and no matter what else they are, they are inventions of Huck by the imagination that invented *Huck.* One open question is whether a Huckleberry Finn allowed to take shape in the mind this way, over an array of narratives good and bad, becomes more interesting, and culturally more telling, than Huck as a literary experience pared down to one text or two.

But if this sounds like academic troublemaking, there are other and perhaps better reasons to try it. *Huckleberry Finn,* according to many respectable readings, is pervasively about cultural habits.[6] If that is so, and if cautions and paradoxes in the first pages can be read as challenging this cultural habit of reading fictions for motives, morals, and truth, then the interpretive process threatens to stall out. To heed "G. G's" NOTICE would mean ignoring well-established and high-minded themes. Yet to ignore the NOTICE and what follows on its heels is to ignore what might be *Huckleberry Finn*'s moral of morals: that inbred habits of interpretation, consistency, obedience to conventions, printed words, and an engraved, stabilized, published Culture, could all be pernicious follies.

Again, acknowledging such dilemmas does not mean Continentalizing *Huckleberry Finn,* for this predicament seems from at least one angle solidly American. If what we have here is a novel's paradoxical anticritique of cultural faculties that make novels possible, then readers of Melville and Wharton and Faulkner have certainly seen that before. What Huck himself seems to want most consistently is a right not to become; and yet when generations of sharp readers discover or impose narratives of becoming in *Huckleberry Finn,* they do no harm. For some of the novel's wonder lies in its power to sustain, with appropriate haphazardness, several identities at once, including a "realistic" tale of a boy's education, and a refusal and satirizing of such intentions. Should there turn out to be several Hucks in this novel, or some sequence of them that cannot amalgamate into one satisfactorily consistent or morally graduated young man, then mingled poignancy and consolation inhere in the motions around him: the onward movement of time, and the boy's own movement through an American landscape as much in turmoil as he. My purpose is to see how Huck and his best narrative do aspire to a condition like that, a release, however ironic, however fated, from all the moral gravities of the earth. I also show that this text implicitly acknowledges, and in odd ways celebrates, a zigzag process of growing up, of learning to tell lies and learning not to, of gaining moral identity, yet *not* sacrificing other psychological possibilities in the process, or losing the endangering, salutary power to shape-shift from one self into some other.

Yet Huck Finn is born, as a figure of that name, in a story about Tom Sawyer. The fact remains that most of Mark Twain's published prose about Huck is sewn into narratives that are more about Tom than about Huck, and that feature Tom Sawyer in their titles. Where is the harm, this time out, in reading *Tom Sawyer* and *Huckleberry Finn* as companion novels, and even (heavens forbid!) as parts of one miscellaneous and uneven tale that seems to roll on even through those detested potboilers *Tom Sawyer Abroad* and the story "Tom Sawyer, Detective?"[7] The question is real enough: if these other works are irredeemably trivial, then the one good work among them might be trivialized by a too-close association. Unfortunately for us, the Mark Twain publications and papers give us more of Huck as an ignoramus, or fool, or ordinary boy—which is to say as a morally incomplete or uncoalesced man—than they do Huck as the achieved moralist, Huck the humanist rebel, or any other Huck celebrated in classrooms and journals for much of the twentieth century. If one can face reading only the published Huck-and-Tom narratives together, *Tom Sawyer, Huckleberry Finn, Tom Sawyer Abroad,* "Tom Sawyer, Detective," things begin to look bleak for a favorite story-of-the-story: that Mark Twain discovered Huckleberry Finn's humanity and moral promise when he sent Huck out on the raft with Jim, and that this was Mark Twain's one true and lasting Huck. But things are what they are: Mark Twain evidently felt no qualms about moving in those embarrassing directions, and whether one likes it or not, Tom, Huck, and even Jim usually go along for the ride. In addition, there are two substantial manuscripts, "Tom Sawyer's Conspiracy" and "Huck Finn and Tom Sawyer Among the Indians," both of them unpublished in Mark Twain's lifetime, tales in which Huck and Tom undergo hundreds of pages of something that looks like further imaginative development.[8] Ragged as some of these narratives are, they are indeed companion tales in interesting ways, in that each of them, *Huckleberry Finn* included, offers a sojourn into nonbeing, a condition beyond the bounds and ground rules of "real life," as Western culture has laid them out, yet also beyond romance and even fantasy, as constructed Western-style literary modes. In *Huckleberry Finn* the attempted escape is even from escapism, from the tyrannies of realism and romance, from "plot," meaning not only from orthodoxies of fiction, but ultimately from orthodoxies of romantic dream. If these companion tales allow us to see that daring attempt a bit more clearly, then time in such dubious company is time well spent.

Tom

When the pupils in Tom Sawyer's schoolroom recite speeches on Examination Evening, the others do "Mary Had A Little Lamb," "The Assyrian Came Down," "Casabianca," and canned orations about Friendship, Melancholy, and the Advantages of Culture. Tom's offering is Patrick Henry's "Give Me Liberty or Give Me Death!" — but he breaks down with stage fright in the middle of it. This is an emblematic moment. Tom's life, as chronicled in the first book about himself and Huckleberry Finn, careens between wish-dreams, anarchist declarations, adventures in quest of ultimate liberty, and bouts of terror when consequences loom. For out in his world of perfect liberty and lawlessness (Tom sees no distinction) waits Injun Joe, and if Tom would try life as a robber, or pirate, or Indian, then the road leads straight into the monster's company.

The most writerly passage in *The Adventures of Tom Sawyer* is the long paragraph that begins chapter 31, the description of Tom and Becky straying very much into the monster's company, of the two children lost in McDougal's cave and gradually understanding the awfulness of their plight, and of Tom consoling the terrified Becky and trying to keep his own fear at bay.[9] As a piece of writing, the passage is especially strong because it is not all horror; or, rather, it is like the best sort of horror writing, as it conveys a touch of pleasure, of fascination with the predicament, dreadful as it is. Tom has here and there wished for death, wished for peace, for platonic or sex-transcending union with Becky, for various sorts of removal from the world, and here he has come upon them all. The two children have wandered away from the others, seeking to be off by themselves, and in some measure to be lost. And when Tom, groping through unexplored tunnels looking for some glint of salvation, comes face to face with Injun Joe, the two of them, boy and grown villain, gazing with shock into each other's candle-lit faces, make more than a catchy tableau for an adventure book, like that kindred moment in which Huck and Pap Finn fall asleep, face to face in the father's cabin, ready to kill each other when Pap wakes up. Injun Joe is death — and Tom looks hard into his face, because Joe is a vanisher, a man who has escaped social identity to become the robber and the outcast that Tom fantasizes about becoming, and the Indian that Tom has sometimes dreamed of being, though Joe himself has had no choice in that matter, and has suffered for his blood in a racist town. Joe is darkness, and in the cave, as elsewhere in the novel, Tom Sawyer can participate in that absolute darkness without losing himself forever in its depths.

Much continues to be done to locate main thematic taproots of *Huckleberry Finn* just about anywhere except in *The Adventures of Tom Sawyer*.[10] Yet for all the failings this novel might have, for those adults who delve into a text whose preface calls it "mainly for the entertainment of boys and girls," parallels run deep: a boy who wants to be nothing confined, and anything but a stable self; a world that makes the quest for perfect, uncompromised freedom terrifying and all but impossible. When the motive is to read *Huckleberry Finn* as a morally superior text about the better boy, Tom gets a lot of bad press, and persuasive readings of Huck's own narrative have made much of Tom as Huck's bad angel, a spirit of malignant childishness haunting the world his friend must pass through.[11] Much of that may be true, and Tom's insistence on tormenting Jim at Phelps Farm, in the closing chapters of *Huckleberry Finn*, is as appalling and tedious as Huck's complicity in the sadistic game, and may convict Tom as bad company for Huck.

Yet when Tom must show courage and act honorably in his own book, he does at least as well as Huck does in his. For instance: Tom Sawyer has much more to lose in saving the neck of Muff Potter, as he does all by himself in a crowded St. Petersburg courtroom in chapter 23 of his own book, than either Tom or Huck does when they resolve to help Jim break out of the Phelps shed, or than Huck does when he decides to keep quiet and protect Jim from the slave-catchers. For Injun Joe will surely try to murder Tom for his honesty, while Huck's momentous decision on the river really preserves the peace and quiet of the status quo, as well as the quiet of his own conscience. There are well-known smaller moments in which Tom is, from the perspective of Huck-preferrers like myself and most other critics, uncomfortably moral or downright heroic: Tom taking a thrashing to protect Becky Thatcher from punishment for tearing a page of her teacher's precious and explicit anatomy book; Tom fearing for the safety of his mortal enemy when Tom learns, after two weeks, that Injun Joe is entombed alive in McDougal's cave.

Trapped in the cave himself, with his beloved Becky, Tom is valorous; there is no way around it. Understanding fully and soberly the fate that impends, and playing no fantasy games to keep the truth at bay, he comforts the shattered Becky and makes sensible forays to find and conserve their candles and hunt for a way out. After considerable struggle and terror he discovers one, comes back for the beloved girl, and saves their lives. Not bad for a boy of eight or nine, a boy doomed, as Mark Twain said, to become one of the one-horse men in the American heartland.[12] Such traces of Mark Twain's contempt for a hypothetical grown-up Tom are comforting to Tom-haters, and something of a counter to the overwhelming fact that Mark Twain came back to work up Tom again and again, in at least five long narratives after *Huckleberry Finn*. And there is additional comfort in this: that between these moments of apparently unbookish, unimitative heroism, Tom is perfectly capable of forgetting everything, all that he should have learned from his troubles, all that there is to fear.

Mark Twain's love-hate relationship with Tom has been amply documented, but the core of Mark Twain's objections seems to be with this prospect of Tom as grown up, or even just a little older, a Tom who has fallen inevitably into some ghastly, permanent state of consciousness, like those through which the younger Tom can float without running around. A return trip through *The Adventures of Tom Sawyer* reveals how much time Tom spends wriggling, fidgeting, dodging about, trying to escape from church services, schoolrooms, work, even life. Because various forms of Tom's recurring death wish are a striking motif in those opening dozen chapters, a case begins to accumulate that in the Tom of *Tom Sawyer* there are at least the rudiments of a thematic comrade for Huck: a boy who can sometimes face hard moral decisions and be selfless; a boy who would escape everything about his world and himself. But for all the episodes and other evidence that would support such a case, and despite the fact that the great exploit that dignifies Huck—his quest to help Jim run from slavery—rattles with absurdity and futility, Tom's fine moments simply aren't so gratifying as Huck's are. One cause of the difference: Tom reaches his moral decisions either instantaneously or offstage, and that readers are never treated to Tom's own account of agonies of conscience, as they are to Huck's. The novel shows us nothing of Tom's decision to risk his life and testify to Muff Potter's innocence. As a suspense device, Mark Twain has Tom return home late at night, "through the window," just before the trial; but when Tom is called to the witness stand the next day, the dramatic effect is surprise. The reader is left to guess that Tom's nocturnal outing was a visit to the nameless defense counsel, and that something of moral consequence, some momentous episode in Tom's moral growth, may have taken place.

But where are the signs that when it comes to moral decisions, Tom Sawyer actually *thinks,* much less learns? His self-sacrifice for the snooping Becky seems instantaneous and instinctual. After one insane "inspiration" to snatch the anatomy book from Mr. Dobbins's desk and run from the school, Tom sits empty-headed, "trembling from head to foot with excitement and a sense of the hopelessness of the situation." Heroics come like a cramp:

> "Rebecca Thatcher," [Tom glanced at her face — it was white with terror,] — "did you tear — no, look me in the face" — [her hands rose in appeal] — "did you tear this book?"
>
> A thought shot like lightning through Tom's brain. He sprang to his feet and shouted —
>
> "*I* done it!"
>
> The school stared in perplexity at this incredible folly. Tom stood a moment, to gather his dismembered faculties; and when he stepped forward to go to his punishment the surprise, the gratitude, the adoration that shone upon him out of poor Becky's eyes seemed pay enough for a hundred floggings. Inspired by the splendor of his own act, he took without an outcry the most merciless flaying that even Mr. Dobbins had ever administered; and also received with indifference the added cruelty of a command to remain two hours after school should be dismissed — for he knew who would wait for him outside till his captivity was done, and not count the tedious time as loss, either.[13]

Weeks of time and dozens of pages flow by between the graveyard murder and Muff Potter's trial for it, and for most of that interval Tom's mind has "drifted away from its secret troubles" (109). Drifted away with a vengeance: the graveyard scene is in chapter 9, and Tom and Huck take their oath of silence and watch the evidence close in around Potter in the two chapters after. But Tom then essentially forgets the ghastly business for ten chapters, during which time he steals away to Jackson's Island — for fun, not flight — plays pirate, plays Indian, is presumed dead by everyone in St. Petersburg, watches himself mourned for and attends his own funeral, returns in glory, teases and courts his Aunt Polly, rescues Becky from a school thrashing, declaims about liberty and death, and finishes up the school year. In the midst of all this rollicking, Tom's cousin Mary offers judgment that "it's only Tom's giddy way — he is always in such a rush that he never thinks of anything" (142). Right enough: Tom Sawyer, in his apotheosis novel, personifies restlessness, turning work into play, reality into dream, and death into life, but also moving from mood to mood, sentiment to sentiment, in a flash, with no psychological transitions and rarely an aftereffect, or an indication that these terrifying lessons have reached him. Only days after being buried alive with Becky and Injun Joe, a nightmare that could cure almost anybody else of interest in caves, Tom and Huck are back in its black horrors, scratching around for the loot of a murderer who has died horribly in this place. Yet to say that Tom's literally incredible psychological immunity, or perhaps superficiality, comments on the shallowness or indomitability of young boys is to read tendentiously, considering how contentedly Mark Twain's omniscient narrative forgets with him.

For between the graveyard murder scene in chapter 9, which brings on Tom's moral crisis about telling the truth and saving Potter (a crisis that Huckleberry Finn does *not* feel) and the courtroom revelation of Joe as the real killer of Dr. Robinson, both *Tom Sawyer* and Tom Sawyer forget about Potter and the impending catastrophe. In addition to playing Indian and pirate, rising from the dead, covering nobly for Becky's voyeurism, and capering in school, Tom does a stint in the local Cadets of Temperance, works up a minstrel troupe, catches the measles, and endures the ill effects of a religious revival on everybody else in town. Then it's back to the moral crisis. What might be bothersome about Tom here, in other words, is his inability to be tormented for more than an evening, to be obsessed or scarred by personal experience. There is no saying that Tom at the book's end is a wit sadder or wiser. Having got everything he wanted, he is perfectly happy and untraumatized, by Joe, the cave nightmare, murder at close range, or anything else he has been through. Tom is so damnably finite, so wonderfully, monstrously resilient; and this can make him charming and exasperating at the same time. He has exactly what he puffs up to wish for in his Patrick Henry recitation, yet something better than Patrick Henry's bargain. For fierce Patrick Henry may have never dreamed that in one life, one imagination, Liberty and Death could so jumble up together as desirable situations, that one human being could achieve liberty tantamount to death, or visit death again and again for thrills and liberation from all that is, including death itself. It is lucky indeed that Tom fumbles the speech before coming to Henry's great, self-committing line, the line that sets liberty and death at odds, defining Patrick Henry for the ages as a covenant with fate, as a personality made of resolves.

Nothing seems to confine or define Tom, not even age or gender. Free of the entanglements of having parents — especially of having a father — Tom is looked after by a loving, indulgent aunt, whom he can evade and bedevil as both son and lover. His midnight return to her, when she believes him drowned, to kiss her on the lips and depart from the house as a figure in a dream, may echo "The Eve of St Agnes" or some sentimental imitation in which the chivalrous beau, dead or alive (or both at once as in this case) returns not to his dam but to his bride. If one wants to read incest themes here, or allegories of gender and power, the way is clear; but it is also possible that in this instant of playing nephew, son and secret lover all at once, Tom escapes from each and all of those identities. At the end of the novel Tom is free of poverty, the banalities of river-town childhood, yet free as well of care for the fortune he has found. In the child-world he has all he needs, more than anybody else he knows; and to boot, he has everyone's envy. The hard letterpress of adult life seems to wait for him; as the novel closes Judge Thatcher has plans to send Tom to West Point, the namesake of that college where Hank Morgan shall manufacture his own supposedly free helots of the New Order; then law school, and then perhaps inevitably, marriage to Becky. But as we leave Tom he is plotting with Huck to become robbers together: rich robbers, on an annuity, robbers who don't even need the cash, but plunder for the joy of plundering and breaking laws. Nor are the boys wedded to that fate either, for the closing midnight blood oath, to be sworn "in the lonesomest, awfulest place you can find" is only a "maybe" event for the coming night. As *Tom Sawyer* ends, no oath has gone unbroken, and a young boy, for the moment at least, has almost unimaginable liberty.

Again, why does this matter? There are comforts in imagining a growing-up without emotional scar tissue, "formative years" that form nothing within, ordeals that leave no trace except money. The Tom Sawyer in *Tom Sawyer* is in many ways nobody, which might underlie the pleasure of this book as a children's novel, and its guilty pleasures as adult fiction. Either way, this is a story about triumph not only over childhood trauma but also over thinking and being. When Tom introduces himself to Becky, he announces to her that Thomas Sawyer is "the name they lick me by. I'm Tom, when I'm good." (80) A long way from being "licked" by experience or moral education, this boy certainly is not Thomas Sawyer; and since he is rarely "good" by local moral standards, he might mean "good" in some other sense: good as a boy of improvisations, a boy as yet un*made*. The fun is that we cannot be sure what he means, or what he is. In *Huckleberry Finn* however, Tom seems more like a somebody, in that Tom is now so enamored of doing things by the book; a good case can be made that Tom's protracted sadistic torment of Jim, and his idiotic endangerment of Huck and himself, indicate doses of Scott, Dumas, and other romancers, readings that seem to have swept him away or "made" him, in the brief time-span between *Tom Sawyer*'s ending and the situation at the start of Huck's own book. On that cause, Tom can be scolded or lamented as malign, a confirmed mentality that Huck must be cleansed of if he is to become interesting, to say nothing of morally mature.

Ultimately a culturally valid reading of *Huckleberry Finn* may have to settle on that text alone; yet what happens to the two boys in their other adventures together — meaning their further adventures as characters in Mark Twain's imagination — can enrich a reading of that text in and of itself, just as a look back to *Tom Sawyer* broadens the possibilities for understanding Huck. For one essential question that *Tom Sawyer* poses about its putative companion volume runs this way: if some part of Tom's triumph is that he can participate in Injun Joe's darkness, ferocity, and moral chaos, *without* giving into it as either a psychological victim or a fellow monster, then is Huck "Tom Sawyer's Comrade" because he has similar immunity? Is Huck's much-touted moral education essentially that he learns to invent or participate in moral life without submitting to *that*? Is remaining free, even of the confinements of maturity and goodness, a value that in *Huckleberry Finn* transcends the value of following the "sound heart," and not the "deformed conscience?" One interesting test of the idea, that the other Tom and Huck texts help enrich the context for *Huckleberry Finn,* is to look at what the boys are like in these other adventures, and what the adventures themselves might suggest about the landscape and lodestones of Mark Twain's imagination.

comrades

Notoriously derived or "smouched" from Jules Verne's *Five Weeks in a Balloon*,[14] *Tom Sawyer Abroad* was written quickly in August 1892 at Bad Nauheim, while Mark Twain was laboring at the manuscript of *Those Extraordinary Twins*. It was planned as the start of a series that many Mark Twain fans are glad didn't go far, a sequence of potboilers that would take Tom and Huck on exploits all over the world.[15] Serialized in the *St Nicholas Magazine*, the story did pick up its admirers then and thereafter, most notably Bernard DeVoto, who among major modern critics has been kindest to it.[16]

With no plot to speak of, and a quick, crude ending, *Tom Sawyer Abroad* seems conceived as, or out of, an array of essentially visual experiences: panoramic vistas and landscapes that the boys move through as witnesses, rather than as participants in action. The experience of reading this novel, if we can even call it such, has less to do with thinking or feeling than with seeing. A return to it brings an impression of a handful of tableaux, moments out of a Delacroix dream, rather than of any firsthand encounter with Saharan Africa, which Mark Twain had never seen, nor of Cairo and the neighborhood of the Pyramids, which a quarter-century earlier he had visited. This seems an imaginative voyage prompted rather by certain galleries in the Louvre, where Mark Twain had gazed at huge romantic canvases of sandscapes and Orientalized life and death, of picturesquely massacred armies and tawny exoticism under bright blue skies, dramatic action observed from a safe and pleasant remove, as from a hill or a passing balloon. It makes as much sense to look at the tale this way as to belabor it for plot or psychological allegory.

As most of the balloon trip passes high over nothing — over the Atlantic Ocean and the widest, emptiest desert on earth — the interludes of color and human action stand out: Huck on the dangling ropeladder, a few feet off the sand, with "a couple of dozen" African lions leaping to get at him; a raid by robbers on a caravan of helpless people and their camels; a tableau of mummified wayfarers, including women and children, caught by some long-ago sandstorm, dried to a crisp, and revealed again after the passage of years; a mirage lake teasing the air-travelers repeatedly until it suddenly proves real; fifty lions brawling over clothing that the three of them have left on this lakeshore. Lions seem an obsession in this tale, almost a dream-motif, and their frequent and incongruous appearances in *Tom Sawyer Abroad* are worth comment. There is additionally a friendly caravan, traveled with for a while at a safe distance of a thousand feet in the air; the Pyramids appear like "three little sharp roofs" in a "soft pinky light" far to the east; the face of the Sphinx suddenly blazes at them through a thick fog, a face like "de biggest giant outen de 'Rabian Nights." And ultimately there is Jim, alone on the head of the Sphinx, clutching an American flag as a swarm of men with guns and ladders scramble up the lion-body to kill him — perhaps the most hallucinatory tableau of all.

It is surprising how little in the way of narrative connects these visual moments. After the mad professor, who owns the balloon, falls from the gondola into the sea, most of the rest, among these tableaux, amounts to digressive interlude: an argument about fleas; a concocted Arabian Nights–style treasure yarn; a speculation about selling African sand at a profit in the United States; a moronic theological debate about whether the deserts of the world were actually created, or just a Genesis leftover; and another debate, equally tedious, about the plausibility of one particular tale from Scheherazade. Nor does Mark Twain show the least interest in ending the narrative smoothly after these reveries and interludes have played out. In the space of half a chapter, Jim floats back to Missouri to find Tom a fresh corncob pipe; Jim is caught in the act by Aunt Polly, and the gloomy boys, found out, are forced to go home. The dreamlike compositions in *Tom Sawyer Abroad* focus in the mind because of this lack of anything between them, anything that could be said to advance plot or characterization. Barely a story, it is a travel tale about visiting essentially nothing: an ocean and a waste of sand, populated by little except the occasional pride of killers, the dead, and some majestic, disturbing icons of both.

Therefore one need not work overtime to grasp a wish-dream that these pages enact, of soaring high and safe above not just human misery, but above complication and entanglement of every sort. The ocean and the desert seem uncluttered and clean, the Sahara antiseptically hot, timeless, and pure, and the human strife on its face inconsequential. One theme here rings much like a theme in *Huckleberry*

Finn: safety has to do with floating, and trouble comes when and if your feet touch dry land, mixing you up again in the dangerous business of being alive on firm earth. The dangers divide about evenly in *Tom Sawyer Abroad.* The boys and Jim face lions twice, and murderers twice, and a ride back up into the blue air is all the rescue required — save once, when Huck must drop into the waters of a variously false and true lake, to rest and "get his pluck up" before climbing the ladder back into the balloon.

The circumstantial evidence of *Tom Sawyer Abroad* therefore has more to do with *where* the boys are, where Mark Twain sends them, than *who* they are. For here Araby is surveyed and lingered over not just as a place, but as a state of consciousness, as well as a state of fiction. The boys do not reflect on their own hair-raising escapes, mourn the loss of home as the winds carry them relentlessly east, or shudder at the absolute bewilderment of soaring endlessly over trackless sea and desert, leaving no trace of themselves. The nameless Professor in *Life on the Mississippi* turns his balloon-ride whopper into a horror story about being free, trapped and lost at the same time; but the Professor is a grown man, reaching for chills into the darkness of a grown-up's all-too-stable identity. The two boys and the freed slave are not frightened by what scares their white elders; Tom and Huck tell stories and argue with Jim and each other like boy-men who are, as Emerson says, sure of a dinner, sure of their place in the world; or, rather, of no need *not* to have such a place just yet.

Here then is a telling connection between *Tom Sawyer Abroad* and *The Tales of the Arabian Nights:* in the voyages of Sinbad the sailor, there is really no Sinbad, at least not by the standards of Victorian and modern storytelling. All this wanderer has to distinguish him is cleverness and a certain unexamined persistence, very like these newer voyagers. The same is true of Aladdin, of Ali Baba, of Morgiana. The essential trait of all these characters is their wish to escape, from poverty, from servitude, from exile, from imminent dangers that pop up without plausibility or warning.

Now Huck is narrating all this, and so meekly and unobtrusively that Huck and his creator are regularly and perhaps rightly lamented by critics for this falling-off, this exploitation of a voice and character that had developed into something wonderful in *Adventures of Huckleberry Finn.* To look for traces of *that* Huck is to be disappointed. When Huck is not busy reporting and admiring Tom Sawyer's prowess as an "Erronort" (River talk for "Aeronaut"), Huck is likely to be talking non-sense, arguing from ignorance, debating absurdities, cooperating in schemes that might be excused as satire on Sunday School theology, backwoods geography lessons, conventions of mapmaking, the revered "stretchers" in the Arabian Nights, and matters of similarly perfect unimportance. Huck does offer one perfunctory compliment to Jim as a man who "inside" is "as white as you be" (326); this praise is won from Huck by Jim's willingness to do more than his share to clean up the leavings of an idiotic plan, belabored in the narrative, about shipping Saharan sand back home to make a profit.

And Jim, who says so little in this narrative, can disappoint as thoroughly as Huck, who says so much, for shoveling sand exemplifies Jim's presence on this trip. He is here to deliver plumb-dumb hypotheses, and now and then blunder comically into the truth; and ultimately he is somebody for Tom to rescue, in what stands for the big finale of this meandering book, the rescue from the Great Pyramid. This is thin gruel indeed, if the Huck expected or insisted on here is the multidimensioned Huck of the raft ride downriver, and if Jim's dignity and sympathetic nature are to be conserved. Yet without maneuvering to boost the reputation of this rightly disparaged book, one must conclude that the whole context is one in which that multisided Huck would be out of place and intolerable as narrator and significant character. Mark Twain has sent his boys and his magnificent black man on the most exotic voyage he ever worked up for them, a voyage *into* the storybooks — which means that even Tom himself is out of place, not just as an American boy but as an imaginative construct.

For what makes Tom Sawyer distinctly Tom is his fervent imposition of storybook fantasy on resistant mid-American "reality," his world-altering insistence that children's picnics are A-rab caravans, that Jim's shed at Phelps Farm is Chillon or the Chateau d'If. But when the A-rab caravans are "real," then Tom cannot be himself, cannot be the romancer, sorcerer, and world-changer, just as Huck cannot signal his full presence by commentary about the Tom Sawyering that American grown-ups are wont to do, dangerously imposing make-believe on the real world. In *Tom Sawyer Abroad* there is little for Tom to make up, and so for himself and Huck and Jim, readiness is all — and all there is to them.

Shameless exploitation, then, of Mark Twain's own best characters? Huck, Tom, and Jim sold out, *as* characters, to a pirated science-fiction thrill show? Fair enough; yet quick judgments like these, convincing as they might be, should not obliterate other indications and possible motives. Also with fairness, one could say that in *Tom Sawyer Abroad,* a Tom–Huck book that followed soon after Huck's triumph and Jim's liberation from slavery and minstrel-show flatness, Mark Twain sends the whole group as far as possible from their place of triumph and liberation, with the effect of liberating all of them from that experience, those definitions, and the potentially oppressive context of The Moral and The Real. Legitimately or not, Mark Twain gathers Tom, Huck, and Jim literally up into thin air and equips them for a romance, refurbishes them all, for a time, as heroes in such a romance, which is to say, heroes whose "character" is largely a capacity to adapt to the perfectly unexpected, stay cool, and take things as they come. In other words, if romance is exploited here for a storyline (if we can even call it so), it is also exploited to allow three characters an escape from being who they are, or rather from what they had become, escape from psychological definitions that overhang them in the mode of realistic narrative. Though Huck rarely talks about life in this travel tale, he offers balloon-high blasts at "civilization" (having evidently learned, in the interim, to spell it right), chiding it more broadly and thoroughly than in his reflections on rafting in his own *Adventures.* His target in *Tom Sawyer Abroad* is the inescapable harm that being on firm earth does to the spirits. Life in a world of human beings means life in which an absolutely free range of moods is lost, and in which the self is confined, *de*fined, and oppressed. There are lions all over Mark Twain's Sahara Desert, where as local fauna they don't belong. Though they do keep the story drifting along by providing cause for narrow escapes, a clue to their thematic value comes just after Huck's hymn to freedom from earthly life itself.

> Land, I warn't in no hurry to git out and buck at civilization again. Now, one of the worst things about civilization is, that anybody that gits a letter with trouble in it comes and tells you all about it and makes you feel bad, and the newspapers fetches you the troubles of everybody all over the world, and keeps you down-hearted and dismal most all the time, and it's such a heavy load for a person. I hate them newspapers; and I hate letters; and if I had my way I wouldn't allow nobody to load his troubles onto other folks he ain't acquainted with, on t'other side of the world, that way.

Well, up in a balloon there ain't any of that, and it's the darlingest place there is.

　We had supper, and that night was one of the prettiest nights I ever see. The moon made it just like daylight, only a heap softer; and once we see a lion standing all alone by himself, just all alone in the earth, it seemed like, and his shadder laid on the sand by him like a puddle of ink. That's the kind of moonlight to have. (294)

　In all of his narratives Huck does gifted observing, yet one doesn't often find him sketching like this, in the eerie style of Henri Rousseau. Daylight is the light of truth, and of course an emblem of literary realism — yet isn't this light better? The self "all alone in the earth," perfectly sovereign, unchallenged, but neither completely alone nor limited by solitude. For close by is the shadow, ink-black, as both companion and other, unsoundable lion-ness conjoined with, though darkly other than, a lion softly and magnificently seen. The moment emblematizes the wish-dream of *Tom Sawyer Abroad,* a sojourn into emptiness, away from the superbly realized America that has made each of these drifting travelers what he is.

　I call this chapter "The Quarrel with Romance," and *Tom Sawyer Abroad,* weak as it might be as fiction from Mark Twain's major phase, serves well to open the issue: Mark Twain's complex relationship to the other great narrative mode of his time. For despite Mark Twain's fulminations about Scott, Tennyson, and popular sentimentality, his quarrel in the major narratives never stays simple. If Mark Twain was an enemy of romance, then he was an enemy who could respect and even envy his adversary, and who could see fit, from convenience or desperation, to make raids on its tricks and treasures. Mark Twain regarded romantic delusion and book-and-chromo-induced senti-mentalism as threats to social sanity, civic peace, individual dignity, psychological freedom, and a basic human capacity to see things as they are. That much is well documented. Yet the absolute refusal of an entire mode can *also* be a species of confinement, and a murderous confinement for an imaginative writer, realist or no. If liberation from the thrall of romance proves a powerful strain in Mark Twain's work, then this other drive seems just as strong, for liberation of the self and the narrative from every doctrinal hold. And if narratives in that cause required forays into romance, and putting characters in literary contexts where, as imaginative constructs, they break aesthetic rules and do not belong, then that kind of marauding was exactly what he did. In *Tom Sawyer Abroad,* Tom, Jim, and Huck are sent on holiday from the literary mode that gave them life; in other works, romance is quarreled with much more elaborately, and here and there varieties of romance are even celebrated for their timeless power. Mark Twain may have been a realist, but realism by no means limits him; and, ironically enough, it was romance that provided escape from the supposedly liberating realist ideology.

mysteries

One other Tom–Huck tale published in Mark Twain's lifetime is a detective story: a shameless potboiler, yes, but also a provocative flight into the world of romance, for "Mark Twain" as a public construct as well as for his two triumphant characters — and perhaps for a private Mark Twain who dreamed them. Desperate for money and goaded back to an old obsession by the Sherlock Holmes craze, Mark Twain went headlong into the detective-story business within months of publishing *Tom Sawyer Abroad,* and over the next four years three long mystery narratives took shape.[17] The first of them, *Pudd'nhead Wilson,* which will be considered in Chapter 4, doesn't involve Huck, Tom, or Jim at all; the second one, "Tom Sawyer, Detective," is a mechanical exploitation of Tom and Huck down at the Phelps Farm again, with Jim left behind in St. Petersburg and out of the action. One other story, "Tom Sawyer's Conspiracy," remained unpublished, unfinished, jumbled, and fascinating, if only for what it suggests about the possibilities of Tom Sawyer's mind, including his evolving and strikingly *un*childish notions of epistemology and human fate, *and* about Huckleberry Finn's reasons for still knuckling under to the younger boy's mercurial leadership. For Tom *is* thinking here, in fits and starts, and not just about romance plots and theatrics and how to impose them on his world. What dawns on him is an intuition about the motions and putative high-seriousness of history, and prospects for some kind of irreverent, imaginative dominion over fate itself. Tom nowhere else seems madder or more profound than he seems in "Conspiracy," and Huck's appreciation of his friend's intelligence, depth, and sudden, brilliant mood-changes — different as these qualities may be from needed prudence and compassion — has better grounds here than in any other work in which Huck plays Tom Sawyer's wide-eyed comrade. This is the most provocative of the Tom–Huck potboilers and the very last of Huck's first-person narratives about Tom and Jim. Though Huck has not grown or changed perceptibly as a character in "Conspiracy," the universe the boys live in has slipped off its axis, and Tom himself has grown not complex, but complicated, becoming a personality with fissures and contradictions so large that talk about boyishness will not explain them away.

Even so, of these Huck and Tom manuscripts, "Tom Sawyer's Conspiracy" is the oddest to contemplate, and potentially the most embarrassing when placed near the great Mark Twain works to which political homage is now often paid, especially *Huckleberry Finn* and *Pudd'nhead Wilson*. If one wants to read either of these texts as "about" race slavery and its terrible moral consequences, then "Conspiracy" makes a good-sized obstacle. The paranoid slave-holding culture of Missouri and Arkansas is spotlit more strongly here than in *Huckleberry Finn*. Abolitionists haunt the woods just across the river on the Illinois shore, and the community, in a "cold sweat" and "considerable worried" about a raid or a rising, stalks the streets in patrols and watches out for strangers. But none of this matters at all to Tom as a moral issue; nor to Huck either, though the time of the action is only about six months after his supposedly uplifting adventures with Jim on the raft. Alas, as "Conspiracy" opens, Huck seems perfectly happy with Tom's "splendid idea" to "get people in a sweat about the ablitionists [*sic*]," trigger more of the violence and mob action that supposedly appalled Huck on his river journey, and endanger the lives of black men and women, including the beloved Jim. Can this be commentary of some sort on Huck's moral malleability, or on the malignant persuasiveness of the Tom Sawyers and St. Petersburgs of the world? Probably not. For the tale Huck tells has shifted far from themes and interests we can discern, or at least argue for, in *Huckleberry Finn*. Jim himself, for example, has been robbed of roundedness and dignity, not by the slave culture he now resides in as a free man, but by shortcuts in characterization. Jim seems at his worst here, more like a gullible minstrel-show fool. Reasoning either preposterously or not at all, he seems sympathetic chiefly as a poor sap who cannot match wits with a ten-year-old white boy, and as someone to be in deep trouble, someone for Tom and Huck to rescue yet again.

The other large-scale embarrassment of "Conspiracy," as a text to be shelved anywhere near Mark Twain's morally engaged narratives, has to do with its address to the paradoxes of racial identity. "Conspiracy" has some bothersome similarities with *Pudd'nhead Wilson*. Once again a tale about race and selfhood ends in a sensational murder trial, and once again an unknown lawyer who "hadn't any business" before in a river town unmasks the true killer in court, this time with invaluable help from Tom, who uses footprints and false teeth rather than David Wilson's fingerprint kit to flush the culprit out. Along the way in the unpublished work, there is much ado about racial masquerading, for profit and for the hell of it: early on, Tom plans to dress up in his minstrel-show disguise to impersonate a runaway slave, be sold to a bounty-man named Bat Bradish, and then be set loose by Huck and Jim, all to stir up trouble about abolitionist raiders. But the plan derails when Huck comes upon a runaway black slave whom this Bradish has acquired half an hour before: a black slave whom Tom spots as a white man in blackface, playing Tom's own scheme "to a dot." Still in blackface, Tom resolves to catch the white man for impersonating a Negro and have him jailed for swindling Bat, as Tom and Huck had planned to do themselves. Bat Bradish is murdered; Jim is accused of the crime, imprisoned, and expected to hang or be lynched; and Tom makes Jim's situation exquisitely worse by spreading a lie that provides Jim with a motive for the killing. The impersonator turns out to be their old friend the Duke, who with the King has conspired to swindle Bradish; the two scoundrels have killed him in making their getaway. So in the courtroom scene Jim is dramatically proven innocent, and when the narrative breaks off, the corrupt, violent race-slavery culture seems to have claimed three more victims: Bradish, the Duke, and the King.

Only with readerly violence, however, can we interpret this story as "about" the moral rottenness of that culture. Though Tom at the outset may be trifling with the powder keg of race relations in his hometown, there is neither malice nor morality in his mind. Tom engages in a classic *détournement,* an act of premeditated, scrupulous anarchy; and if trouble for the town's values and complacency comes as a side effect, then that trouble signifies no righteous assault by Tom on ingrained depravity and race slavery. His conspiracy has much more to do with disrupting social order of any and every sort, and with jarring all logical expectations, the narrative rituals of court trials, and other adult pathologies. As the "Conspiracy" accelerates, everything is trivialized: slavery, abolitionism, racial identity, personal safety. It is an uncomfortable fact that more race-swapping and racial impersonation go on here than in *Pudd'nhead Wilson,* so much more that its potential thematic importance in "Tom Sawyer's Conspiracy" evaporates in a comedy of smoke and mirrors. Race here looks very much like a gimmick to propel a tricky detective yarn. Denied dignity before the frame-up and even after, the Jim we are offered seems naive to the point of psychological nonexistence, dutifully assisting Tom's show-off embellishments of the case against him. For it is Jim who supplies his plot-happy young friend with a convincing motive for a crime Jim did not commit, a motive that almost hangs him. And as for Huck, the noble "sound heart" who now and then in other tales has been able to see social depravity steadily and whole, Huck is won over to Jim's persecution more solidly than he ever was while tormenting him at the Phelps Farm. Huck's one show of remorse for helping in the conspiracy evaporates in a moment, when Tom promises romantic glory for everybody:

> "There's our old Jim, the best friend we ever had, and the best hearted, and the whitest man inside that ever walked, and now he's going to get hung for a murder he never done, I just *know* he never done it, and whose fault is it but this blame conspiracy, I wish it was in — "
>
> "Shut up!" he says, "you can't tell a blessing from a bat in the eye, I never see such an idiot — always flying at everything Providence does, you ought to be ashamed of yourself. Who's running this conspiracy? — you? Blame it, you are hendering it every way you can think of. Old Jim get hung? Whose going to let him get hung, you tadpole?"
>
> "Well, but — "
>
> "Hush up! there ain't any well about it. It's going to come out all right, and the grandest thing that ever was, and just oceans of glory for us all — and here you are finding fault with your blessings, you catfish. Old Jim get hung! He's going to be a hero, that's what he's going to be. Yes, and a brass band and a torchlight procession on top of it, or *I* ain't no detective."
>
> It made me feel good and satisfied again, I couldn't help it. It was always just so. (184–85)

And when elegant schemes fail, it is Tom, not Huck, who shows greater anguish about Jim's plight, and who vows to save his friend or blow his own brains out. Veteran Tom-haters can find much here to suggest that his pain is only self-pity, embarrassment, and book-borrowed sentimentality. Yet it is Tom, and not Huck, who eventually does rescue Jim and sets things right, with considerable help from what the King calls "a righteous overruling Providence," a track of far-fetched coincidence that carries the two boys and the ex-slave into deep trouble and out again.

And what exactly does Tom Sawyer mean by "conspiracy?" Jim has happened upon Bat Bradish's body a moment after Bradish is murdered, and fallen over the corpse; just then witnesses have come by to see what they think is the end of a fatal struggle; later on, by a "mortal piece of good luck" the boys find an abandoned skiff, with the oars ready in the locks, just when they need to slip back to town. Soon after that, on a wild-goose chase to locate Burrell's Gang on Fox Island, the boys board a riverboat and Huck literally stumbles over the sleeping Duke on the forecastle, which results in talk about Jim, a counterplot contrived to sell Jim down the river at a profit rather than see him hanged, and a scheme by the con men to show up at the trial to lay claim to Jim — and therefore to be on hand for their unmasking as murderers. And throughout there are strange tirades by Tom, about this "conspiracy" as a thing apart, a dark plan that no human has conceived, and that runs along all by itself.

Against "Tom Sawyer's Conspiracy," crass exploitation has been a versatile charge: exploitation of Mark Twain's established and popular characters, of the slavery crisis and the drama of abolitionism on the borders of North and South, of skin color as a treacherous sign of identity, of outrageous coincidence to keep a detective story boiling along, of social, moral, and psychological enigmas for the sake of selling a page-turner. Yet before this tale joins the record as damning evidence about the intentions of *Pudd'nhead Wilson,* and whether or not that novel can be plausibly read in this context as a satire or fable or sustained commentary on anything, we need to look at the hazy presence of "Conspiracy's" ulterior narrative. As the plot takes unpredictable turns, and as Huck, Jim, and Tom are sacrificed to it as characters, there comes a sequence of moments in which Tom and others puzzle over individual agency and Providence. In the opening pages a farcical exchange starts between Tom and Jim on the question of fate, a burlesque of Christian debate about free will:

"Jim, Providence appoints everything beforehand, don't he?"
"Yessah — 'deed he do — fum de beginnin' er de worl'."

"Very well. If I plan out a thing — *thinking* it's me that's planning it out, I mean — and it don't *go;* what does that mean? Don't it mean that it wasn't Providence's plan and he ain't willing?"

"Yessah, you can 'pen' 'pon it — dat's jes' what I mean, every time." . . .

"Well, then, it's right for me to go ahead and keep on planning out things till I find out which is the one he wants done, ain't it?"

"W'y, sutt'nly, Mars Tom, dat's all right, o'course, en ain' no sin en no harm — "

"That is, I can *suggest* plans?"

"Yassah, sutt'nly, you can *sejest* as many as you want to, . . . but doan you *do* none of 'em, Mars Tom, excep' only jes' de right one — because de sin is shovin' ahead en *doin'* a plan dat Prov'dence ain't satisfied wid." (135)

This goes on for a while, with Tom winning the argument, and Tom and Jim consenting to proto-dadaist disruption of the town's peace and safety, chaos for its own sake in the name of History and its inscrutable motions. In an aside, Huck credits Tom with conceiving, there and then, "the idea" for the American Civil War, and with giving the idea up magnanimously to please the worried Jim. In Huck's account, satire flickers in something like a classic Huck-manner, with his apparently guileless praise triggering perceptions that Huck does not, or may not, consciously intend. Satire then, but satire of what? Of the madness of civil wars? Of mayhem in ostensibly Christian cultures? Of the mangling of history in the individual mind, or the hopelessness of conserving truth and passing it onward intact? All of the above, perhaps. Yet beyond them all perhaps this too: that the madness of Tom Sawyer's conspiracy, stirring up trouble and danger for their own sake, has more in common with the way things go, historically and culturally, than our chronicles usually admit, and that the idiot troublemakers of the world have not only more effect, but more right to recognition as "agents of Providence," than the solemn, world-historical figures lauded on public monuments. In subsequent episodes, Tom Sawyer, who has set out to foment "conspiracy" for the hell of it, apprehends with delight that hell, or the Holy Angels, or the King's proverbial "overrulin' Providence" may be as crazily conspiratorial as he is, and that Huck, Jim, and Tom himself are not plotters at all, but half-blind agents of some larger plan — a cosmic "conspiracy" dishing out joy, misery, and suspense with no clearer motive than Tom has — nothing more moral than making human experience into an outrageously plotted yarn, a narrative that thrills by surprise, bizarre coincidence, and the confounding of all sane expectations.

Isaac Bashevis Singer was fond of saying that humanity was created because God likes stories. The theme mustering in "Conspiracy's" opening pages, and popping up repeatedly thereafter, seems to be that God or Providence or the dark powers that govern experience are fond of turmoil, and contrive to make life dangerous, coincidental, even logical, yet beyond comprehending. As Tom recognizes that each successive plan of his has derailed and crashed, he rejoices as Huck despairs. Tom talks like a happy acolyte in the great mysteries:

> But Tom's face lit up pious and happy — it made me shiver to see it; and he give Bill a dime, and says, quite c'am —
>
> "All right; run along; we are a coming." Bill cleared out and we hurried up, and Tom says, kind of grateful, "Ain't it beautiful, the way it's developing out? — *we* couldn't ever thought of that, and it's the splendidest design yet. *Now* you'll be trustful, I reckon, and quit fretting and losing confidence." (184)

Three chapters on, Jim's plight has so compounded and darkened that Tom must now keep his hands entirely off the pilot-wheel of "his" conspiracy, knowing full well, as even Huck now understands, that the narrative of their commingled lives is writing itself:

> "All right, then, we ain't fools, but ain't it lucky that we went down the river when there warn't the least sense in it, and yet it was the very thing that met us up with the King and the Duke, and we can see, now, Jim would be hung, sure, if it hadn't happened. Huck — something else in it, ain't there?"
>
> He said it pretty solemn. So I knowed he had treed the hand of Providence again, and said so.
>
> "I reckon you'll learn to trust, before long," he says.
>
> I started to say "I wisht *I* could get the credit for everything another person does," but pulled it in and crowded it down and didn't say nothing. It's the best way. After he had studied a while he says —
>
> "We got to neglect the conspiracy, Huck, our hands is too full to run it right."

> I was graveled, and was agoing to say "Long's we ain't running it
> anyway — 'least don't get none of the credit of it — it ain't worth
> the trouble it is to us," but pulled it in and crowded it down like I
> done before. Best way, I reckon. (204–5)

This is really Huck's marker in "Conspiracy," this instinct to "crowd
down" any urge to resist Providence or the inherent chaos of the human condition. In the first pages of the tale he announces his mood,
or more accurately his motto for this tale:

> Me and Jim and Tom was feeling good and thankful, and took the
> dug-out and paddled over to the head of Jackson's island early
> Saturday morning where we could be by ourselves and plan out
> something to do. I mean it was Tom's idea to plan out something
> to do — me and Jim never planned out things to do, which wears
> out a person's brains and ain't any use anyway, and is much easier
> and more comfortable to set still and let them happen their own
> way. (134–35)

Staying with such stoicism, rolling with the trouble caused by Tom's
plans, blind chance, or malignant or beneficient will, Huck may seem
more clearly defined as a character here than Tom Sawyer. As he leaps
from infantile egotism to heroic compassion, from sadistic delight to
self-sacrifice, from idiocy to brilliance and back again, and up and
down between despair and faith in the way "things" are going, Tom
shows in comparison a blur of psychological states. Tom's treatment of
Jim in this story — always with Huck's acquiescence — seems unprece-
dentedly depraved and matchlessly noble. He shows callousness and
brutality outstripping anything he does or suggests doing in other
narratives. Even so, Tom's bursts of anguish and compassion for Jim,
and Tom's subsequent efforts to right all wrongs make Huck's go-
along attitude look not just weak but reprehensible. "ACTION IS CHAR-
ACTER" vows a flagging Scott Fitzgerald, in a note to himself about his
last, unfinished novel;[18] an assumption that propels and informs "Tom
Sawyer's Conspiracy" seems to be that action of nearly any sort, physical, social, psychological, political, *replaces* character, and replaces it
with something possibly better, more free to ride out and comprehend
the storm-tides of the human situation. For this consummate non-
Tom, this contradiction-laden, stoic-malignant, monster-saint Tom
Sawyer, solves the murder and saves Jim from both the rope and the

Cotton South, and does so because his brains, bouts of stupidity, and unstable psyche make him a wind harp for the breezes of providence. Tom is the one human being in town who can comprehend the way "things go," aid and abet the cosmic nondesign, and exploit small developments along the way. A local detective named Flacker builds a ludicrous narrative out of the available evidence, deducing that Jim and two unknown dwarf accomplices, "one cross-eyed and t'other left-handed" (201) are henchmen in Burrell's Gang, because a detective, says Huck, will "read every little sign he come across as if it was a book" (202). Neither the structure of this narrative nor the world it presents have much in common with "a book," meaning some tale in which events are not only plausible but make a species of sense, and in which a protagonist or even a detective has understandable motives and a more-or-less stable identity. In contrast, "Conspiracy" drifts into open combat with detective-story etiquette, with conventions of storytelling as Mark Twain knew them, with its own characters as Mark Twain had previously made them, and with Providence and chaos as mysteries representable on the page.

This view seems to scour a minor manuscript for high-serious sig-nifications. But the disruptions in "Conspiracy" shed light on bet-ter and better-known works, including the original *Tom Sawyer* book, *Pudd'nhead Wilson* and the Mysterious Stranger tales, and even *Adven-tures of Huckleberry Finn*. In *Tom Sawyer Abroad*, "Tom Sawyer, Detec-tive," and "Tom Sawyer's Conspiracy," Tom Sawyer is a wish-dream, as much so as Huck ever was for Samuel Clemens, and Mark Twain's various remarks about Tom being a weak or unpromising protagonist, refer to a Tom Sawyer he never created, a Tom grown up, losing not only his social liberty and the confidence that goes with it, but also the psychological liberty of an unstabilized identity, a self that can dwell in fantasy and fact together, forget the most grievous trauma, and im-provise happily into the future. Over the course of these five narra-tives, horrendous things happen to Tom. Orphaned as a small child, he has seen midnight murders in graveyards and been chased by kill-ers; he has been buried alive, watched his own funeral, and heard plagiarized elegies for his insignificant self. He has seen one scheme of his after another run afoul, bringing misery to himself and the few friends he has—and none of this affects his morale or his psyche for more than the occasional half-hour. If Tom is a big part of Mark Twain's dream of boyhood, that dream was more heretical than a celebration of "innocence" or nostalgia for simpler times in a cultural history. The abiding wish in these Tom Sawyer–Huck Finn stories is for some state before one became, and for keeping that precious incompleteness amid terrors and catastrophes that rain down to form and *de*form everyone else. Only in one of these narratives, *Huckleberry Finn,* does Mark Twain gaze into the catastrophe of becoming, a tragedy to which he almost sacrifices his best and most famous hero.

But of these sequels and unpublished manuscripts, the Tom–Huck story written closest in time to *Adventures of Huckleberry Finn* is the fragment called "Huck Finn and Tom Sawyer Among the Indians." Apparently begun while *Adventures* was still being readied for the press, "Indians" was perhaps intended to be the "lighting out" for the Territory that Huck proposed in his famous closing lines.[19] In "Indians" Tom and Huck head West, with Tom full of sentimental-romance ideas about the Plains nations, full of Fenimore Cooper, that is; and Huck seems once again the compliant sidekick. Though one of the themes here involves the vast difference between the Real West and Cooper's wilderness, what unfolds in "Indians" is a restyled *Last of the Mohicans,* with bad savages making away with Jim and a beautiful white maiden, and a modernized Hawkeye named Brace Johnson leading the pursuit. Tom and Huck tag along with this hero, who is handsome, quick, noble, brave, consummately male, and wise in the Red Man's ways. True to form, Tom's delusions get the rescuers into trouble, but this is trouble of a gruesome high-adventure sort, and the tale is patently not centered on Tom's rude awakening to truth. Jim is again the captive, as he is in "Tom Sawyer Detective" and "Tom Sawyer's Conspiracy," for Mark Twain evidently liked having Jim in bondage of some sort, with Tom and Huck plotting to rescue him, and Tom in charge. But the manuscript breaks off before anyone is rescued, and it seems to be failing in any quarrel it engages in with Fenimore Cooper and romance about American Indians.

Some of these features may merely signal Mark Twain indulging in old tricks as he tried to turn out a potboiler. Harder to dismiss, however, is the fact that in "Indians," as in each of these other tales, Huck is back to being the go-along, generally happy and worshipful in that role, and apparently unaffected emotionally, morally, or in any other way, by his river journey with Jim. Though in this tale Huck does correct Tom once in a while, Tom does almost all of the grand-scale thinking. Moreover, Tom does the moralizing as well in both "Indians" and "Conspiracy," and what psychological struggles there are in these tales belong to him. It is Tom, not Huck, who sees the mutilated bodies of Buck, Sam, and Bill. It is Tom who resolves to rescue Jim, a resolve to which Huck assents without fervor; and it is Tom who feels (this once, in all these narratives!) humiliation at having believed the romantic lies in his Cooper novels. Huck opens the touchy question:

> Once I said:
> "Tom, where did you learn about Injuns — how noble they was, and all that?
> He give me a look that showed me I had hit him hard, very hard, and so I wished I hadn't said the words. He turned away his head, and after about a minute he said "Cooper's novels," and didn't say anything more, and I didn't say anything more, and so that changed the subject. I see he didn't want to talk about it, and was feeling bad, so I let it just rest there, not ever having any disposition to fret or worry any person. (50)

Though this moment is like none in *The Adventures of Tom Sawyer*, or *Adventures of Huckleberry Finn*, or any of the published work involving Tom, it has no ramifications. The bloody adventure from here on does not pause again to glimpse or speculate about Tom Sawyer's inner life. And as for Jim, the unhappy truth is the same as in the other published and unpublished sequels and potboilers. Jim never again regains the measure of humanity and dignity he achieves and holds in *Huckleberry Finn*. In *Tom Sawyer Abroad* he is comic relief and something to rescue from a swarm of murderous Egyptian natives; in "Huck and Tom among the Indians" and "Tom Sawyer's Conspiracy" he may be construed as a victim of Tom, or race prejudice, or some other social or moral ill, but only in a sentimentalized reading that coaxes stubborn texts into harmony with the novel everybody loves.

Yet what difference does this make, that the unfinished, unpublished Tom-and-Huck stories don't support a case that Mark Twain had deep-lying moral preferences for Huck, or lasting contempt for Tom Sawyer, or even that Huck, out beyond the bounds of his *Adventures*, doesn't talk and act as morally grown-up and psychologically strong as we might want, if only for reassurance that his river education has stayed with him? A contrarian reading of Huck in this context — the context of the other Hucks and Toms that Mark Twain dreamed up before and after — holds that Mark Twain did indeed keep faith with his most memorable character, or rather with one quality in Huck that by the evidence mattered most to him: the power to be, first and last, a boy *sans qualités*.

running from the angels

If that sounds like heresy, then heresy has the advantage of taking us closer to fundamental strengths and resilience in this novel: its wit, its energy, and its many-sided suspense. It isn't morally or structurally disastrous that Huck never gets caught by anything for long, not even by his own "sound heart," which moralist readings of the novel make much of, and which Mark Twain himself remarked, in his always-quoted, paradoxical description of Huck as a boy with a sound heart and a deformed conscience. If Mark Twain meant to offer a handy distinction, then the action of the novel muddles it admirably. Having reached the apparently momentous decision to help Jim to freedom and "go to hell!" in the cause of intuitive goodness, Huck still proves capable of collaborating in swindles, even of the young and the innocent. If the credulous rubes of Pokeville deserve gulling, and if the mean-spirited, voyeuristic town of Bricksville deserves everything it gets from the Royal Nonesuch, then what of the plot against the bereaved Peter Wilks family? It matters that Huck participates in this con game more actively than in others in the book, and that he blows the whistle on the Duke and the King only after days of complicity. The delay does much more than percolate an intrigue in the novel. For suspense has been building about Huck himself, as the plot against the orphan girls grows more sinister. And there is lingering suspense about Huck even *after* he hides the money in the dead father's coffin and writes Mary Jane a note about the con men: suspense not about this exploded scam, but what might follow in a darkening succession. After all, it isn't moral principle that turns Huck against the plot, so much as the prettiness and spirit of Mary Jane Wilks, who seems to appeal to Huck's hormones and sympathies more effectively than do the middle-aged career criminals with whom Huck schemes his way down the Mississippi. Even so, an altogether different sort of suspense also looms in these pages, not just about Huck's morality but about Huck as a sustainable voice and character, and whether both of them, the fabricated and the counterfeited narrative, will finally come completely apart.

Such dangers—which are after all exhilarating, and part of the fun of reading this book—seem rooted quite a way back in the tale. Where exactly things do start going awry, in structure or in that basic plausibility that supposedly identifies realistic fiction, matters less than the moment where the novel begins flaunting its own truancies. In chapter 20, the Duke is interrogating Huck about whether Jim is really Huck's slave or an exploitable runaway; and Huck's answer, which "settles" the Duke, unsettles everything else: "Goodness sakes, would a runaway nigger run *south?*"[20]

We never hear a decent answer to Huck's question, which is at once rhetorical and reflexively embarrassing to Huck as Jim's companion and rescuer, to Mark Twain as plot-crafting novelist, and possibly to us readers, if we haven't minded the "Notice" at the start of the book, which warned us to leave logic and reasonable readerly expectations behind. When Huck and Jim somehow miss the confluence with the enormous Ohio River in the middle of the night, what seemed at the time to be the main plot-current of the novel—the quest to take Jim into free territory—takes a pratfall. There may be no shock in that. The gestating detective story evident in the first half-dozen chapters has also (luckily) collapsed, and vaguely picaresque adventures after the escape from Pap have vaguely promised that the central agon of the book might be something different: perhaps a liberating move *past* plot, past sense, past all reason-contraptions at the heart of the novel, and into "plot" based on character, with "character" founded in the charms and perils of the moment at hand.

Regardless of when this or that section of the novel was actually penned,[21] the fact remains that Mark Twain chose to contrive a riverboat out of the darkness and run over and wreck his two protagonists, their raft, and the discredited plot less than two pages after delivering the news that the crucial turn toward freedom has been missed. Huck is sent for an adventure alone among the Grangerfords and Shepherdsons, an experience whose importance in this plot against plots will become clear in a moment. When Jim and the raft are restored to the tale in chapter 19, the Duke and the Dauphin join them not five pages later, and it is their arrival that assures that the narrative will escalate the war on narrative convention.

Only a few paragraphs before the moment when Huck, under cross-examination, implicitly ridicules what he and this novel have ostensibly been up to, the Dauphin lays out the new ground rules for drifting down the Big River: ground rules not only for social order, but also for identity—all in one of the supremely dadaist comic passages in *Huckleberry Finn*. Apparently strangers to each other, the two con men have jumped aboard with angry locals in hot pursuit, and in a "What got you into trouble?" exchange, they have each attested to being professional frauds. Only then does the younger fraud go into his Duke of Bridgewater act, as much for the gray impostor as for Huck and Jim. When concocted identities begin to fly, neither man believes the other for a moment, yet for at least three reasons each man's pretenses are resisted only briefly and feebly. First, the boy and the slave must be awed and subjugated so that the two usurpers can take over the raft. Second, each impostor is putting on a professional show for the other impostor's benefit, signaling not only what talents he has for deception and how he now means to use them, but also how far he will go in fakery for the sake of gain. Yet there may be something further, neither for Huck's benefit nor for the other man's, but rather for each faker's own gratification: a sacramental casting-off of every old mask and self, and a confirmed readiness to assume new ones. When late in the afternoon the old, bald cheat declares himself "the late Dauphin of France!" he is certainly one-upping the Duke in the game for control on the raft, but he does more than that. Like a partner in a game of bridge, the older man is accepting, endorsing, and raising the Duke's bid: to play-act before Huck and Jim, to do make-believe together for whatever profit the southward ride might afford, and to put away any interest in the truth.[22]

At this point, what the Dauphin has *not* said matters considerably: not scorning the Duke's claim to royal rank, the King has responded, as it were, in the same suit. Details in the contract have yet to be settled, for the Duke at first hears the raised bid poker-style, not bridge-style, and misunderstands this offer of collusion and a truce about truth. The King has to come closer to spelling out the pact, but again the language in his peace offering has layers to it. The posturing that has been going on is at once subtle and ridiculous. Each man knows the other's complete fraudulence, and certainly they have been sizing each other up *as* frauds, looking for depth and thoroughness in the counterfeit, searching opportunistically for weaknesses, but searching also, as it turns out, for an ally in deceit. Even so, the King's peace has breathtaking dimensions:

> "Like as not we got to be together a blamed long time, on this h-yer raft, Bilgewater, and so what's the use o' your bein' sour? It'll

only make things oncomfortable. It ain't my fault I warn't born a duke, it ain't your fault you warn't born a king — so what's the use to worry? Make the best o' things the way you find 'em, says I — that's my motto. This ain't no bad thing that we've struck here — plenty grub and an easy life — come, give us your hand, Duke, and less all be friends." (747)

On the face of it, this is a pact among career criminals, a declaration of war on everybody else, and a proclamation of stoic antistoicism. Yet even on the surface (given what happens soon after) the king's "motto" hovers between significations. By "make the best" he seems to mean both to accept meekly and outrageously exploit, and so his "motto" means this: leave things as they are, but also overhaul them for personal gain. A man who is not who he says he is, and who may not be anyone at all, certainly can intend both things at once, and this friendship, founded thus on two reciprocal lies (or rather on *four,* since each confirmed liar agrees here to feign belief in the other man's patently fraudulent identity) is also founded on a doctrine with two opposite meanings. When the pact is made, it is joined immediately by Huck and Jim, who in turn become frauds to protect themselves and keep the peace. For in the next moment Huck tells the con men an elaborate lie about being an orphan heading for an uncle's Louisiana plantation, and about Jim as Huck's own slave and personal servant.

Huck's raft drifts south as a carousel of imposture, and for ten chapters the truce stays unbroken, with the King's bizarre rule holding sway: that until further notice everyone aboard can be whoever and whatever they want. It is telling that even in private, even when they believe that neither Huck nor anyone else can hear them, Bilgewater and the Dauphin address each other by those preposterous titles or variations on them, never resorting to actual names, never demanding those real names from one another. Moreover, in "Tom Sawyer's Conspiracy," which apparently unfolds months later, these two are still, not only to the world but to one another, the Duke and the King. Do they *have* other names? Have they forgotten what they are? Does either of them believe for a moment that his ludicrous lie has fooled another con-man? The pact they have made is a lasting friendship without a shred of honesty. A translation, then, of the King's Peace: each man should regret, and then forget, the fact that fate has assigned him a particular station in life — which means that each of them has chosen one fraudulent identity instead of some other, and that on this river one pretense is as good as any other. Having resolved to accept without question each other's humbug, these shape-shifters can set about accepting "things as you find 'em," which means imaginatively transforming themselves further, to victimize any gullible soul they find.

Before this Quadruple Alliance of deception, Huck has made his way simply, via one alias at a time. Hereafter, until he sheds the King and the Duke and arrives at the Phelps Farm, he must keep two impersonations going at once, one inside the other, just as the two con men do.[23] Huck has to play whatever supporting role they assign him in a given scam — stage roustabout, British serving boy, or mum audience, concealing what he knows about the unfolding scam — and for their eyes only he must play orphan boy heading for Uncle Ben's farm with his trusty slave. So whenever these four are gathered together, nobody is who they really are, and when they work the shoreworld, no one they meet (with the exception of one insistent doctor named Robinson in the Wilks neighborhood) insists that they come clean. The double-masquerading keeps up even after the Duke and King are gone and Tom Sawyer arrives on the scene; thanks to a misunderstanding by Mrs. Phelps, Huck becomes Tom, Tom becomes Sid, and Jim becomes an escaped slave with a fictitious $200 reward on his head, and all of them are actors in a protracted, pointless game of Romantic Prisoner.

Huck proves ready for all that, as Huck's adventures before the coming of the royalty have polished him in the art of lying, and more thoroughly than in the value of standing up for friends and truth. A classic interpretation holds that Huck does this masking for self-preservation, and that this continuing motive makes him more virtuous than grown-ups who play make-believe for profit or power. Though that reading seems solid as far as it usually goes, there are twists to Huck's masquerading, in that the "self-preservation" he engages in also means self-erasure, and not just as a means but also as an end. Intrusive, dangerous grown-ups must be kept at bay or got rid of, as well as some inconvenient or dangerous Huckleberry Finns: impersonations, personalities, personae that sour and turn lethal quickly, and that whisper in chorus a warning that being somebody — anybody, even oneself if one *has* a self — means big trouble.

Having murdered himself to escape from Pap, Huck's first impersonation overreaches his talents, and implies that more is under way, in this masquerade, than hiding a fact that some small sliver of the world classifies him as a somebody named Huckleberry Finn. For reconnaissance on the Missouri shore, Huck doesn't need to change sexes; his night visit to the Loftus house requires no disguise, for Mrs. Loftus is a stranger. But a strong theme in chapter 11 is that Huck and Jim have to conceal themselves literally and absolutely from the world. When Huck is found out — at least as a male — by Judith Loftus, he retreats into a male alias, which also fails to convince her. He is routed from the house, ignominiously yet still in masquerade, as a something called Sarah Mary Williams George Elexander Peters — the "Elexander" being tossed into the name-string by this woman who realizes she can lay whatever names she likes on this absurdly hermaphroditic child that cannot keep track of its own pretenses or even of its sex. Huck runs for Jim and the raft, and together they push off in the night, running silent and showing no lights; as Huck exclaims to Jim, "they're after us!" They? Not just slave-catchers and bounty hunters; and not just the social disruptions connected to Huck's murder-charade. "They" now includes Huck's own ghost, because Huck Finn dead has become more worrisome to his home town, and therefore to Huck himself, than was Huck Finn in life. "They" means everybody: the Huck Finns of St. Petersburg, the dead Huck whose body (everyone thinks) rots on the bottom of the Mississippi, the murder that Huck has faked so well and that in freeing him of one self menaces him with these others. Out in the dark woods and closing in, there is Huck the slaughtered boy and Nigger Jim the escaped and murderous slave; and the living Huck and the gentle Jim must "hump" to leave them all behind.

Though Huck can make good his escape from accumulated identities, his near namesake, Buck Grangerford, cannot, and Buck's failure costs him his life. Over the decades a web of thematic connections has been woven between the Shepherdson–Grangerford chapters and the surrounding narrative;[24] many of these connections have to do with the destruction of children, psychologically and in the flesh, by the social airs and vicious make-believe of the adults they must live with. Buck accepts the feud as an absolute reality of life, or at least of his life, and knowing too little of the world beyond, he cannot see hypocrisy and waste in these intermittent slaughters that are deeply tangled with family history and dignity. The deadly dream pervades the world of the Grangerfords, yet really there are no dreamers, except perhaps the morbid-minded and now-dead Emmeline. The rest of the family, especially Buck, have blindly accepted somebody else's detestable fantasy as truth, have accepted that to *be* means to be a Grangerford and to live and die in preposterous conflict. Buck dies because all other possibilities have been sacrificed for this; Huck almost dies because as "George Jaxon" he has nearly become one of them, not merely through living in their house, but through the motions of his mind. In a well-known passage, ludicrous but also chilling, he has tried to talk himself into admiration for Emmeline's sick "crayons" and ghoulish poetry. Admiring the "aristocracy" of Colonel Grangerford and his tawdry, pretentious parlor, Huck feels duly humbled to be in such a home. His indoctrination does not go on long, for when Buck and his cousin Joe are slaughtered as the feud flares again, Huck is driven back to the river, to the raft, Jim, and safety. Yet safety from what? Though Huck calls himself "powerful glad to get away from the feuds," George Jackson is also left behind on that bloody riverbank, the boy who has almost affirmed this monstrous narrowing of life, and who has been killed, not just as a masquerade but as an identity, by the murder of his double before his face.

The ending of the Grangerford–Shepherdson episode may make it the ghastliest in *Adventures of Huckleberry Finn*, and though the feud has to figure in any thorough reading of this novel, so also does its tonal dissonance in the text. *Huckleberry Finn* may have tragic elements, moments that even figure in the tragic mythologies of the United States;[25] yet Huck's narrative, staying true to a dream of absolute freedom, refuses the confinements of tragedy. If by consensus somber themes in the book involve disguises and false identities, then part of the novel's unsmotherable gaiety follows from how easily all the raft-riders, after this bloody interlude, can get away with being somebody else. There seems no limit to the realism-cracking insanity of these deceptions; hereafter, on the river and on the Arkansas shores, anything goes. For a profitable while at least, the shorefolk will believe whatever they are told; and to read their gullibility only as satire on backwoods intellects is to read only a part of what is here. When the Duke paints Jim blue, dresses him in a "curtain calico gown, a white horse-hair wig and whiskers," and parks him on the raft as a "Sick Arab — but harmless when not out of his head"; when Huck is marketed to crowds as Adolphus the English servant boy from Sheffield, when the Duke plays a just-now-reformed pirate returning from the Indian Ocean, and when the two con men fool a town for three days as a world-famous

Shakespearean acting troupe, the novel has left realism far behind, and pole-vaulted into tall tale and whopper.

Yet *who* is telling these whoppers? Huck's voice never falters, and he is never nudged aside so that some narrative presence behind him, a Mark Twain voice, can insert something outrageous, dropping the Huck persona for the sake of a Southwest joke. An ungainly paradox in the novel begins to build soon after the arrival of the con men. We have this eminently plausible boy and the unforgettably convincing landscape he moves through; here too is this recurring business of putting on disguises that cannot possibly work, and of getting away with most of them, at least long enough to make money. Ways have been found through this conundrum, many of them involving focus on theme and a letting-go of questions about realism. Yet what may be most real about this visited America is not its gullibility or ignorance or stupidity, but its collective, disease-like dissatisfaction with things and people as they are, as bounded anyhow, even by common sense. The outrageous naiveté of the Pokevillers, the Bricksvillers, the Phelpses, and even the smart Wilks girls is a diminished concern in reading *Huckleberry Finn*, because what is foregrounded is this wish-dream of self-escape, of becoming somebody else with the impulsive choice of a new name, the concoction of a shabby, far-fetched disguise — and of actually getting away with it.[26]

Masquerades are surfaces, unless they penetrate deeper, down into the consciousness that does the masquerading. That can be a dangerous indication, in a supposedly realistic narrative that sacrifices plausibility as a principle of form, and that therefore relies on a voice, a controlling consciousness, to keep the novel within the bounds of *psychological* realism. As evidenced by a century of good conversation, *Huckleberry Finn* has proved important to this culture as a record of a self undergoing creation or transformation, a self becoming distinct and real, indistinct as such terminology might be.[27] To assert that there is really no construable "Huck" here, or that Huck turns out to be more a "they" than an "he," is to serve no purpose and read reductively, as reductively, in fact, as elaborate arguments that make Huck's morally charged moments and adventures add up neatly. Huckleberry Finn can be an eminently plausible self, all the more so because as a fourteen-year-old boy he shows signs of moral anarchy even *after* those crises in which his moral nature and fate would seem tempered and confirmed. Though such relapses and outbreaks make Huck's *Bil-*

dungsroman less tidy, they make both novel and protagonist more *real*, to the extent that structural and modal troubles caused by "stretchers" in the plot are made trivial. Recognizing this deeper fidelity to realist values requires another round of letting go, this time involving Huck at Bricksville and thereafter, and even Huck in high-drama moments of moral reckoning. What is given up, however, is a too-pat fable of his awakening; what is gained is Huck, as a boy whose psychological dimensions, possibilities, and verisimilitude are unprecedented in American fiction, and who as a cultural icon is worthy of the role.

By the Bricksville episode I mean the threefold sequence in that locale: Sherburn's broad-daylight, main-street killing of a harmless drunk named Boggs; the showdown a few minutes later between Sherburn and the irresolute lynch mob; and Huck's trip to the circus when the mob breaks up. Peculiar things happen to Huck in a short space. As a backstage part of the conspiracy to bilk audiences with fake Shakespeare, he goes on a binge of watching, and what he watches, with his usual reserve and impartiality, can be a bother to moralist interpretations. Having gawked at the killing of Boggs, Huck follows the mob to Sherburn's house; and then it's off to the Big Top. The urge is strong to see thematic continuity, indications that this sequence adds up to something more than a series of local spectacles. Much is made, therefore, of Huck's moment of concern for Boggs's daughter, and his empathy at the circus for a man who lurches out of the grandstand, ostensibly another local drunk, but to Huck perhaps an unconscious reminder of the just-dead Boggs. The staggering man is loaded aboard a wild-looking horse, and though they plunge around the ring perilously, the rider turns out to be an accomplished clown-acrobat with the troupe. The scene is a joke on Huck, who alone in the raucous crowd has fretted for a moment about the clown's safety, and there is an implication that Huck is the only white male in Bricksville with a touch of compassion, a capacity for sorrow at the brutalities that pass for entertainment hereabouts.

Even so, this is a *moment;* and if there are moral parallels or lasting psychological effects to be traced among these three crises — Boggs's murder, Sherburn's abortive lynching, and this circus deception — those parallels and effects are not self-evident in the motions of Huck's mind and certainly not foregrounded in his narrative. Huck recollects all this, obviously, and keenly, for the whole book is recollection. Yet Huck's psychological journey through Bricksville, as reexperienced in his narration, shows Huck's attention shifting freely and wholeheartedly to fresh disasters when the latest ones are barely over, and with no palpable aftershocks or moral imprints in his thinking. In fact there is eerily scant evidence of Huck's continued curiosity about the outcome of what he sees. He never wonders, for example, what happens to Boggs's suddenly orphaned and devastated daughter. And if Colonel Sherburn has told the mob how a true gang of lynchers should come for him in the dark, and bring a man along, then will they indeed come for him on the next night, or the next? Does the law ever bother Sherburn for murdering an unarmed man in broad daylight, before a swarm of witnesses? Does Sherburn stay in the village and go perhaps to the circus or the Royal Nonesuch?

The point is this: that when Huck himself moves on to the *next* spectacle, his interest in painfully unfinished human dramas seems to end. Boggs and his daughter have each given Huck a spasm of horror and pity. Sherburn has won a minute of confused admiration, having shown an adulterated dignity, as a cold-blooded killer and as the only ready man in his showdown with hesitant avengers. The last sentence of the scene — the last instant in which Huck seems to think of it on his river journey — resounds with paradox: "I could a staid, if I'd a wanted to, but I didn't want to." Huck means what he says, and in at least two ways; and the two ways collide head-on. He runs from the mob and Sherburn because what he has seen here of monstrous courage and civic cowardice, and especially of nobility, opportunism, and cruelty commingled in this man on the roof. Huck has been dizzied with possibilities beyond his imagining, having to do with the inscrutable and disintegrated self. Sherburn astonishes not only because he coldly kills but also because, ripe with years and a species of grandeur, Sherburn is a perfect enigma, without evident motives for killing, for staying, or for being in this town at all. Sherburn represents a darkness of supreme amorality, a darkness that Huck does not want to gaze into. Yet Huck's curt excuse for leaving the scene, psychologically as well as on foot, implies more: that Huck is himself still free enough, uncongealed enough, to make his escape quickly from the presence of Sherburn's terrifying brand of absolute freedom, never moralize about it, and thereby conserve his own psychological liberty. In a sense he conserves the reader's own liberty in the process; a reader of this account stays quite free to interpolate more profound and lasting response in Huck — or less. One can hear in this recollection a sound of soul-shaking events fixing deeper in Huck than Huck's words go, and confirming psychological and moral lessons that Huck has already learned. But one is also at liberty to hear nothing of the sort.

In other words, moments like these in *Huckleberry Finn* reaffirm Huck as a boy who can confess and conceal in mingled, tangled ways, who can be profound at one moment and trivial the next, and whose psychological and moral nature cannot be fixed and mapped. This is the Huck that matters, as a breakthrough in American realistic narrative, and as an American cultural icon. A core of pleasure in these episodes — for pleasurable they are in peculiar and perhaps embarrassing ways — is that they hover between spectacle and catastrophe, and that their telling hovers between moral engagement and mere watching. There is no saying for sure if and how they function in the transformation and conservation of the psyche of Huckleberry Finn, this boy who is threatened as much by himself (including his putatively *better* self) as by the world and its deformed moral lessons.

The notorious pair of angels that Jim sees hovering around Huck's head, one of them black and one white, have been wrung hard for significations:[28] the black angel is Pap, or Miss Watson's hypocrisy, or the race-slavery moral system, or Tom Sawyer, or some amalgam of these and more; and the white angel is paradoxically Jim himself, or Huck's sound heart, or a powerful goodness that must be found intuitively rather than culturally defined. Yet a more complete reading of Jim's prophecy, and of Huck's predicament, must countenance a possibility that in this novel, for this particular boy, each of these angels is a menace. Each of them threatens Huck with the disaster of becoming, with subjugation of self to something other, some external presence, code, or force. The wish-dream of freedom in this novel is fervently dreamed, and so jealously that even goodness seems a danger to it, should goodness manage to overtake and define a child's identity.

Which is to say that once Huck resolves to resist his deformed conscience, to "go to hell" taking a stand against the corrupt value-system of the prewar American South, the narrative enters a crisis, though the decision itself seems to assure that the great crisis has passed. If Huck becomes irretrievably good he shall cease to be free. This raft of his will be swamped with moral identity, and the wish-dream escape from everything, even the self, will go overboard. Cheer as we do for Huck's decision to stand by his friend Jim and defy the slave-system, and the hypocritical morality of Miss Watson, and whatever social or moral

bugbears we want to see outfaced here, a reading of *Huckleberry Finn* as
an essentially moral fable, reaching a culmination in his lie to the slave-
catchers or his tearing up the note to Miss Watson, has trouble navigat-
ing a paragraph that comes immediately after the pursuing white men
depart:

> They went off, and I got aboard the raft, feeling bad and low,
> because I knowed very well I had done wrong, and I see it warn't
> no use for me to try to learn to do right; a body that don't get
> *started* right when he's little, ain't got no show — when the pinch
> comes there ain't nothing to back him up and keep him to his
> work, and so he gets beat. Then I thought a minute, and says to
> myself, hold on, — s'pose you'd a done right and give Jim up;
> would you felt better than what you do now? No, says I, I'd feel
> bad — I'd feel just the same way I do now. Well, then, says I, what's
> the use you learning to do right, when it's troublesome to do right
> and ain't no trouble to do wrong, and the wages is just the same? I
> was stuck. I couldn't answer that. So I reckoned I wouldn't bother
> no more about it, but after this always do whichever come hand-
> iest at the time. (714)

Huck's decision *about* his decision seems vague, and yet (or *therefore*)
this is another moment that saves the novel, as it indicates how this
new moral instinct, psychological turning point, or whatever it is, shall
matter in the creation, de-creation, or constant re-creation of somebody who for only a fraction of the tale calls himself Huckleberry Finn.
This is Huck's true declaration of independence from both the dark
angel *and* the white, from both Miss Watson's defining morality and
from the consequences, to the self, of standing against it, however
important that decision might be to Huck's personal charm and to the
moral dimensions of his narrative.

The passage commonly paired with this one, for the sake of map-
ping out a Pilgrim's Progress reading of *Huck,* is the "All right, then,
I'll *go* to hell!" passage in chapter 31, where Huck tears up the message
about Jim's whereabouts. One authoritative college text, partial to
hand-on-the-sleeve footnotes, advises students to flip straight to this
moment from the crisis in chapter 16, and reassures in small print that
the boy's trouble over his note to Miss Watson should be construed as
"Huck's famous crisis of conscience."[29] Chapter 31 is the most storied
in the novel, having become a kind of *les stances du Huck,* signifying an

arrival of heroic tragedy in the backwoods and the American vernacular, something no Royal Nonesuch could ever achieve. With disarming simplicity Huck describes himself going through moral agonies like a protagonist in Corneille or Racine. He prays fruitlessly; he looks hard at his world-besotted self and his accumulated social obligations; he soliloquizes about how he has come into this trouble. Then, true to the etiquette of classical tragedy, he comes to a firm decision — and then, with a consummately theatrical turnabout, he resolves on the opposite course.

This scene (and it does recall a dramatic monologue) can be lauded for many reasons, as it seems true that nobility has found right here an American voice, that tragedy or some shred of it has been deftly translated into our landscape and experience, and that new claims are being staked to a grand tradition, with Huck as our very own El Cid or Tennysonian Arthur, someone whose nobility sprouts admirably from an American time and context. The earlier decision to help Jim, or at least not to turn him in, was made in a rush and under the pressure of hostile company. But this later scene is tranquil, the thinking intense, deliberate — and the sound heart scores its clearest victory over the deformed conscience.

In such a victory, however, crisis brews, having to do with a drama yet to unfold. This drama involves the conservation of Huck as both a dynamic *and* an emblematic character, a dynamic consciousness that has *not*, like Le Cid or Tennyson's Arthur, taken a set shape in a wax museum of neoclassical virtuous men. Like those conventions about the slave-catcher episode, readings of chapter 31 often pull up short; again, a paragraph that follows, just after the famous "All right, then, I'll *go* to hell!" can bump a firmly moralist reading off-balance:

> It was awful thoughts, and awful words, but they was said. And I let them stay said; and never thought no more about reforming. I shoved the whole thing out of my head; and said I would take up wickedness again, which was in my line, being brung up to it, and the other warn't. And for a starter, I would go to work and steal Jim out of slavery again; and if I could think up anything worse, I would do that, too; because as long as I was in, and in for good, I might as well go the whole hog. (835)

These follow-up ruminations, coming on the heels of the dramatic resolution to be good, might matter centrally to the intention of

Huckleberry Finn; at those moments when he seems to be morally re-deemed, Huck is immediately rescued as a free self. That is what this passage seems to be for: a return of Huck to that pre-moral condition in which he can think and do whatever he wants, free of the grip of even his own slowly coalescing moral system. Even so, in this novel no restoration of Huck's anarchy, and no celebration of it against in-exorable forces of culture and growing up, stands as a point of arrival. The paradox is that like any ideology that Huck has dealings with, personal anarchy itself threatens identity; and as an incarnation of un-becoming, Huck must ultimately transcend even anarchy as a confine-ment. Huck may be drifting psychologically as well as physically, but both psychologically and physically he is going *somewhere.* There is enough direction in Huck's experience, and in his inner life, not only to keep chaos in check, but also to instill pathos and that measure of tragedy that counter, complement, and subvert the subversions of *Huckleberry Finn,* keeping the narrative free even from doctrines of absolute freedom.

Mark Twain's greatest novel never implicitly denies the reality of the self. It does, rather, affirm refuge from the self's cultural definitions. In just that way, perhaps, it also provides a little comfort for us identity-besotted Americans. Having celebrated Huck's psychological holiday for so many decades, we have rationalized our pleasure by talking incessantly about the novel's thick-woven moral fabric, and taken our cues from these travels of Huck, along the great river, and in his own mind. Such movement does have great thematic importance, but per-haps of a different sort. Should hard-core contrarian readings hold that there are several different Hucks in this novel, and that they do not amalgamate into one consistent or morally schooled boy, then such readings must face the poignancy of certain motions that engulf him: the motions of time, and the journey downriver through dan-gerous landscapes. Even if Huck's moral growth is suspect, or uncer-tain in its staying-power, he is certainly getting somewhere physically. Moving deeper into the American South is analogous here to moving deeper into trouble, farther from friendly faces, farther into violence, confusion, and brutality, especially against Jim, his one real friend on the journey. The Duke and the King grow more vicious with each new scam; Jim has been drifting farther from freedom and his family; and Huck himself, who can feel, at least intermittently, "free and easy and comfortable" on his raft or in the woods near home, finds himself beached in strange country, with his friend locked up, with a false identity imposed upon himself, and with Tom Sawyer again running Huck's life.

The motion within Huck is much harder to map: on his way down the river, he has made moral decisions essentially on his own, without pressure from Tom, Mis Watson, organized religion, or freestanding ethical codes. Yet that evident change in Huck's nature, consoling as it may be from a moral perspective, cannot be affirmed without complications. For one, a consoling, appalling possibility cannot be driven out, that Huck has really learned nothing of consequence from the mayhem he moves through, even though he does supposedly write it down and count it as significant personal experience. But significant exactly how? The answer is and is not available: Huck's narrative repeatedly hints that he comprehends more than he says he does, that some side of the boy's consciousness recognizes and finds importance in the stupidity and violence he must endure. Yet what is the essential and recurring lesson that Huck's experience teaches him? What Huck has seen all the way down the river, as early as the cabin days with Pap, and as late in the book as the shooting of Tom at Phelps Farm, is *consequences*, consequences of being too much, too firmly, one sort of human personality. Games, make-believe, postures, and pretenses are constantly getting out of hand; people wed themselves to intentions — noble, depraved, childish, deliberate, thoughtless, original, plagiarized — and run into unexpected but plausible calamity.[30]

I am suggesting that the ultimate danger Huck is schooled in is this danger of being stuck, and of letting any social role or demeanor, even that of confirmed reprobate (like his father) or young *pícaro* (like himself on much of this southward flight) overtake the identity. Comically, pathetically, people on the river pay for letting that happen; and Huck himself has suffered whenever that fate has closed in upon him. And fate it is: if growing up is a choice of nightmares, a diminution of possibilities, then the alternative Huck sees is worse, and there is no implicit hope in *Huckleberry Finn* that time will provide recourse or any wider choice. The fate of staying Huck is epitomized by his own Pap, who has followed the "easy and comfortable" life and the path of moral anarchy all the way to monstrous adulthood. Alcohol has played its part, and a streak of innate cruelty. But there is no avoiding a whispered foretelling in Pap of some twenty-years-older Huck, sweet-natured or otherwise, persisting in rascality and disconnection long beyond a time when any of that could be charming or even sane. Pap Finn represents possible consequences of staying Huck, staying free; other folk on river and shore represent consequences of being too firmly anyone else.

This is why thematic and psychological uncertainty prove to be such saving graces in *Huckleberry Finn,* as the novel's provisional refuge from catastrophes of becoming, and from catastrophes of remaining loose. It matters that we *not* know the full impact of Huck's moral experience; it is important that we cannot say for certain who or what this boy shall become. In such vertigo, comedy and darkness whirl together, and the whirling sustains, however transiently, a sort of hope. One of Mark Twain's familiar jokes as a platform speaker involved comparing his own ethics to George Washington's: "George Washington," he liked to say, "could not tell a lie. I can, but I won't!" Like many of his well-remembered quips, this one spins in a way that recalls moral dislocations of *Huckleberry Finn.* There is a joke here on Mark Twain himself as a "shifty" platform comic, outlandish in his praise for himself and therefore not to be trusted. But there is a nudge here at George Washington as well, Washington as another lifeless cultural icon like the Emerson hinted at in the Whittier Birthday Speech, a great man looted by mythology and his own achievement, even of the human capacity and liberty to lie. And there is a swipe as well at what passes for moral education in the United States, that process of oxidizing heroes and authors down to calx, of denying iconic figures and the individual self their birthright powers to *remake* the self, honestly or otherwise, and reimagine the world. When Mark Twain says "I can, but I wont!" we have no assurance that he won't, and keen expectations in fact that he *will,* for in his mouth the phrase becomes one of those infinite regressions. If Mark Twain *can* lie, then his promise that he won't can be a lie; and if we all can lie, then what assurances can we give one another that at any moment anybody is telling absolute truth, unless we affirm that indeed we *cannot* lie, that we lack the gift or the skill, or that we have learned the George Washington lessons well in school — in which case, we are lying truly. Round and round: Mark Twain's jest delights because in its moment, speaker and audience leap free together, free from a constructed world of grave oaths and solemn assurances, of having to trust what we see and hear: all the suspicious others, and even the dark self.

As a narrative, *Huckleberry Finn* aspires to a condition like that: release, however ironic, however fated, from moral and psychological gravities of living on the earth, even as this novel affirms a zigzagging process of growing up, of learning to tell lies and not to, of gaining some inevitable and ultimately essential species of moral identity, yet not sacrificing other possibilities in the process, nor a power to shape-shift from one self into another. Guilty or not, the pleasurable thought is that Huck remains to the end, and on through the other Tom–Huck manuscripts, as polymorphic as a "real" boy can be, and that many selves may travel in this one body, and under this one name.

days of yore

Huckleberry Finn suggests the anxieties of a writer bothered not merely by romantic delusion but also by paradoxes in the truth, and in the realist mode where truth supposedly is best presented. The "real" world of *Huckleberry Finn* is animated by dreams and fabrications, some of them deadly, yet some of them ultimately essential to keeping life bearable, and a boy, a novel, and a grown-up author imaginatively and ideologically free. If there are *literary* morals in *Huckleberry Finn,* one of them surely has to do with the perils of imagining in modes; and no mode, not even realism itself, is endorsed as essentially valid or safe. Even so, if realism for Mark Twain was a paradoxical process, he liked to cast romance as the worse adversary, and as a storytelling challenge that brought down both his wrath *and* his admiration. His complex quarrel with romance carried Mark Twain deep into its hostile territories on several occasions.

In popular fiction from Radcliffe and Lewis straight through to the end of the nineteenth century, one homeground of the Anglo-American romantic novel remained the England of the Middle Ages and the Tudors. In Mark Twain's own heyday, the prose fiction that he found so damnably and enviably popular, and to his own temperament inescapably seductive, clanked about in chain mail, brandished broadswords, and fainted in furbelows. Charles Reade was a leader in a buzz of such novelists, and in the 1880s Reade was making a fortune. Given Mark Twain's competitive instincts and his drive to get rich, it is no surprise that from the start of that decade, in the canon of the great American realist, we find a good deal of romantic costume-drama, some of which, including *A Connecticut Yankee* and the completed version of *Number 44, The Mysterious Stranger,* figure regularly in theoretical discussion of Mark Twain's work; others, like *The Prince and the Pauper, A Personal History of Joan of Arc,* and *1601,* readers have often preferred to pass by.

Judging by the response of Mark Twain's best critics, *The Prince and the Pauper* is an embarrassingly "well-made" tale, in a Victorian-drama sense of the phrase. Not only a romance by common definition, it is also a doubles-story, and in literary criticism doubles-stories have been talked almost to extinction, thanks to the installation of Freud and Lacan in college English departments. Tales of this shape supposedly suggest anxieties about the id, the unconscious self, the repressed alternative personality whispering or howling for escape, and about public and private lives, bifurcated sexuality and gender confusion.[31] Insofar as Mark Twain's critics have countenanced *The Prince and the Pauper,* they have sometimes followed such lines of thought, and debated what this doubles-tale might say about Clemens's double-self—his private and public identities, or the lingering poor boy within the great writer and the erstwhile tycoon. Nonetheless, those who doubt such dimensions in a tale for children have well-marked alternatives.[32] Since disinherited princes and knights, changelings in royal cradles and nurseries, high-born souls traveling perilous roads incognito, fiancées in the thrall of usurpers, and miraculous rescues from mortal trouble are the stock-in-trade of historical melodrama, it seems fair to hold that Mark Twain as an author-entrepreneur was trying his hand at doing what Reade did, and Lew Wallace, Sardou, Victor Hugo, and others who had won not just riches but delirious praise from a worldwide public, praise such as Mark Twain had not heard (at least before *Huckleberry Finn*) for any work of his own.

As another subscription-trade entertainment, *The Prince and the Pauper* disappoints critics who for good reason decline to see more in it, or make more of it. Even so, its cultural staying-power is unquestionably high, as witnessed by the dramatizations, live-action films, animated features, and picture-book versions this supposedly feeble story continues to inspire. As some species of entertainment the novel unquestionably works, and perhaps works too well to make trouble-loving professional readers happy. We run a risk of probing too deep when looking into such a book for hints about Mark Twain's mind, or the yearnings of an American public that self-evidently likes this book enough to make it a standard. The question is modest, yet stubborn: Is there anything really special about *The Prince and the Pauper,* other than its coming from Mark Twain's hand?

Much of the romantic appeal of doubleness has to do with worlds within, psychological or moral possibilities that, but for some fluke, might go undiscovered, unnamed, or forever restricted. In a good nineteenth-century Anglo-American doubles-story, whether it be "William Wilson" or *The Strange Case of Doctor Jekyll and Mr. Hyde,* "The Secret Sharer" or "The Jolly Corner," the wastrel, killer, mutineer, or rampaging hedonist can be found out and at least for a while released into the open air. And though the ending of such a tale might aspire to tragedy, one consoling implication can linger: that the self is possibly bigger than it seems, perhaps wilder and more terrible, but admirable in at least its dimensions and consequences. A grim prospect, however, that keeps cropping up in late-century variations, by authors like Conrad, Wilde, James, and Stevenson, is that the self is *not* transcendent but only dangerously malleable, down to the core, transformed and victimized by fate, peculiar chemicals or dark magic; and that identity might be manufactured by such things, by social forces and external influence.

So *The Prince and the Pauper* is one such late-century story about doubles and mistaken identities, and therefore one of an unevenly distinguished group of Anglo-American fictions (more American, this obsession, than Anglo). But if the book has distinguished kin, so what? The critical talk about *Prince* has often been hesitant, even dismissive. The consensus seems to be that this is a slick children's story, a potboiler of the stock well-made sort, with little to distinguish itself except some inert foreshadowings of interests that intensified later in Mark Twain's career: the injustices of the English monarchy, the miseries of the poor, the callousness and corruption of the titled classes, and perhaps the storytelling possibilities of setting resourceful boys adrift with dim prospects, many enemies, and one true and misvalued friend.

But *The Prince and The Pauper* does have peculiarities; it is a doubles-story of a different hue, even amid the variety that flourished in Mark Twain's prime. And a bit like *Huckleberry Finn,* Mark Twain's romance of Tudor England does remain at odds with stage and screen versions that have helped bring the story back to popularity repeatedly in the past century. Indeed, this novel is less a novel of education than it is a tale of self-loss and vanishing, in some ways more suggestive of Kafka's "The Metamorphosis" than of *Oliver Twist, David Copperfield,* or other tales in which boys wander London streets, seeing and feeling the injustice of the commonfolk world, and thereby learning to be humble and good. Though we can see elements of that schooling in the tale of the displaced young King Edward, they must contend with a great deal of narrative interest in *non*being, in coming untethered from the clothes, context, and ceremony that make kings and knights and poor boys what they are. Though the tale attends more to King Edward's vagabonding than to Tom Canty's masquerade as a prince and a monarch, the parallel tales, as far as they are so, are not just about coming away from home and being mistaken for someone else, but also about coming apart.

Like Tom and Huck, Tom Canty is essentially fatherless; John Canty, his biological sire, enters Tom's life only now and then as a menace and a usurper, having bludgeoned to death an impoverished old priest called Father William, who has taught Tom a smattering of reading and Latin and Greek, along with a few rudimentary courtesies and a touch of compassion, and has been the best "father" Tom has known. As for the other boy, with his mother long dead, Edward's closest ally and confidant in the palace is the Earl of Hertford. Canty has no family; Prince Edward has no parents; the ragged knight Miles Hendon has spent years in a foreign dungeon, not knowing that his own father and mother have died in his absence.

Orphaning the three major characters seems more than a gambit for keeping the plot lean and uncomplicated. The exhilaration of the tale has to do with new identity and new life. Tom accepts the chance wholeheartedly when it comes to him, and he is nearly destroyed by taking it, reaching a psychological abyss in the hour before he is rescued from the coronation, really the obliteration of himself by the acquired identity of Prince Edward. For his own part, Edward resists his new life at every turn, and because he does so he too is constantly in danger, from John Canty, from tramps and ruffians and the people they rob, from angry housewives, a justice of the peace and officers of the law, and most gravely from a mad hermit, who alone among the folk Edward meets in his adventures, actually believes that the young king is exactly who he says he is—and intends therefore to slaughter Edward as the heir of the villainous Henry VIII, despoiler of the Holy Catholic Church.

This moment of Edward's near-immolation is a tableau, paused over voyeuristically by the narrative. Bound, gagged, and writhing on a bed, the rightful king of England whimpers as the crazed hermit raves and gloats, this hermit who thinks that he is "naught but an archangel—I that should have been Pope!" Murder is interrupted by the arrival outside of Miles Hendon, who by the laws of romance seems the correct rescuer. Yet deceived by the hermit, Hendon rides away again, leaving Edward to be saved by the worst possible savior, John Canty, who thinks he is rescuing his own son Tom. So for a moment we have an inside-out Sacrifice of Isaac. A man-child, bound hand and foot, is posed tableau-fashion with an old man with a dagger and murderous intent; but the old man and sacrificer is the angel this time, and the rescuer is the father, who is nonetheless doubly *not* the father. For not only has John Canty mistaken Edward for a mad Tom; he has killed the Tom's good surrogate father, the priest who taught the real Tom the values Tom eventually needs to be a good king — meaning a good *impostor* king — a better king than the real king would have been if he had not lost his identity and his home, and gone wandering about as — well, not Tom, but nobody.

Am I making the moment stranger than it really is? Possibly. But judgment of that has to be grounded in a sense of whole novel's convolutions, and of its disruptions about this matter of who is really who. In Tom Stoppard's absurdist anti-drama *Rosencrantz and Guildenstern are Dead*, Rosencrantz (or maybe Guildenstern, for these wanderers too are so much "doubles" that they aren't quite sure themselves which one is which) asks the passing Player King, master of the wandering troupe headed for Elsinore, "What exactly do you *do?*" This is the answer:

> We keep to our usual stuff, more or less, only inside out. We do on stage the things that are supposed to happen off. Which is a kind of integrity, if you look on every exit being an entrance somewhere else.[33]

Riddling, in a play full of riddles that cannot quite be worked out, which may be the point (if there can be a point) to a drama that subverts customary and complacently accepted distinctions between drama and real life, and assumptions that everything on the stage or off can be forced to make sense. But if the Player King's answer is not a good answer, it catches at least one good question. When dramatic or literary artifice commingles with life, or with history, or with values that thoughtfully or otherwise we like to call realistic, what then is the mix, the result? A fanatic about history, especially English and European history, to the extent that he fiddled for years with perfecting a History Game[34] (a cumbersome ancestor of Trivial Pursuit) and railed at romantic and sentimental writers for playing loose with historical fact, Mark Twain in *The Prince and The Pauper* makes an actual king into the central character in a very tall tale, and swaps him off the throne in favor of an impostor, who is an unwilling, unwitting player-king. The real king — "real" in the sense of being an undisputed figure from history — becomes in the streets of London an unwilling impostor himself, a poor boy named Tom Canty, except that he doesn't accept the name, the identity, or the social station, and proclaims to almost everyone that he is Prince of Wales, and later that he is the rightful King Edward VI. And so the historical Edward becomes not merely a mystery boy but a lunatic; whether they "know" him as Tom Canty or not, everyone, including his guardian Miles Hendon (who eventually discovers that he is no longer himself — but more about that later), thinks that the king is mad. Back in the palace, everyone assumes that Tom Canty is Edward the Prince or Edward the King, but a prince or a king who has lost his wits, a mad boy on the English throne. In fact (if one can possibly get away with such a phrase) the one man in the world who believes that Edward, the "real" Edward, is indeed himself or at least what he says he is, believes himself an avenging archangel and tries to slaughter Edward for being King Edward. *The Prince and the Pauper* keeps to the usual stuff, more or less — only inside out.

Tom Stoppard did not write *The Prince and The Pauper.* In several ways, however, this children's story, whose simple, strong premise has fostered its translation or mistranslation to screen and picture-book, turns loops that take it out into a deep left-field of doubles-stories, where wide-wandering and exoticness are the norm. On one level the novel is manufactured history, loaded with quotations from real historians and upholstered with detail to give it a feel of authenticity but also of heightened fraudulence. That is a familiar and small paradox. These made-up adventures of actual historical figures, and these words conjured for them to speak, are familiar literary license; Shakespeare, Scott, and Browning, who all on occasion do the same thing, provide reassuring company, though Mark Twain's posturing elsewhere as champion of uncosmetized historical truth sets him a little apart, and makes this venture an anomaly. But within the large and rather commonplace paradox of romance-realism and make-believe history, there are others that though smaller in scope, do tighter, more surprising tumbles in the mind.

For instance: though Tom and Prince Edward, thanks to a joke that goes too far, are mistaken not merely for each other but for each other as mad, the psychological experience sketched in for each boy, in his new and frightening circumstances, is absolutely opposite, and with opposite ramifications. Though the main attention of the narrative is on Edward-as-mad-Tom, it is Tom who undergoes, or at least begins to, a Shakespearean tragic transformation, while Edward's misadventures make him a shadow version of a tragic hero, or one of Shakespeare's less interesting classical-model protagonists. Tom veers toward a complete self-loss, or self-reinvention, into the public role that fate has handed him. By the end of the story, Tom is becoming a King Edward in truth, not only fancying and embellishing the opulence and pomp of the life that has snared him, but ultimately denying his own real mother on the streets of London as he makes his way to the Westminster coronation — which is to say, to his petrifaction into the identity of King. Edward therefore saves Tom's life in the halls of Westminster Abbey, saves him from becoming another stone effigy like those in the aisles all around the coronation throne, or another suit of empty armor like the one in which Edward has hidden the Great Seal of England: a rigid, hollow self that history, custom, and brutal necessity have contrived.

Edward's danger is Tom's inside out. Because he knows perfectly well — dangerously well — who he is, Edward is constantly in trouble with people who don't believe him and also from people who do. The moral lessons of ordinary life he learns only with peril and suffering, and his one genuine ally accepts and defends Edward as a "king of shadows and dreams," not quite mad, yet not genuine either, a creature in some zone between fraudulence, delusion, and honest truth. So Edward, like some preteen Cato or Coriolanus, is nearly destroyed because he will not change; and for his part Tom is nearly undone because deep within he veers close to changing absolutely.

I referred to Miles Hendon, the ragged knight who befriends the dethroned Edward, as having some part in fostering the Tom Stoppard funhouse-qualities of this book, as another nonperson in a bewildering array. Hendon himself has been disinherited while fighting overseas and languishing in a foreign dungeon, yet Hendon is not a refurbished Ivanhoe. Miles Hendon is rather Ivanhoe turned inside-out. In Scott's romance, having been disowned by his father Cedric, Ivanhoe returns from the Crusades in disguise, first as a palmer, then as an unknown knight with "Desdichado" (wretched one) inscribed on his shield, a faceless suit of armor within which rides a willful man. Hendon comes home to his estate as himself, and is denied to be himself: by his own brother Hugo, by his fiancée Lady Edith to whom Hugo is now married, and by the remaining servants of the house, Miles's father and mother having died in his absence. All of that would imply that Hendon's brother and bride are denying themselves as well, or some great part of their own identity.

It turns out that Edith is lying both as the former beloved and as the happy wife, having been forced to marry Hugo and hating him thoroughly. So Miles, having returned home as himself, finds that he is now nobody, and is jailed with Edward for impersonating himself; or, rather, both of them are jailed as a pair, a player-king and a player-knight. In *The Prince and the Pauper* there is no dignity to disinheritance, and no plausible recourse. There is no joust, no romantic identity as the boy or man of mystery. Hendon recovers himself by a fluke: going to the palace on a whim, he is discovered accidentally by the whipping-boy who has heard of Hendon from the rediscovered king, and Edward back on his throne restores Hendon's lands, lady, and title by royal decree. It matters that when Edward first meets Hendon, the just-returned knight is living in rooms on London Bridge, a place between places. It also matters that one of the tour de force passages in the novel, a passage in which Mark Twain's gusto as a writer seems to reach a peak, is about this somewhere that is nowhere, a centuries-old nontown of perpetual transition, where people live and die without going anywhere, or really being anywhere, and feel endangered by the prospect of stable dry earth and identity:

> The Bridge was a sort of town to itself; it had its inn, its beer houses, its bakeries, its haberdasheries, its food markets, its manufacturing industries, and even its church. It looked upon the two neighbors which it linked together, — London and Southwark — as being well enough, as suburbs, but not otherwise particularly important. It was a close corporation, so to speak; it was a narrow town, of a single street a fifth of a mile long, its population was but a village population, and everybody in it knew all his fellow townsmen intimately, and had known their fathers and mothers before them — and all their little family affairs into the bargain. It had its aristocracy, of course — its fine old families of butchers, and bakers, and what-not, who had occupied the same old prem-

ises for five or six hundred years, and knew the great history of
the Bridge from beginning to end, and all its strange legends;
and who always talked bridgy talk, and thought bridgy thoughts,
and lied in a long, level, direct, substantial bridgy way. It was
just the sort of population to be narrow and ignorant and self-
conceited. Children were born on the Bridge, were reared there,
grew to old age and finally died without ever having set a foot on
any part of the world but London Bridge alone. Such people
would naturally imagine that the mighty and interminable pro-
cession which moved through its street night and day, with its
confused roar of shouts and cries, its neighings and bellowings
and bleatings and its muffled thunder-tramp, was the one great
thing in this world, and themselves somehow the proprietors of it.
And so they were, in effect — at least they could exhibit it from
their windows, and did — for a consideration — whenever a returning king or hero gave it a fleeting splendor, for there was no
place like it for affording a long, straight, uninterrupted view of
marching columns.

Men born and reared upon the Bridge found life unendurably
dull and inane, elsewhere. History tells of one of these who left
the Bridge at the age of seventy-one and retired to the country.
But he could only fret and toss in his bed; he could not go to
sleep, the deep stillness was so painful, so awful, so oppressive.
When he was worn out with it, at last, he fled back to his old home,
a lean and haggard spectre, and fell peacefully to rest and pleasant dreams under the lulling music of the lashing waters and the
boom and crash and thunder of London Bridge.[35]

Overblown though this might be, it is certainly the cadenza passage
of *The Prince and the Pauper,* a celebration and a shiver about a historical place and a dreamed condition of perpetual nonarrival, a life
literally on the road. The oddness in the prose is symptomatic of
Mark Twain's narrative style throughout the novel, a style genteel and
Anglo-mannered, sometimes well past the point of affectedness. If the
London Bridge meditation recalls Scott, Leigh Hunt, or Dickens more
than it does the Mark Twain voices of *The Innocents Abroad* or *Roughing
It,* then other longish passages in *The Prince and the Pauper* sport similar
encumbrances, yet without so much color and flash. Chapter 17 opens
like a humorless counterfeit of Reade:

Miles Hendon hurried along toward the Southwark end of the Bridge, keeping a sharp lookout for the persons he sought, and hoping and expecting to overtake them presently. He was disappointed in this, however. By asking questions, he was enabled to track them part of the way through Southwark; then all traces ceased, and he was perplexed as to how to proceed. Still, he continued his efforts as best he could during the rest of the day. Nightfall found him leg-weary, half famished, and his desire as far from accomplishment as ever; so he supped at the Tabard inn and went to bed, resolved to make an early start in the morning, and give the town an exhaustive search. As he lay thinking and planning, he presently began to reason thus: The boy would escape from the ruffian, his reputed father, if possible; would he go back to London and seek his former haunts? no, he would not do that, he would avoid recapture. What, then, would he do? Never having had a friend in the world, or a protector, until he met Miles Hendon, he would naturally try to find that friend again, provided the effort did not require him to go toward London and danger.

It seems a plausible guess that as a stylistic outing, *The Prince and the Pauper* was at least partially an I-can-do-it-too demonstration for the sake of literary respectability, proof that this popular Missouri-Washoe-pilot-journalist-comedian could lay on the stylistic sauce just like the revered romancers on the Anglo-American scene — meaning those British writers whose names were being intoned in American schoolrooms. Yet imitation, even for show or monetary advantage, can have other sides and motives, just as a put-on can mean not only mockery but obliteration of the mocker. And aside from proving, or rather showing off, a knowledge of broader lexicons and sidelights of English history and everyday life, this "long, level, direct, substantial bridgy" lie that Mark Twain tells may signify what the Bridge itself seems to mean for Miles Hendon and the displaced Prince Edward.

realism, romance, and dynamite

The Prince and the Pauper may be about many things that critics have sometimes grudgingly conceded it might be about: the plight of the poor, the need of lawmakers to feel the edge and bite of law, the need of the highborn and comfortable to understand the suffering all around them, and to apprehend the "there but for fortune" condition that many of us are in on this earth.[36] But this book is also about limbo, about how easily the self can slip away, or be obliterated precisely because it will *not* slip, about the perils of being incompletely made, and of being made too solidly and well. And if any of this rings true, then one extractable theme of the novel might be that there is no extractable theme, because the self is mystery, neither illusory nor real, just as the "real" and historical people in the novel are neither fact nor illusion. At the same mirror, in the same moment, a real prince and a dreamed-up boy can stand together and admire what they see in the glass, because each of them is "truly" like the other, history-book true, and yet a shadow of a dream. The first of two Old England novels that Mark Twain published in his lifetime, *The Prince and the Pauper* ransacks the trick-bag of romance while raising a fuss against the mode. Though injustice, squalor, ignorance, and degrading social habit move through the foreground — as satire, at least in part, of the popular-fiction taste for glorious, tidy days of yore — the plot of the novel owes nearly everything to the sort of romantic story structure that was selling so well, and that Mark Twain liked railing against. In that simple way, the story of Tom and Edward is a prelude to *A Connecticut Yankee in King Arthur's Court,* for that ambivalent quarrel with romance radiates with higher intensity in the tale of Hank Morgan and the Lost Land. But this inchoate question about selfhood also prowls there, in the later work, and as a heightened presence. After *Huckleberry Finn,* Mark Twain's meditations on the contingency of selfhood, and on the contingency of literary modes, grow both surer, more complex, and more self-aware, and in *Yankee* the literary and psychological crisis achieve connections that are unprecedented in Mark Twain's fiction.

Before *Yankee* there had been several all-out uprisings against the romantic mode, campaigns that seem meant to drive its bad habits clean out of the American sensibility — and out of Mark Twain himself — and supplant them with plain-language representations of experience as ordinary people knew it. The adversary, in such fiction, often proves to be the personality seduced by romance, by sentimentality, by literary culture heavily and mindlessly ingested. That is not a theme of any consequence in *The Prince and the Pauper;* but *Huckleberry Finn,* as I have suggested, presents romance as trouble, in the form of Tom Saw-

yer and his insistent fantasies. Even so, it is not easy to find in that
text, or in Mark Twain's commentary about it, evidence that he as yet
recognized the difficulties in being "The Boss" of the new American
realism. There was much to learn, about how a creed of fidelity to the
facts and common sense is neither simple nor pure, how mysteries
lurked among his own assumptions about "reality" and truth, how
the *representation* of truth can never escape the pull of romance. Further, the grand-scale ideas that now overtook him, and against which
he seemed, in his last quarter-century, to have so little immunity —
traumatizing new doctrines about human nature, society, and consequence — threatened the coherence of the stories he wanted to tell,
and endangered the prospect of getting them told. There were failures coming, the most spectacular of them being *A Connecticut Yankee*,
Mark Twain's boldest attempt to reckon with romance, with the problem of defining an identity, and with the potentially devastating impact of new idea-systems upon the self.[37]

If *A Connecticut Yankee* will no longer "wash" as a defense or an
indictment of either the Hank Morgan mentality or headlong pragmatism, then perhaps we can reread it in ways truer to the biographical
record, and to the abiding sense that something big is at stake here —
for Mark Twain, and possibly for the moral status of the American
novel. It is possible to do, in other words, what Everett Carter called for
in his 1978 "The Meaning of *A Connecticut Yankee*": find a "significance" in keeping with what we know of this author and his intentions.
One can do so by accepting a possibility that critics have been uneasy
about: that *A Connecticut Yankee* is not held together by a consistent or
distinct narrative voice, or sustained by the presence of a protagonist,
as *Huckleberry Finn* is sustained. To give up on Hank as a coherent
narrator is not to give up on the novel, nor be left speechless about
how it works, insofar as it does. One can look instead toward more
constant presences in the tale, motifs in the plot, the humor, the satire,
and the declamations this narrator (whoever he is) indulges in all the
way through.[38] My premise is this: the novel makes war against every
conceivable enemy of absolute personal integrity, and attempts to
name and overthrow the pernicious force that sustains them all. Mark
Twain's resentment here encompasses the enslaving stasis of religious
practice, of political and social institutions, of modes of warfare, of
manners, dress, and above all of the self — everything, including the
conventions and confinements of narrative. His wrath about fixity

leads him, inevitably, into a dilemma about the nature of identity, about finding and expressing the self as it might exist out beyond the touch of civilization, and about the incompatibility of such perfect freedom with the demands of narrative, as well as with life in any human society. Mark Twain spent years laboring to make a far-fetched story speak social and moral truth, telling a tale about a long-ago, never-was place, as a commentary on a contemporary world, and writing a novel that voiced not only opinions about social justice, but anxiety about the nature of identity, of freedom, and of narrative as a consequential act. In other words, the anomaly of "moral, Realistic fiction" is the treacherous ground upon which the novel shudders.

Begin where *A Connecticut Yankee* itself began, with famous lines in one of Mark Twain's notebooks:

> Dream of being a knight errant in armor in the middle ages. Have the notions & habits of thought of the present day mixed with the necessities of that. No pockets in the armor. No way to manage certain requirements of nature. Can't scratch. Cold in the head — can't blow — can't get at handkerchief, can't use iron sleeve. Iron gets red hot in the sun — leaks in the rain, gets white with frost & freezes me solid in winter. Suffer from lice & fleas. Make disagreeable clatter when I enter church. Can't dress or undress myself. Always getting struck by lightning. Fall down, can't get up. See Morte DArthur.[39]

Some of the ambitions of *A Connecticut Yankee* are already suggested in these lines: not merely Hank Morgan's ludicrous trek in full armor with Sandy in tow, but also the conflicting motives that underlie and undercut the novel. The ironic joke here certainly has to do with the Bergsonian principle of rigidity. To imaginations nurtured on romantic fiction, or its elder sister the Continental romance, the knight-errant represents power, dignity, perfect freedom, and mastery of the world. But Mark Twain's comic knight is perfectly powerless, and cannot even blow his nose. Less obvious, perhaps, is the fact that the satire is not against heroism, or boyish dreams of power and freedom. It aims instead at the cultural icon for that yearning. The "dream" that triggered the novel is as much a wish-dream itself as it is a parody of chivalric fantasies, and underneath the comic discomforts, this dream seems as strong as any that motivates Tom Sawyer. The difference is that Mark Twain fantasizes better than Tom does, imagines the details of knight-errantry as Tom cannot. The dream means this: that the problem with heroism and chivalry is the iron suit. A perfect fantasy would be of a knight who *can* get to his handkerchief, scratch, be comfortable as well as marvelous, heroic, envied — a knight free and luxurious as no storied knight ever was.

If Hank Morgan and his novel are born here, then the wish-dream kept not only its shape but its centrality to what followed. Major episodes are organized around this dream of rapprochement between chivalric glory and what Hank calls "solid comfort," and *Connecticut Yankee*'s expressions of this dream suggest an obsession with it. Once Hank is packed into his steel suit and committed to his quest with Sandy, Sir Bedivere happens by in comfortable, flexible armor, and Hank leers at the superior design:

> How stately he looked; and tall and broad and grand. He had on his head a conical steel casque that only came down to his ears, and for visor had only a narrow steel bar that extended down to his upper lip and protected his nose; and all the rest of him, from neck to heel, was flexible chain-mail, trowsers and all. But pretty much all of him was hidden under his outside garment, which of course was of chain-mail, as I said, and hung straight from his shoulders to his ancles; and from his middle to the bottom, both before and behind, was divided, so that he could ride, and let the skirts hang down on each side. He was going grailing, and it was just the outfit for it, too. I would have given a good deal for that ulster, but it was too late now to be fooling around.[40]

Later on, after the experience in slavery, Hank's trial, and his death sentence, Mark Twain assigns the rescue to "five hundred mailed and belted knights on bicycles!" who come racing in well ahead of schedule; Hank has given up hope, assuming that his help will ride horses, as usual, and be heavily armed. In the following chapter Hank reaches his apotheosis as a knight himself, defeating a swarm of English chivalry in one quick fight. As the most victorious, potent, and heroic knight ever, he wins a "thunder-crash of applause," and surpasses any glory that Tom Sawyer dreamed of — and Hank does it all in togs absolutely opposite to the dream's iron:

> And then out I came. But I didn't get any shout. There was a wondering and eloquent silence, for a moment, then a great wave

of laughter began to sweep along that human sea, but a warning bugle blast cut its career short. I was in the simplest and comfortablest of gymnast costumes — flesh-colored tights from neck to heel, with blue silk puffings about my loins, and bare-headed. My horse was not above medium size, but he was alert, slender-limbed,· muscled with watch-springs, and just a greyhound to go. He was a beauty; glossy as silk, and naked as he was when he was born, except for bridle and ranger-saddle. (431)

Flesh-colored, these tights let Hank be as naked as his horse, and still, like his horse, have natural dignity. In the first chapters of "The Tale of the Lost Land," nakedness means powerlessness, humiliation. Captured by Sir Kay, Hank has been stripped "naked as a pair of tongs" for display as a prize to Arthur, Merlin, Guinevere, the knights and ladies of the kingdom. At that moment there is no question that a suit of armor means dignity and strength, and nudity abject defeat. And so Hank's last great "effect" in King Arthur's court is to turn these symbols around. Nakedness becomes the sublime chivalric style. After a few minutes in the lists, Hank envisions himself as an illustration in a children's book by the likes of Howard Pyle. "Across my mind," he muses, "flitted the dream image of a certain Hello-girl of West Hartford, and I wished she could see me now." *A Connecticut Yankee in King Arthur's Court* never stops being a wish-dream of glory, no matter what other themes assert themselves, or undercut that dream in the novel, and no matter what happens to spoil that glory after Hank achieves it, and after Mark Twain lives it vicariously through his hero. The fantasy that makes the book a popular if odd choice for young readers is of the self adored, as the bravest, wisest knight in the age of chivalry. What always blocks the way is the iron raiment of social and artistic and psychological convention. The heavy metal that children in Mark Twain's own century regarded as the garb of heroism exemplifies all the other hobbling habits, the habits of thought, the moral systems, the social institutions, the popular literature that Mark Twain had to live with, just as it does the confinements of the never-land where Hank Morgan wakes up.

Because the narration rails about the ills of a class system and an established church, the novel's wider war, on every species of moral, psychological and artistic confinement is partially drowned out by the invective against medieval and modern Britain. But *A Connecticut Yan-*

kee's satire seems almost boundless in scope. Certainly Camelot represents a wellspring of romantic falsehood, and so the novel can be read as an indictment of mode that Mark Twain had long derided. Yet as *A Connecticut Yankee* unfolds, its targets expand to encompass any system or thesis that threatens liberty or ultimate fluidity of being, everything that might conceal the truth about the self *from* the self. As a result, and whether or not such resentment is thoughtful, or more akin to blind rage, the narrative must seek to make good its escape from conventional form, even from a coherent narrative voice, and try to sustain itself by the ferocity of its own attack. Structures, consistencies, codifications, predictabilities, rules, regulations, illusions of personal integrity—all merge into one adversary, one immense threat to the possibility of absolute freedom, of truth, and of fictions that seek, one way or another, to dream and to tell the truth at the same time.

Romantic fiction is not a mode whose definition Mark Twain troubled over; when he refers to it, he usually means overblown tales of bold warriors, fair ladies, extravagant emotions, magic, and derring-do. No more esoteric definition suggests itself in his canon, just as his conception of "Realism" seems no more precise than the intention to convey truthfully the experiences he knew firsthand or accepted as possible, and the inner life experienced by more-or-less ordinary folk. And so Camelot is made the home of all the lies that Mark Twain links to the romantic sensibility. The Round Table world is a place of filth and ignorance; and Merlin, whom Tennyson had recently promoted to Grand Master of romantic daydreams, is portrayed here as a third-rate vaudevillian. England is a place of such misery, brutality, and wrong that King Arthur, without Hank's help, cannot begin to transform it. And Hank conversely is the realistic sensibility incarnate (again, in that loosely bounded way in which Mark Twain thought about realism).

It is tempting to say then that battle lines on literary modes are drawn in the novel, and that the dubiousness of what follows shows Mark Twain's failure to stick to one strategy. But the complexities that ensue in Mark Twain's quarrel with romance do not seem accidental. Having set himself a paradoxical task, he keeps at it to the end. As the story was taking shape, Mark Twain wrote to the ever-anxious Mrs. Fairbanks (who was dismayed by the reports reaching her about the gory, irreverent nature of Twain's recent platform readings from a "work in progress") that his intent was actually to pay homage to

Thomas Malory.[41] The implication is that massacring knights with Gatling guns (an idea hit upon early in the writing process) and dwelling on the sordid side of the Middle Ages was, somehow, a salute to the grandsire of romantic nonsense. That inference is not so bizarre as it might seem. There is more evidence, in fact, that the book has at heart such a contradictory wish than there is that the novel fails to be consistently anti-romantic. Homage is paid indeed: as a tradition that cannot be refused and routed by a little pragmatic thinking, romance is both a problem and an advantage for the novelist, whether realistic or not in his inclinations. As a mode, romance is an absurdity, a thing of beauty, an opportunity, and a threat. Its multiplicity is portrayed for the visiting realist in Hank's first moments in the Lost Land:

> When I came to again, I was sitting under an oak tree, on the grass, with a beautiful and broad country landscape all to myself — nearly. Not entirely; for there was a fellow on a horse, looking down at me — a fellow fresh out of a picture-book. He was in old-time iron armor from head to heel, with a helmet on his head the shape of a nail-keg with slits in it; . . . and his horse had armor on, too, and a steel horn projecting from his forehead, and gorgeous red and green silk trappings that hung down all around him like a bed-quilt, nearly to the ground.
>
> "Fair, sir, will ye just?" said this fellow.
>
> "Will I which?"
>
> "Will ye try a passage of arms for land or lady or for — "
>
> "What are you giving me?" I said. "Get along back to your circus, or I'll report you."
>
> Now what does this man do but fall back a couple of hundred yards and then come rushing at me as hard as he could tear, with his nail-keg bent down nearly to his horse's neck, and his long spear pointed straight ahead. I saw he meant business; so I was up the tree when he arrived. (51–52)

Hank has company in this tree, company in the form of Mark Twain himself, the storyteller who understood that for all its falsehood, romance is too handsome a mode to be supplanted; that is, unless realism can borrow from romance to strengthen its own claim. Hank will never win a joust as a mechanic and a foreman in a factory; he has to concoct some way to become a knight himself, just as Mark Twain, foreman of American realists, treed by centuries of romantic storytelling, must adulterate his narrative, brew a tale exotic and potent enough to outface the lies of chivalry and medieval splendor, offer the world a hero, and do all this without recourse to the worst falsehoods about heroism, the lies still flourishing in popular fiction.

The mingled nature of *A Connecticut Yankee* therefore runs deeper than a few discordant episodes and shifts in Hank Morgan's voice and mentality. The novel is saturated with doubleness: for all its violence, filth, and incorrigible stupidity, this "Lost Land" of chivalric Britain may be more vividly imagined, and therefore more acceptable as a *fantasy*, than the Camelot of Tennyson's *Idylls* or most other versions of Arthur's story, back to and including Malory. The wish-dream I spoke of partly accounts for this surprise. Through the mechanism of Hank, Mark Twain is out to dream himself into someone greater than Lancelot or Merlin, to be first among heroes in the most storied of kingdoms. The cold rooms and the dog-ravaged banquets only make the dream more intense, though they satirize the upholstered Pre-Raphaelite imaginings that boosted the popularity of chivalric fantasy in Mark Twain's lifetime. But more important than either of these effects is what they accomplish together, as they blend in a mode which escapes both romanticism *and* realism. This is, in other words, a reflexive narrative, demonstrated by the fact that the novel goes beyond *Huckleberry Finn* and *Pudd'nhead Wilson* in making storytelling itself a subject, offering an array of lessons (some comic, some not) about the craft, of telling a story, and about the storyteller's difficult obligations to an audience, to truth, and to his own paradoxical identity.

Connecticut Yankee as a story about storytellers: they turn up constantly in the novel, occupying many social positions, and embodying several relationships between narrative and truth. As the knight who trees Hank at the outset, Sir Kay is a lively storyteller in his own right, and the captured Yankee must listen to himself portrayed, at Arthur's court, as a "tusked and taloned man-devouring ogre." "Never was there such a country," he observes, "for wandering liars," Merlin and Sandy being champions in the national competition. But to complicate matters there are also characters whose tales are apparently to be heard without judgment. There is, for example, a story told by the young man saved from the rack, who recounts his own valiant refusal to confess his poaching. A young priest tells of a destitute young mother about to be burned for witchcraft; a woman dying of smallpox recounts the family's story of serfdom and excommunication. Hank's own newspaper chimes in with breezy accounts of tournaments, miracles, and battle; and to Clarence, who has tales to tell of this or that event in the kingdom, falls the task of narrating the Malory-story of Lancelot, Guinevere, and the death of Arthur at the hands of Mordred, and finally of ending the history that Hank cannot finish. With all this narrating going on, to be evaluated in so many different ways, there are nonetheless four preeminent storytellers in *A Connecticut Yankee,* including two liars central to Hank's life in Camelot. Although they differ little in the repetitiousness and the excess of the stories they tell, they are worlds apart in their motives for the telling, and that difference further clarifies the novel's perspective with regard to romance, its moral effects, and its intentions. As the first professional romancer Hank meets, Merlin represents the darkest side of the art, not only in the clumsiness of his tales, but in the baseness of his designs. There are only two motivating forces behind his romantic lies: self-aggrandizement and malice. Nearly everything that Mark Twain found wrong with romance can be found in Merlin. His tales promote superstition and confusion in his own world; they frighten children and gullible adults; they frustrate the search for truth, foster injustice, pump up his own "stock" in Arthur's court—and they bore people silly. On hand as the old wizard launches a "quaint old lie" in the royal banquet hall, young Clarence has that irreverent accuracy of judgment that Mark Twain celebrates in boys as a species:

> "Who is it?"
>
> "Merlin, the mighty liar and magician, perdition singe him for the weariness he worketh with his one tale! But that men fear him for that he hath the storms and the lightnings and all the devils that be in hell at his beck and call, they would have dug his entrails out these many years ago to get at that tale and squelch it. He telleth it alway in the third person, making believe he is too modest to glorify himself—maledictions light upon him, misfortune be his dole! Good friend, prithee call me for evensong." (71)

It takes Hank a little time to endorse Clarence's low opinion of Merlin, for the Yankee finds the story "simply and beautifully told." Before long, however, Hank is echoing Clarence's curse, recognizing Merlin as an enemy of truth, peace, and progress in the Lost Land—and romantic lies as his black magic. Hank observes that "the big miracles, the ones that have won him his reputation, always had the luck to be performed when nobody but Merlin was present." When Merlin fails with the Holy Fountain, he concocts a story about an unbreakable curse by the "most potent spirit known to the magicians of the East"; having stolen Hank's lasso in the tournament, he covers the theft with more nonsense, that this rope "belongeth to the King of the Demons of the Sea." What adds interest to Merlin as the embodiment of pernicious romance is that somewhere in a career of lying he has lost track of the truth. Does he actually believe that his "veil of invisibility" will give Sir Sagramour protection against Hank, that a pinch of smoke-powder and a few incantations can save his tower, or that a spirit has put a curse on the Fountain? There is no way of telling: Merlin has so muddled the truth with fantasies and exaggerations that he can recognize reality no more. Confounding not only the world and the truth but himself as a storyteller, Merlin is literary romance at its self-destructive worst.

When she first encounters Hank, Sandy too has mislaid the truth in her own stories, and she has the ill effect of forcing the Yankee out of his comfortable home and his enterprises and off on a quest. "It may be," Hank muses after questioning her, "that this girl had a fact in her somewhere, but I don't believe you could have sluiced it out with a hydraulic; nor got it with the earlier forms of blasting, even; it was a case for dynamite." Her detachment from reality seems as complete as Merlin's; and to the company of this "blatherskite" Mark Twain sentences Hank, thereby allowing Sandy to be the most long-winded romancer in the novel. The fact that Hank not only endures Sandy but marries her has caused problems for critics, who have variously interpreted this somersault in Hank's affections as a sentimental lapse on Mark Twain's part, or a hint of Hank's love for power and his need for fawning, simple-minded companionship. But while Hank's marital bliss with Sandy comes as a surprise, his reconciliation to her as a story-teller unfolds with care. This is possible because Sandy is an innocent. Her romantic fictions are endless and, like Merlin's, they hopelessly mangle the facts of any case; yet there is no hint of ulteriority behind these embellishments, not even the faintest of selfish purposes. The stories Sandy tells, innocuous, straightforward, predictable, are the humblest sort of entertainment, harmless fictions that one can listen to, sleep through, interrupt at will, even believe in (up to a point) with ease and safety. Exasperated by her at first, Hank is afraid to say anything that might "set her works agoing"; soon, however, he finds that the innocence of Sandy's narratives allows some sport with them, with her, and no offense taken, no harm done at all, not even to the flow of the tale. Sandy is not the charlatan-romancer, the storyteller who exploits tradition for the sake of deceit or personal gain. She embodies the tradition at its *best:* endless, repetitious, pure, an unsilenceable presence in the literature of the world. The satire of the realist might confound the conspiring romantic liar; but not the simple, ancient romance, fresh as it flows from the spirit of Malory. The only thing for the confirmed realist to do is relax and get acquainted. Hank can wade in and out of Sandy's narratives like a child at play in a stream:

> "Man of prowess—yes, that is the man to please them, Sandy. Man of brains—that is a thing they never think of. Tom Sayers— John Heenan—John L. Sullivan—pity but you could be here. You would have your legs under the Round Table and a 'Sir' in front of your names within the twenty-four hours; and you could bring about a new distribution of the married princesses and duchesses of the court in another twenty-four. The fact is, it is just a sort of polished-up court of Comanches, and there isn't a squaw in it who doesn't stand ready at the dropping of a hat to desert to the buck with the biggest string of scalps at his belt."
>
> " —and he be such a man of prowess as ye speak of, said Sir Gawaine. Now what is his name? Sir, said they, his name is Marhaus, the king's son of Ireland, — "
>
> "Son of the king of Ireland, you mean; the other form doesn't mean anything. And look out and hold on tight, no, we must jump this gully. . . . . . There, we are all right, now. This horse belongs in the circus; he is born before his time."
>
> "I know him well, said Sir Uwaine, he is a passing good knight as any is on live, — "
>
> "*On live.* If you've got a fault in the world, Sandy, it is that you are a shade too archaic. But it isn't any matter." (175–76)

Indeed not. As a romancer who can neither be stopped nor insulted, Sandy soon shows Hank the advantages of making a pact with her naive, fantastic imagination. After hours of her convoluted talk, Hank thinks of Sandy as the "Mother of the German Language"; but soon he has cause to applaud her as the mother of advance men and publicity agents. She is better than Hank himself at keeping the dangerous Morgan le Fay cowed and compliant, for Sandy knows the power in the mere mention of "The Boss"; when a half-dozen knights on the highway surrender to Hank, who has been blowing pipesmoke through his helmet, it is again Sandy, not Hank, who knows what to do next. In a naive, romance-ridden world, a naive romantic intelligence sometimes passes for pragmatism. Blatherskite or not, Sandy has gifts that a writer could covet, realist or otherwise. Because she understands intuitively how *others* understand the world, she can use that psychology to get Hank what he wants, and do all without compromising her innocence.

While Sandy may be translucent, a character she nonetheless is, not a walking symbol for a literary mode. Yet in this novel, which of all Mark Twain's longer tales seems the most elaborately symbolic, the essence of Sandy is her special moral orientation to romance, just as Merlin is defined by why and how he exploits his own imagination. Sandy seems first and last a version of the storyteller, a romancer whom this skeptical, pragmatic stranger first laughs at, learns to respect, then loves and marries. Sandy's nature and fate would matter little, however, were it not that Hank's own style as a storyteller provides commentary of its own about the various breeds of romance and realism, and their entanglements as literary modes.

It should be clear that by "Hank," I have meant Hank Morgan and Mark Twain together, for discussions of this novel have had mixed luck in establishing the moral differences between them, and because the history of how Mark Twain wrote the novel makes the argument for their separateness difficult. And unproductive — for it is the *changefulness* of the narrative voice that seems interesting, not only for its surprises, but for what those changes mean. One such transformation is Hank's reconciliation to Sandy's kind of romantic sensibility, not merely as personified in herself, but as embodied in her world. The scorn that Hank first feels toward Camelot gives way to a bemused acceptance of at least some of its customs, and of its myths and fantasies. Hank blows up Merlin's tower for practical reasons: to take revenge on Merlin, secure his own reputation in the kingdom, and scare off a curious horde. But later in the novel he restores the Holy Fountain chiefly for the Tom Sawyer delight of putting on a big show:

> About two hundred yards off, in the flat, we built a pen of scantlings about four feet high, and laid planks on it, and so made a platform. We covered it with swell tapestries borrowed for the

occasion, and topped it off with the Abbot's own throne. When you are going to do a miracle for an ignorant race, you want to get in every detail that will count; you want to make all the properties impressive to the public eye; you want to make matters comfortable for your head guest; then you can turn yourself loose and play your effects for all they are worth. I know the value of these things, for I know human nature. You can't throw too much style into a miracle. (265)

What follows is more than the triumph of a sometimes childlike Yankee. It is an ecstasy of one Missouri storyteller, "glorying" in the detail he can spill onto the page, in the cleverness and the joke of his German incantations, the Greek fire, pocket batteries, wires, pumps and pipes. The narrative here reads like a rapturous wish-dream. The first newspaper in the kingdom brings even higher excitements for Hank, who can now confess to pleasure in residing among Malory's Dark Ages:

> I knew, then, how a mother feels when women, whether strangers or friends, take her new baby, and close themselves about it with one eager impulse, and bend their heads over it in a tranced adoration that makes all the rest of the universe vanish out of their consciousness and be as if it were not, for that time. I knew how she feels, and that there is no other satisfied ambition, whether of king, conqueror or poet, that ever reaches half way to that serene far summit or yields half so divine a contentment. (308)

Hank learns to relax and enjoy his place in the realm, to respect and love some of the folk he had regarded as "white Indians." These changes might imply that Mark Twain himself, in the course of writing the book, had to lay aside some of his own severity on the subject of romance as an enemy of truth and an evil in fiction. But more instructive than any perceived continuity or evolution in Hank's account is its dissonance. Readers of the novel have troubled over the contradictions they find in Hank's personality: here he seems a fierce democrat, there a bloodthirsty totalitarian; variously callous and bathetic, he hates the veneration of the few, and gloats over the veneration of himself. Such discord can perhaps be addressed, if not explained, as various sides of one complex psyche. But moments like this one are hard to put away:

Consider the three years sped. Now look around on England. A happy and prosperous country, and strangely altered. Schools everywhere, and several colleges; a number of pretty good newspapers. Even authorship was taking a start; Sir Dinadan the Humorist was first in the field, with a volume of gray-headed jokes which I had been familiar with during thirteen centuries. If he had left out that old rancid one about the lecturer, I wouldn't have said anything; but I couldn't stand that one. I suppressed the book and hanged the author. (443)

Or this, from a time when Hank is supposedly at a humanitarian white heat. Immediately after saving a mother from the stake, he is sponsoring "a general jail delivery at Camelot and the neighboring castles." The immediate problem however is bad music at a royal banquet:

The poor queen was so scared and humbled that she was even afraid to hang the composer without first consulting me. I was very sorry for her—indeed any one would have been, for she was really suffering; so I was willing to do anything that was reasonable, and had no desire to carry things to wanton extremities. I therefore considered the matter thoughtfully, and ended by having the musicians ordered into our presence to play that Sweet By and By again, which they did. Then I saw that she was right, and gave her permission to hang the whole band. This little relaxation of sternness had a good effect upon the queen. A statesman gains little by the arbitrary exercise of iron-clad authority upon all occasions that offer, for this wounds the just pride of his subordinates, and thus tends to undermine his strength. A little concession, now and then, where it can do no harm, is the wiser policy. (198)

This isn't Hank in a spasm of blood lust, or a glimpse into his totalitarian heart. This isn't Hank Morgan at all, but Mark Twain the platform comedian, scuttling his protagonist, the moral consistency of the fiction, the integrity of the satire and all that, for the sake of one good "whopper." Such moments foster the argument that Hank's good intentions have given way to techno-barbarism, that he is sinking lower than the civilization he would correct:

There was hardly a knight in all the land who wasn't in some useful employment. They were going from end to end of the country in all manner of useful missionary capacities; . . . they went clothed

in steel, and equipped with sword and lance and battle-axe, and if
they couldn't persuade a person to try a sewing machine on the
instalment plan, or a melodeon, or a barbed wire fence, or a
prohibition journal, or any of the other thousand and one things
they canvassed for, they removed him and passed on. (444)

In a moment the narrative is back in the reins of Hank-as-moralist,
with noble plans to overthrow the Church and institute universal suf-
frage, "given to men and women alike — at any rate to all men, wise or
unwise, and to all mothers who, at middle age, should be found to
know nearly as much as their sons at twenty-one," and deriding Clarence because "he never could be in earnest" about social and moral
reform. While these are difficult moments in the narrative, in a sense
they do not violate Hank's characterization, because Hank is a miscel-
lany. Sentimentalist, moralist, show-off, egotist, democratic Everyman,
jokester, mass-murderer — the problems with Hank, and the major
structural and moral problems in the novel, grow from Mark Twain's
anxiety about the nature of the self, and from his uncompromising
idea of freedom as a way to find that self, and to sustain a novel about
both the hope and the terror in being alive.

A *Connecticut Yankee* apparently plunged Mark Twain into deep consideration of the effect of culture on the mind, the beginning of an
inquiry that would both trouble and enrich his fiction, his essays, his
private writings until the end of his life. If there is a baseline to Hank's
thinking, about where he is and what he is doing, it is found in passages that take the following theme:

> Inherited ideas are a curious thing, and interesting to observe
> and examine. I had mine, the king and his people had theirs. In
> both cases they flowed in ruts worn deep by time and habit, and
> the man who should have proposed to divert them by reason and
> argument would have had a long contract on his hands. For in-
> stance, those people had inherited the idea that all men without
> title and a long pedigree, whether they had great natural gifts and
> acquirements or hadn't, were creatures of no more consideration
> than so many animals, bugs, insects; whereas I had inherited the
> idea that human daws who can consent to masquerade in the
> peacock-shams of inherited dignities and unearned titles, are of
> no good but to be laughed at. The way I was looked upon was odd,
> but it was natural. (111)

Hank offers a similar judgment about the woman he is going to marry; as he moves toward matrimony he begins to see himself as only another victim of cultural brainwashing:

> Being awake, my thoughts were busy, of course; and mainly they busied themselves with Sandy's curious delusion. Here she was, as sane a person as the kingdom could produce; and yet, from my point of view she was acting like a crazy woman. My land, the power of training! of influence! of education! It can bring a body up to believe anything. I had to put myself in Sandy's place to realize that she was not a lunatic. Yes, and put her in mine, to demonstrate how easy it is to seem a lunatic to a person who has not been taught as you have been taught. (236–37)

Between these passages falls Hank's climactic soliloquy on the nature of the self. More than a flash of cynicism from Mark Twain's pen, it seems a motto for the novel: the moral and psychological version of the dream from which all began, of a lost man suffering under the burdens that supposedly define and flatter him, as a creature of consequence to the world:

> Oh, it was no use to waste sense on her. Training — training is everything; training is all there is *to* a person. We speak of nature; it is folly; there is no such thing as nature; what we call by that misleading name is merely heredity and training. We have no thoughts of our own, no opinions of our own: they are transmitted to us, trained into us. All that is original in us, and therefore fairly creditable or discreditable to us, can be covered up and hidden by the point of a cambric needle, all the rest being atoms contributed by, and inherited from, a procession of ancestors that stretches back a billion years to the Adam-clam or grasshopper or monkey from whom our race has been so tediously and ostentatiously and unprofitably developed. And as for me, all that I think about in this plodding sad pilgrimage, this pathetic drift between the eternities, is to look out and humbly live a pure and high and blameless life, and save that one microscopic atom in me that is truly *me:* the rest may land in Sheol and welcome, for all I care. (208)

Our thinking is not our own; our ideas are not ourselves; they are only another way of deceiving ourselves, of keeping up delusion not just of importance but of coherence. In a narrative as diverse as *A Connecticut Yankee,* no single passage can be picked out as the central idea behind the book or its structure, or even the paradox behind the book or its structure, or even the paradox behind the force of its rhetoric. But there are reasons why the "microscopic atom" passage stands out. One sees the collision here of ideas that oppose each other throughout the book: the reformist impulse buries itself in the perceived futility of trying to reform anything. The celebration of individuality and free choice collides with the idea that most of what we are is nothing but social automation; history-as-progress encounters history as futility; the storyteller as independent, corrective, creative consciousness faces the possibility of the storyteller as machine. No other single passage in the text has this kind of scope. Further, the sentiments expressed here and implicit in the peculiar form of the novel give each other a kind of sanction. In light of this puzzlement about man, the final affirmation of the one small and evasive particle of the genuine "me," the changefulness of Hank seems a quest to evade exactly this kind of cultural and psychological entrapment in characterization, and in stifling ideas about plot, unity, form of any kind, whether of romance, realistic fiction, satire, farce, of anything else. The preaching in *A Connecticut Yankee* aims at all restrictive habit, belief, social institutions; it celebrates freedom as the highest good, and the very way it *defines* freedom evades complications, abstractions, confinements. A matter of kinesthetics in the first notebook entry, freedom remains so throughout the novel. It is comfortable clothing, soft chairs to sit in, a bed free of lumps and vermin; it is decent windows to look through, bicycles and agile horses to ride and the liberty to ride them anywhere. The enemy is dungeons, chains, slave collars, bad armor, disease, hunger, poverty. There is nothing theoretical about any of this. In the course of the novel, however, as the complications in the idea of absolute freedom begin to assert themselves, the idea of freedom as a possibility, and of the abolition of all confining finitude, encounters the problem of the mind.

For the mind proves to be the inexorable confinement. No physical improvement of life, not even an education at Hank's West Point can make a difference in recovering the one true self, in regaining some unrestricted condition of being that everyone loses in "training," in growing up, in being alive. The freedom Hank yearns for is an impossible, uncompromised freedom from everything; the artistic freedom

Mark Twain wants is an equally impossible freedom from every imaginable kind of restraint — even, it turns out, from consciousness. Hank's numerous moments of sensuous and emotional delight in *A Connecticut Yankee,* the "glorying" he experiences in the years of complete mastery of his world, are a part of the novel's appeal as a wish-dream; but the ultimate sort of freedom that Mark Twain yearns for, as an identity, as a storyteller, necessarily eludes him: as a condition it lies out beyond the reach of fiction. Yet the aspiration itself is an organizing force in the novel: it pervades *A Connecticut Yankee,* present in one of the most disturbing leitmotivs in the narrative, a bizarre metaphor for the ultimate escape, and as it were, for the motions of the novel itself. I mean the presence, nearly everywhere in the book, of blasting powder, dynamite, rockets, grenades, and high-explosive destruction.

Hank begins setting off bombs and grenades almost immediately after his arrival in Camelot: blowing up Merlin's tower is his first public act as Arthur's chief minister, and it cues the first of his arias of delight in demolition, which grow more intense and unsettling as the novel goes on. From that moment, bombs and fireworks are in Hank's pockets, in his adventures, and on his mind; they become the second great obsession in the narrative. The Holy Fountain is actually restored with stone, mortar, and a water-pump; the rockets and Roman candles provide a show, but Hank is disappointed that he cannot solve the problem with something more lethal:

> I almost regretted that my theory about the well's trouble was correct, because I had another one that had a showy point or two about it for a miracle. I remembered that in America, many centuries later, when an oil well ceased to flow, they used to blast it out with a dynamite torpedo. If I should find this well dry, and no explanation of it, I could astonish these people most nobly by having a person of no especial value drop a dynamite bomb into it. It was my idea to appoint Merlin. However, it was plain that there was no occasion for the bomb. One cannot have everything the way he would like it. (255)

Afterward, Hank's history rumbles with detonations: he blows up three knights with one of his grenades, and delights in the rain of metal fragments and bits of flesh:

> When they were within fifteen yards, I sent that bomb with a sure aim, and it struck the ground just under the horses' noses.

Yes, it was a neat thing, very neat and pretty to see. It resembled a steamboat explosion on the Mississippi; and during the next fifteen minutes we stood under a steady drizzle of microscopic fragments of knights and hardware and horseflesh. I say we, for the king joined the audience, of course, as soon as he had got his breath again. There was a hole there which would afford steady work for all the people in that region for some years to come — in trying to explain it, I mean; . . . (317–18)

And one recalls Hank's pleasure in Clarence's defenses for the Sand-Belt cave:

"Well, go on. The gatlings?"

"Yes — that's arranged. In the centre of the inner circle, on a spacious platform six feet high, I've grouped a battery of thirteen gatling guns, and provided plenty of ammunition." . . .

"Well, and the glass-cylinder dynamite torpedoes?"

"That's attended to. It's the prettiest garden that was ever planted. It's a belt forty feet wide, and goes around the outer fence — distance between it and the fence, one hundred yards — kind of neutral ground, that space is. There isn't a single square yard of that whole belt but is equipped with a torpedo. We laid them on the surface of the ground, and sprinkled a layer of sand over them. It's an innocent looking garden, but you let a man start in to hoe it once, and you'll see." (467–68)

In the battle itself one sees more of what looks like childish glee at mass death by high explosives, and the destruction not just of Hank's enemies, but of the world he has built from almost nothing. The novel that began in a dream of confinement ends in a vista of homogeneous protoplasm. The "Tale of the Lost Land's" closing episode achieves this grotesquely apt antithesis to Mark Twain's first idea, represents an absolute human formlessness to set against the dream of human fixity. In *A Connecticut Yankee*, dynamite represents the kinesthetic return to that "one microscopic atom that is me," the spectacular, instantaneous negation of feudalism, the established church, modern civilization, and the trained, conditioned, armor-laden, deluded self — everything that threatens "me," confines it, frustrates its return to a pure and supremely free condition. All the rest can go to Sheol, and with high explosives Mark Twain sends it there. In other words, the dynamite seems an analogue for Mark Twain's narrative process in the novel. The book is his own peaceful field of glass-cylinder torpedoes, the prettiest garden of them that he ever planted, a narrative that can shift without warning from satiric realism to romantic sentiment and suspense, to lessons in political economy, lectures on religion and science, frontier humor, slapstick, and finally holocaust. Like a good piece of platform humor, the novel tries to sustain itself on a sequence of surprises, on no continuity except surprise and shock.

One effect of such an arrangement is the "entertainment" Mark Twain promises in the first draft preface of a *Yankee:* the popularity of the novel over the past century will bear that out. Another is the undoing of narrative voices. The narration is fragments; the Mark Twain of any given moment speaking freely, without restrictions of tonal or moral consistency, seeking both the one right voice in himself, and a way of storytelling that can express his rising suspicions about form and coherence of any kind. But a frustrating tautology lurked in Mark Twain's path, and the anomalous conclusion of the book suggests that he saw it. Although the idea of killing off an army of knights stretches back to the "Sir Robert Smith" sketches and drafts that preceded Hank Morgan, and was not a plot twist he was forced into later, two characteristics distinguish the Battle of the Sand-Belt from its preceding forms. First, there is the introduction of all the dynamite, slaughtering thousands of knights, digging a ditch twenty-five feet wide and a hundred feet deep around The Yankee and his band of boys, and destroying every trace of his achievement. The other is the entrapment of Hank by the flood, the ditch, the wire, the mountains of dead. Sir Robert Smith always won his battle; but Hank loses everything, checkmated by the extreme of human form and the extreme of formlessness, by armored corpses and protoplasm. To see the ending this way is not to make Mark Twain a mechanical allegorist on the nature and restrictions of fiction, or the book into a novel that dynamites its own meaning and its own form. The implications of knighthood and grenades seem deeply connected to every self-professed concern in the book: hatred of a stifling society and of the tedious lies of chivalric romance; the fear of self-loss under social reflexes; and the exhilaration of destroying a bad world suddenly, utterly, and of wiping out the always-limited self and starting over. Regardless of what moral judgment one makes about Hank, it must be said that he fails because the world is too much for one man to change. Conversely, the novel ends up trapped in a cave of its own: resorting to a new narrator, then to a spell out of an old romance, then to a frame-tale narrator, then to an ambiguous fade. It all seems an attempt to hustle the reader out of the novel, to keep him moving so quickly from one time, place, and voice to another that the questions of what has happened, thematically as well as in the action, will be lost in the rush. An effort like that has to fail, because the orthodoxies of storytelling cannot be supplanted by a fiction of sheer surprise, a fiction whose very skepticism about the self militates against everything that fiction was in Mark Twain's century. After the last shock must fall a silence, in which the light show of dynamite turns to smoke and chaos; in which the constantly changing narrative voice seems incoherent, and in which the story can seem pointless. The deepest issue in *A Connecticut Yankee* is a marvelous failure; after the surprises there is only Mark Twain's confusion, after the disturbing question, only this bewilderment. The rest of his career would be spent on a quest to find forms that could work both as literature and as explorations of who and what we really are, celebrations of life and profound doubts of its reality, its coherence, and its consequence.

Chapter 4

The Wilderness of Ideas

Mark Twain's work after 1890 sails into choppier waters, which is one reason why studies of the canon regularly treat its last twenty years as a separate phase. Those years have been read as a closing act in an epic life-tragedy, or as a time of desperate experiment, a time in which Mark Twain's rising pessimism struggled against imperatives he apparently continued to feel: to entertain his public and to affirm *something,* if not actually celebrate life.[1] But dividing Mark Twain's career into theater acts might prove exactly the wrong thing to do, if we want to see one essential quality of this writer and his work: Mark Twain's continuing resistance to categories and boundaries, and to the hemming-in of life and identity itself to suit the formulations and mental habits of his time. I have been spotlighting a troublemaker side of Mark Twain, focusing on his delight in subverting the ground rules for literary art and all definitions of the self. In turning now to works from the swarm of manuscripts after *A Connecticut Yankee,* I shall show how this mischief transforms and compounds along with Mark Twain's evolving desire for absolute liberation as a writer and as a human being. Psychological, political, and metaphysical fixations that appear in the late work seem to me subordinated to, and symptomatic of this drive, this desire. Enormous new doctrines inundate Mark Twain in the 1890s and after. My premise is that these prostrations can be understood better as episodes in Mark Twain's larger adventure, his quest to imagine who and what we human beings can be — and what we inescapably are.

Nonetheless, near the turn of the century Mark Twain's mind was much on the move, like the culture in which he was saturated. Looking at his continued rebellion against the self's confinement, therefore, should not mean downplaying the importance of either that culture or his personal experience. Fine studies have been written of Mark Twain's life between *A Connecticut Yankee* and the end, including readings that see the cultural pressure upon him as overwhelming, and that accordingly interpret some of his work as revealing essentially the ideology of a late Victorian bourgeois.[2] In a forest of short tales, tirades, polished narratives and mongrel manuscripts, much evidence can be found to secure such interpretations. Yet what can go unnoticed, especially in determinist commentary, are indications that as a literary artist Mark Twain could be keenly self-aware, and aware as well of his waning century as a Mardi Gras of intellectual contrivance and excess. In Britain and the United States, this decade became a high tide for "isms": scientific, pseudoscientific, political, and literary formulations, many of them totalizing, some of them quite seductive. Although Mark Twain's psychological and artistic struggle in these years included troubles about the orientation of the self to received doctrines, neither the published work nor the biographical evidence require us to read the later Mark Twain as a helpless prisoner of strictly middle-class, capitalist, and male mind-sets. We can find richer explanations of Mark Twain's cultural importance, and of the impact of his culture upon him. Complex works from this period gain in resonance when they are allowed to reveal a mind in combat not merely with confining and *de*fining dogma, but also with the very *idea* that a given formulation, or any culturally fostered swarm of them, ought to transform, limit, or define an individual self. Mark Twain's combat is Fabian, often confused, and artistically dangerous, full of retreats and surrenders as well as all-out insurrections. So much the better: a self-conscious, turbulent, ingeniously heretical Mark Twain remains much more interesting to his culture, as an artist of mythic proportions, than a Mark Twain rolled flatter by received idea-systems in his time, or by formulaic reading in our own.

Mark Twain ages and passes away in a storm of his own manuscripts, only some of which he actually sent to press. Others he abandoned, or finished but buried in his papers because he was uncertain about their fitness for his public; still others he seems to have written as a private catharsis, perhaps to give name to inchoate hopes or rages, or to blow off other kinds of steam. Some sketches and tales he apparently tin-

kered with throughout those last two decades—years that may not
have been, in important respects, only a slide into despair and artistic
impotence.[3] He had lost his fortune by 1894, but with royalties and a
triumphant world tour Mark Twain made enough money to pay his
debts, buy another estate, and live handsomely there and at other
exclusive addresses until his death. He was bereft of old friends, and
his cherished Susy, and Livy, and finally Jean; yet amid those losses he
apparently had steady and compassionate company, the consolation of
work, and apparently a ration of happier days. No surprise, therefore,
that biographers have had fallings-out in computing Mark Twain's
Misery Index, or telling how dead-earnest this pessimism was that
supposedly—and paradoxically—fostered so much writing.

Mark Twain's intellectual and spiritual *unrest* in these years interests
more than debate about whether to gauge his late life as fundamentally happy or sad. I have proposed that Mark Twain's turmoil provides
part of the pleasure of his writing, and part of his legacy to America, as
a culture still embroiled in defining itself as something undefinable,
unfinished, and yet mysteriously whole. The work after 1890 includes
narratives that seem well-crafted, and others that seem botches and
potboilers. There are fables, and polemics that turn against themselves, subverting the very themes they champion at the start. And
there are notorious emulsions of great darkness and buoyant good
cheer. I must be drastically selective here in walking this terminal
moraine of Mark Twain's writing, but not, I hope, arbitrarily so. Because Mark Twain as a writer took an inherently bigger risk, obviously,
in works he resolved to publish than in works he decided not to, and
because material that reached market in his lifetime has figured more
in making his reputation than what he did not send to press, I shall
begin by focusing on a handful of the published materials. At the end
of this chapter there are speculations about two peculiarly similar
works, and what happens when they are looked at as possible phases of
the same long meditation. Issued as a short book shortly before Mark
Twain died, one of these stories, *Extract from Captain Stormfield's Visit to
Heaven,* has been largely overlooked. The other, about a Mysterious
Stranger named Number 44, a tale that Mark Twain tried several times
and that did not reach print accurately until half a century after his
death, has grown large in our thinking about his late-life beliefs and
artistic intentions. First, however, let us look at a familiar pairing, two
great river-town narratives, and observe how each challenges the social

perceptions that set each in motion, subverts basic rules for the framing of narratives, and jolts deep-lying American assumptions about the nature of identity. In each of these works, Mark Twain's quest, whether successful or not, is to affirm unindoctrinated, nonideologized sides of the self. He seems to demand a prerogative of American prose to sport with totalizing formulations yet remain free of their thrall. If we can read these works as creatively unstable, they gain not only in general interest but also in intellectual integrity, and in their relevance to larger social crises, certainly at the end of the nineteenth century, and also perhaps at the close of the twentieth.

As Mark Twain's fiercest, most finished satires of small-town life on the shores of the Mississippi, "The Man That Corrupted Hadleyburg" (1900) and *Pudd'nhead Wilson* (1894) have been compared often, for self-evident reasons.[4] The erstwhile Hadleyburg and the Dawson's Landing of *Pudd'nhead Wilson* have clearer social hierarchies than other American towns Mark Twain wrote about, and fuller complements of pretentious or hypocritical First Citizens and families. In each tale interknotted secrets must not only be found out but also untangled from one another; moreover, these mysteries ultimately can find release only in a mass meeting. In *Pudd'nhead Wilson* the big scene is a court trial, and something like a Dionysian festival in "Hadleyburg"; at both gatherings mighty people are brought low, and humble folk raised up — ironically and unhappily — in civic esteem.

So the detective story makes another comeback as a Mark Twain obsession, and the plot gimmickry in weaker Tom Sawyer narratives creaks again in these two works, running none too well in the case of *Pudd'nhead Wilson*. There might be philosophical or psychological dimensions to Mark Twain's interest in detective stories (a possibility to be raised with *Pudd'nhead Wilson*); and changelings, stolen daggers, identical twins, mysterious sacks of money, and thrilling last-second revelations flourish in Victorian popular fiction, including of course novels now regarded as classics. Yet *Pudd'nhead Wilson* can be set in more interesting perspectives than either the crowd of Mark Twain's other whodunits and river-town stories, or a quick tour of nineteenth-century pop culture. To edge only a few steps away from these two texts, one can interrogate them as artifacts peculiar to the 1890s, and take cues from the fact that structural and thematic unities were just then coming under unprecedented challenge as aesthetic virtues. In other words, if formal or thematic trouble in "Hadleyburg," or mysteries and plot-holes in the tale of Dawson's Landing can be explained, or in some measure excused, by the state of Mark Twain's bank balance, his family troubles, his psychological turmoil, or his professional envy of Robert Louis Stevenson and Conan Doyle, then they might also be explained in terms of a cultural milieu that by the end of the nineteenth century was in full upheaval. The record reveals clearly that Mark Twain was having personal difficulties; but it also indicates that he was tuned in to the arts and intellectual life of his day, knew acutely what sort of decade he was living in, and understood what insurgencies were mustering against conventions of representation. In the art of Anglo-American fiction certain questions were cropping up everywhere: What now were the moral obligations of the storyteller? And what legitimate place, if any at all, could serious ideas hold in a work of imaginative literature.[5]

In the world of the arts, strange business had long since begun, and stranger things were everywhere under way. The London and New York literary scenes of the early 1890s had been ruffled by *The Picture of Dorian Gray* and Wilde's brazen preface, refusing realism, romanticism, moralizing — and literary refusals. The Impressionists, once so shocking, had been flourishing in the Paris salons for at least fifteen years; Van Gogh and Seurat had already made their mark as renegades and died young; Pater's call for fiery intensity as the sine qua non in art and life was now a quarter-century old. The French Symbolists, many of them gone for decades, were finding vogue even in Boston; Zola had reached international fame and prosperous middle age, and Swinburne's and Whistler's best work was twenty years behind them. This was the decade of *The Awakening*, of "Heart of Darkness," *Ubu Roi*, *McTeague*, *The Interpretation of Dreams*, of Beardsley's *Salomé*, Munch's *The Scream*, and of Henry Adams, self-styled Yankee archetype, lying on the floor (so he said) of the Paris Exposition, his historical neck broken by forces utterly new. As a world traveler and adventurous reader, Mark Twain knew firsthand about such things, and about the upheaval they represented. He had dined and visited with people who were bringing this about;[6] he had wandered through Western Europe as it fermented through symbolism, decadence, late romanticism, nihilism, literary naturalism. He had corresponded with some of the daring folk on the English and American artistic and literary scene. All of this may have had no effect on Mark Twain's affiliations with American-style realism; as we have seen, those affiliations had always been not only loose and supple, but also self-evidently aware that "realism" (not as his rule book, but as his mode) encompassed the opposite narrative strategies I reviewed in Chapter 1. Mark Twain had no need to catch up with Mauve Decade paradox; the Mauve Decade was only catching up with him.

the trap of the written word

Some of Mark Twain's stories from the 1890s and after can be read as crucibles in which literary conventions react with ideas and modes that intend the overthrow of those same conventions. It is a commonplace that *The Importance of Being Earnest* and *Arms and the Man* keep faith with the trumpery of the well-made play even as they enact aesthetic and moral subversion of that kind of drama. Do "Hadleyburg" and *Pudd'nhead Wilson* have something like within them? Conventions reified as well as undone? Are these narratives also profoundly works of the Anglo-American 1890s, sensitive to disruptions under way in the literary culture of the wider world?

As a well-made story, "The Man That Corrupted Hadleyburg" rates as Mark Twain's shrewdest, belying claims that shapely plot designs embarrass his storytelling and debase his intentions. Symmetries are certainly here, for better or worse. At the start of the tale and at the close, "Hadleyburg" is panned across cinematically as a prideful, smooth-surfaced American village. "The most honest and upright town in all the region," as the place is styled in the opening lines, weathers its crisis and becomes "an honest town once more," as the last line says — though this last line is both an English sentence and a nonverbal illustration, with the old and new civic mottoes inscribed in circles hooked together like a barbell, a colophon that seems to advertise the story's comforting geometry. But as an interpretive help the figure certifies nothing. In fact the trouble is epitomized in the mirror-image opening and closing, and in this mirror image at the bottom of the story's last page. "Lead us not into temptation"; "Lead us into temptation": the town motto has shifted slightly, radically, enigmatically, and questions boil up as to what "honest" meant in the story's first line, or here at the end, where Hadleyburg, a "whole town," becomes "an honest town once more." The closing phrase about the place never being caught "napping again" looks suspicious too. What sort of "napping" seems intended here, and what has it to do with the farce that breaks loose in the story's middle? Even the reference to the whole "town" can mystify: Who or what was or is this place called Hadleyburg? Is it the nineteen "Symbols" humiliated in the mass meeting about the sack of gold? That seems a poor guess, because the stranger's design encompasses more than these folk. As his advisory to the meeting declares, "I wanted to damage every man in the place, and every woman — and not in their bodies or in their estate, but in their vanity — the place where feeble and foolish people are most vulnerable." Yet if the con artist means what he says, then how would bringing down the Symbols, whom the public of Hadleyburg seem fed up with anyway, do such intended universal "damage?" The stranger has meant to teach the town, whatever it is, a lesson; but who has learned what in this experience, or learned surely? Perhaps one lesson of the fable-like tale amounts to this: that *no* lesson, whether punitive, moral, social, or psychological, is really worth taking to heart. With good reason, "Hadleyburg" is often linked with the Mysterious Stranger tales that Mark Twain wrestled with in his last years; in those tales as well, one remarkable quality is how the havoc that breaks out complicates or overwhelms the moralizing. The company this story keeps in late-work collections does not in itself simplify its reading.[7]

Begin again: "The Man That Corrupted Hadleyburg" is a story about a story that brings down the social and moral hierarchy of a town. The story that works this mischief is a story about civic goodness, an unknown Samaritan, and miraculous recompense. Everything about that story — which an unseen somebody who calls himself Howard L. Stephenson lays out a little at a time in notes and postscripts — is *false*, including the treasure for which nineteen reputations are risked and eighteen brought to public grief. There was no good deed that set all this in motion, no gift of twenty dollars to a destitute man, and no "kind and sage advice" dispensed with the money. It turns out that there was no Howard L. Stephenson either, and perhaps no initial ill turn to foster his vengeful fantasy of a good deed. For like a true put-on artist, the author of the all-disrupting tale ultimately effaces himself. Signing only one document with the Stephenson alias, he signs no others, allowing his handwriting to be his trademark, and letting his tales, letters, and notes of instruction be the sum of his identity. The frame narrator of "Hadleyburg" intimates that the town's moral and social Samson may be in the town hall as the meeting unravels, possibly as the smooth collector of curiosities who blackmails the Symbols into paying nearly forty thousand dollars to buy the gilded lead in the sack, to keep it from being peddled to the world as souvenirs of their humiliation. But all of this is left in Hawthornian umbras of possibility. The teller of the story of kindness and treasure, with its supposedly secret addenda, and addenda to addenda, and eventual disclaimers, stays a shape-shifter and a put-on artist in essence, known only in a shadowy way by his plotting, his indefinite and dubious grievance, his skill at spinning yarns, his remorse at implicating two people he eventually thinks blameless, his ignorance of their actual complicity, and his final failure to know the good and the disastrous effect of what he has engineered.

So part of the experience of reading "Hadleyburg" is meeting a man who isn't there, enjoying his mischief, and then wishing he would go away. Yet Howard L. Stephenson, or whatever his name is, blends into larger motions in this tale, which slides far from individualized characterization, from distinguishable people, personalities, and names, and toward a dream of protoplasmic group-identity, a dream that offers solace, and humor, and a chance for recovery from crises of the distinct, the established, and the known. Mark Twain has the dynamite torpedoes out again, and the main event of "Hadleyburg" is the obliteration of a caste system and a set of identities, throwing an American town back into something like primordial community. The longest scene, the town meeting, is a movement backward in the history of dramatic narrative, all the way home to the dithyramb, the form ancestral to satire, tragedy, and other specialized and conflicting structures with which life and conflict are represented. A disgraced parson named Burgess presides, more or less; an aged, impoverished, cornered couple, the Richardses, cringe in the masses below; and nearly everyone else blends into "a cyclone of voices" that usurps the meeting from Burgess, gleefully "outs" the self-compromised Nineteen, and makes of the night a festival from preliterate times. Song and poetry generate tribally, ecstatically, with fresh verses spilling in from around the raucous room. There are no bards, no designated authors; Hadleyburg in its delight has leaped back to an age before such nonsense began, before there were authors to be caught in the webs of their own utterance. Hadleyburg as pre-Thespian chorus has no trouble making verses or finding inspiration on the spot:

> "Five elected! Pile up the Symbols! Go on, go on!"
> " 'You are far from being a bad — ' "

"Name! name!"

" 'Nicholas Whitworth.' "

"Hooray! Hooray! it's a symbolical day!"

Somebody wailed in, and began to sing this rhyme (leaving out "it's") to the lovely *Mikado* tune of "When a man's afraid of a beautiful maid"; the audience joined in, with joy; then, just in time, somebody contributed another line —

"And don't you this forget — "

The house roared it out. A third line was at once furnished —

"Corruptibles far from Hadleyburg are — "

The house roared that one too. As the last note died, Jack Halliday's voice rose high and clear, freighted with a final line —

But the Symbols are here, you bet!

That was sung, with booming enthusiasm. Then the happy house started in at the beginning and sang the four lines through twice, with immense swing and dash, and finished up with a crashing three-times-three and a tiger for "Hadleyburg the Incorruptible and all Symbols of it which we shall find worthy to receive the hall-mark to-night."[8]

To read this night as a catharsis of gleeful malice, or as an affirmation of human frailty, is to understand part of what is going on, yet not quite enough of it. The good humor and fellowship of "the house," welcoming the truth about the civic reputation, make it clear that revenge on the elite is not exclusively or even primarily what it wants. By freeing themselves from the high-toned oppression of the Symbols, from the repulsive equation of wealth with superiority of character, and also perhaps from a moral pomposity that has infected everyone, the people in this house — momentarily at least — unburden themselves of even more. Out the windows go social and political hierarchy, religious rituals and high-seriousness (which they summon for the sake of parody). For one evening, these Hadleyburgers obliterate their separateness from one another, and even the confinement of their very names. One buoyant affirmation in this tale is that for *this* night at least, one ordinary American Hadleyburg has become a people, free not only of an ersatz community they have inflicted on themselves by venerating these Symbols, but also of so much that obstructs and divides collective *humanitas* in modern America.

As Chair of the meeting, Reverend Burgess is a fitting nonleader because of his disgrace. He shouts for order occasionally, voices the crowd's warm feelings toward "poor" Edward and Mary Richards, and takes it on himself to conceal their damning claim on the gold. But otherwise he is the servant of the multitude. The one named ring-leader of the festivities is the man named Jack Halliday, introduced as "the loafing, good-natured, no-account, irreverent fisherman, hunter, boys' friend, stray-dogs' friend, typical 'Sam Lawson' of the town," a would-be king of fools who after years as a civic nobody finally gets his feast day. Yet after making the wisecrack that triggers the festival, and contributing one improvised line to the *Mikado* parody, even Halliday disappears in a tide of namelessness, and it is *A Voice, A Powerful Voice,* a *Tornado of Voices* (just so, capitalized and italicized) that take matters out of the hands of the Chair, the town jester, and everyone else of name—except of course the Symbols, who are being pilloried for being Somebodies. The *Mikado* song is the beginning of revels that make "Hadleyburg" a stand-out and a delightful puzzle among Mark Twain's so-called dark writings. The crowd sings its travesty four more times later in the evening; meanwhile, acting as one, they conduct business vigorously, with blinding efficiency, with fervor akin to both worship and blasphemy, and with nobody in charge:

> At this point the house lit upon the idea of taking the eight words out of the Chairman's hands. He was not unthankful for that. Thenceforward he held up each note in its turn, and waited. The house droned out the eight words in a massed and measured and musical deep volume of sound (with a daringly close resemblance to a well-known church chant) — " 'You are f-a-r from being a b-a-a-a-d man.' " Then the Chair said, "Signature, 'Archibald Wilcox.' " And so on, and so on, name after name, and everybody had an increasingly and gloriously good time except the wretched Nineteen. Now and then, when a particularly shining name was called, the house made the Chair wait while it chanted the whole of the test-remark from the beginning to the closing words, "And go to hell or Hadleyburg — try to make it the for-or-m-e-r!" and in those special cases they added a grand and agonized and imposing "A-a-a-a-*men!*" (423–24)

A too-settled social order gives way to folklife, to a springtime of human society in which collective talk and humor flow free, overcoming repression, inhibition, and decorum. It is a springtime with power and identity residing nowhere and everywhere, and art and culture invented in and for the moment. The almost-nobody who signs himself "Stephenson" has not dreamed of that, for Stephenson too is self-confined as these people for an evening are *not,* confined by resentment and the elaborations of his own plot, like a writer entangled in the moral ramifications of his own fiction. Stephenson's story brings down a world, yet in the wreck that world escapes the dominion of the storyteller, and "Stephenson" is left as exactly what he says he is, "a disappointed man." Actually his tale has slipped farther from his grasp than he knows, and to the end he has no clue about the consequences for the Richardses, or for the well-intentioned, long-suffering Reverend Burgess.

The paradox here for Mark Twain as a writer involves this particular dream of primordial freedom — from social conformity, from culture-founded ideas, and from selfhood as a modern construct — represented as a dream of *oral* discourse, of talk and song, but *not* of writing. Written words in fact prove part of Hadleyburg's crisis: Stephenson's sting amounts to a fabric of written messages, instructions from nowhere, private counsel with no counselor around to explain further, words that trigger fantasies of good deeds long ago, words that can be misconstrued and turn poisonous if pondered too long. The nineteen letters that the Symbols give Burgess are the petards that hoist them, or all of them except Richards, whom Burgess saves by concealing the letter — and whose letter about the concealment twists in Richards's mind until it drives him insane. Nineteen people in the town of Hadleyburg read a written message, pick up the pen, write something down, and are toppled by doing so. The twentieth and last catastrophe, which befalls Burgess, is deathbed testimony with the dead weight of a legal document. And of course Stephenson, once he has written out the pages of his scheme and delivered them all over town, can do nothing when the plan spins out of control and injures people he had not intended to harm. Writing is dangerous business, civilized business, even writing meant to upend a civilization's barriers against the primal freedom of the individual self.

The disasters that befall three victims of Stephenson's game make a story within and after the story of "Hadleyburg," a coda to a narrative that itself breaks past several mirage endings. The town meeting, at which the Symbols are all (but one) unmasked, takes exquisite turns after the moment when other Mark Twain court scenes wrap up. Appointed by the crowd to auction the bogus treasure, Halliday sells it to a speculator in rarities who has appeared from nowhere; reselling it to a Symbol named Harkness who wants to corner and suppress the evidence, the speculator gives $1500 to the devastated Richardses, promising to bring the rest of their ten-thousand-dollar windfall on the following morning. Then with another round of the *Mikado* song, the meeting adjourns. Yet after this *gamos,* where nearly everyone has a thrilling recess from being anybody, part 4 of "Hadleyburg" enacts a sober return to the world as known, a world of identities and their consequences; in this last part of "Hadleyburg," dreams that had flourished in part 3 wither. To feel the chill of this anticlimax, we must understand what these three people might represent, as personalities beyond reach of liberation, closing a tale in which a fantasy of perfect freedom is conjured up, yet never affirmed.

Edward Richards, "poor Richards," bank cashier and perfect citizen to receive Stephenson's big sack and his daisy chain of instructions, is paradoxically both the most sympathetic character in "Hadleyburg" and the most dangerous. He proves lethal to himself, to his gentle wife Mary who dies of chagrin on the same night he himself dies of delirium and paranoia, and also to the ruined Burgess, who apparently suffers ruin again, in this town, by the last oral testament of the dying madman. Edward Richards can be both gentle old man and destroyer, can be counted on by Stephenson to do what he is told, and also to break the trust in due course, because Richards is habit incarnate, and because self-pity, guilt, and regret are his constituting habits, along with unthinking obedience. When he receives the sack and the instructions, Edward hurries to publish the note in the local papers without thinking twice, believing himself *ordered,* albeit anonymously:

> Mrs. Richards said,
> "If you had only waited, Edward — if you had only stopped to think; but no, you must run straight to the printing-office and spread it all over the world."
> "It *said* publish it."
> "That is nothing; it also said do it privately, if you liked. There, now — is that true, or not?"
> "Why, yes — yes, it is true; but when I thought what a stir it would make, and what a compliment it was to Hadleyburg that a stranger should trust it so — "
> "Oh, certainly, I know all that; but if you had only stopped to

think, you would have seen that you *couldn't* find the right man, because he is in his grave, and hasn't left chick nor child nor relation behind him; and as long as the money went to somebody that awfully needed it, and nobody would be hurt by it, and—and—"

She broke down, crying. (399–400)

Mary is telling her husband what the two of them shall be from now until the night of the meeting. From the habit of obedience, and of ordinary domestic life and guilt and want, they move straight into pathologies of unhappy solitude:

Richards and his old wife sat apart in their little parlor—miserable and thinking. This was become their evening habit now: the life-long habit which had preceded it, of reading, knitting, and contented chat, or receiving or paying neighborly calls, was dead and gone and forgotten, ages ago—two or three weeks ago; nobody talked now, nobody read, nobody visited—the whole village sat at home, sighing, worrying, silent. Trying to guess out that remark. (404)

Alone, meek, frightened, and short of cash, the Richardses are pitiable, in a limited way: limited because it is their nature to perseverate, to fix in one psychological state until some external force knocks them into another. Psychological loops of self-pity and self-recrimination cause Edward to turn Burgess's message inside out, and take the disgraced man's reassuring note to them as a sarcastic threat, intimating that Edward's dishonesty, concerning both the Stephenson letters and the unspecified frame-up of Burgess years before, will be the talk of the town. Edward Richards can never escape the oubliette of himself, which is why he cannot avoid doing harm to his benefactor, to the man who has tried to save him from both poverty and public scorn. Edward and Mary are the "nice" people of Hadleyburg; by the misunderstanding throng they are huzzahed into silence when Edward tries to speak, to dodge his own entrapment by Stephenson's ruse. Niceness and meekness are the public identity they *cannot* escape, an identity as inexorable as their injury to Burgess. Poverty and pain they also cannot escape, even with forty thousand dollars in freely offered checks under Edward's pillow. They are trapped because they have become people, complex yet stable identities, with habits of public citizenship and private agony. And for his part, Burgess remains the scapegoat of Hadleyburg no matter what he does, or does not do. That is the role the culture has assigned him, along with a name, an ethos, a memory, neighbors, an identity in a world of other women and men.

As the town's one confirmed noncitizen and refuser of seriousness, even Jack Halliday has discomfiture in due course, when he suspects that the normally too-stable identities in Hadleyburg are coming un-stuck, and that folk of public repute and rigidity seem suddenly as happy and unpredictable as he. Halliday has fun with the general despondency, triggered by Stephenson's first round of messages: the woe about not knowing the right words to win the money. As an inter-textual parody of David Wilson and his fingerprint kit, Halliday fakes a camera, stops passers on the street, and pretends to catch them in their set and uniform moroseness. The moment underscores a con-trast between Halliday and Wilson: Wilson's fingerprinting and filing are a potentially serious business that nobody in Dawson's Landing can fathom, a catching of unchanging truth about people, an unheeded mark of selfhood that ultimately can vindicate or condemn. But Halli-day's likeness-taking is bogus; his role as a character is to dispute com-monplaces about identity and challenge limiting definitions of self, rather than set up more categories. His spirit is not malicious, and his motives are never clearer than these, perhaps because clear motives would make him unfit for his task in this narrative. Motives, after all, would make Halliday as defined as these others — and potentially as narrow and brittle. Soon after, when general happiness breaks out (as Stephenson's follow-up note is received secretly and widely), Halliday is astonished, yet his astonishment is mixed with enthusiasm for what-ever is going on, as it reaffirms flux and life in the human spirit, the discontinuities in which he revels:

> He noticed that the faces of the nineteen chief citizens and their
> wives bore that expression of peaceful and holy happiness again.
> He could not understand that, neither was he able to invent any
> remarks about it that could damage it or disturb it. And so it was
> his turn to be dissatisfied with life. His private guesses at the
> reasons for the happiness failed in all instances, upon examina-
> tion. When he met Mrs. Wilcox and noticed the placid ecstasy in
> her face, he said to himself, "Her cat has had kittens" — and went
> and asked the cook; it was not so; the cook had detected the
> happiness, but did not know the cause. When Halliday found the

duplicate ecstasy in the face of "Shadbelly" Billson (village nick-
name), he was sure some neighbor of Billson's had broken his leg,
but inquiry showed that this had not happened. The subdued
ecstasy in Gregory Yates's face could mean but one thing — he was
a mother-in-law short; it was another mistake. "And Pinkerton —
Pinkerton — he has collected ten cents that he thought he was
going to lose." And so on, and so on. In some cases the guesses
had to remain in doubt, in the others they proved distinct er-
rors. In the end Halliday said to himself, "Anyway it foots up that
there's nineteen Hadleyburg families temporarily in heaven; I
don't know how it happened; I only know Providence is off duty
today." (409–10)

In Jack Halliday's view (which is to say, in this moment of reflection
by a man who makes fun of rigid identities) it is a duty of providence to
keep everybody else earthbound, meaning stuck in their usual selves.
That Jack Halliday seems a cousin to David "Pudd'nhead" Wilson is
axiomatic: as outcasts in their respective rigid towns, and assigned
the social identity of the fool and the loser, the two men bide their
time until a day when they assist in toppling a social order, at least
for an hour or two. In some respects, however, they work opposite
magic. Halliday's anti-mission is to ridicule and undermine assumptions about selfhood, and promote their disruption. David Wilson,
however, spends his youth puttering with one unglamorous method
of *establishing* identity, of proving — beneficially or otherwise — who
is really who, and settling at least one question about individuality
that arguments about race, class and gender cannot come close to
resolving.

the markers of the self

In each case the trouble is started by somebody else. Tom Driscoll and
his mother Roxy unwittingly drop a bomb on the social order of Dawson's Landing; Stephenson takes aim much more deliberately at the
fabric of Hadleyburg. And in each case the end results, assisted by a
town fool, are unexpected, a disruption in which not only social hierarchies but also literary modes, fin de siècle doctrines, and clashing
intuitions about reality and the individual psyche collide in an exhilarating mess. Here, then, is a respectable reason for Mark Twain's return to the well-made play tradition and its cousin the mystery story. In

these crowning revelations, of supposedly true identities, long-lost parentage, concealed heroics or depravity, one fantasized moment can both reassure and horrify. When worlds are known or set right with last-second miracles, a narrative can whisper that there is truth, and that truth will "out" somehow. But it can also whisper that without such miracles of luck and genius, truth (if indeed there is any) will *never* out, or that in the adulterated "reality" of mystery stories and cunningly wrought tales, we only pretend to see into the hidden life of things. Or to try a perspective based more squarely in the time: when the bootprint, the telltale signature, or the lost dagger, handkerchief, false teeth, or Miss Prism's old leather handbag "prove" that a mild-looking man is a monster, that the accused wife is virtuous — or as in the great stage comedy of the decade, that the carefully facetious Bunburyist is not only named "Earnest," but *is* earnest, and has been unwittingly earnest all the while, then for an instant the represented world both spins faster and stops dead. If the lunatic, the lover, and the poet remain unknown but for such paltry objects and the deliriously lucky interpretation, then which is finally the "real" man or woman? A concealed self revealed in the last act and the final chapter? Or the lifelong, world-fooling, and even *self*fooling disguise? In other words, do these amazingly unmasked characters merely stand revealed as they always were? Or do they also, in that instant of revelation, become somebody else, or nobody at all?

One happy effect from the theory crises of the last three decades is that totalizing, winner-take-all readings of complex and troubled novels have given way to healthy pluralism, and that a little heretical talk about such texts can be understood as enriching other strong readings, not portending their overthrow. Politicized times may require that *Pudd'nhead Wilson* be interpreted first and last as political satire, with emphasis on moments that configure the narrative as a hot, if thoroughly confused, quarrel with slavery, with racial discrimination, with agrarian capitalism, with pretensions and bigotries of antebellum small-town life. One recent collection of essays on *Pudd'nhead Wilson* shows those intentions consistently: as a novel about American public troubles in the 1890s, *Pudd'nhead* is read as saturated with determinist doctrine, with ironic response to the Plessy–Ferguson case, with recognitions that race slavery was not really over, and with miscegenation fears fueled by Mark Twain's brush with the pseudo-Darwinist and eugenicist doctrines then rattling in the popular press.[9] Though some of these readings clash, they can make sense together when seen from a slight remove, because they portray Mark Twain and his narrative as heavily engaged in his country's front-page legal and social controversies. The stubborn interpretive conflict, however, has to do with how sure we can be about the steadiness and strength of Mark Twain's views on the social inequality of the races, on the worth of lineage and family prestige, or on the prospects for interracial harmony or a multicultural United States. Within *Pudd'nhead Wilson* there are indeed characters and plotlines bearing satiric weight, the satire having to do not only with race consciousness, but with race *and* consciousness, and the impact that skin color, even of a hypothetical sort, is expected or required to have on the individual self. Even so, it could be a mistake to hear such themes in the novel as discrete, or even as dominant. The larger experience of *Pudd'nhead,* rising from its array of characters and from its small tales and large ones, may show designs or anti-designs all its own.[10]

More than a decade ago, Hershel Parker returned to the manuscripts, typescripts, and correspondence in which *Pudd'nhead Wilson* took its ungainly shape, and traced the hopscotch, backward, inside-out, "jack-leg" way in which Mark Twain produced the novel. Then with meticulous fury, Parker demolished a generation of commentary that had revered *Puddn'head* as a Fabergé egg of noble and flawlessly realized intentions.[11] That was the end of the innocence; nonetheless, coming years after Parker's whistle-blowing, the recent political and cultural interpretations of this novel do not connive to glue broken icons back together. They seem to originate, rather, in a simple assumption that I am accepting as well: paste-job or not, an interesting text may resonate with certain deep chords struck by the age and culture in which it was written, and we can try to read that text just so, as a cultural artifact, and as the artifact of one preeminent American career and possibly archetypal mind, rather than as some perfect and premeditated achievement in literary form.

There seems no point, therefore, arguing how many separate stories can be distilled out of *Pudd'nhead Wilson.* Tom Driscoll and the slave nicknamed Chambers — whichever is which — and Roxy, and their mutual catastrophe hold the foreground. Though Pudd'nhead himself seems to come and go, the novel is named for him, and called his "tragedy," either by Mark Twain's decision or merely his assent. Further, by his own confession and the manuscript and typescript evidence, the Italian Siamese Twins originally dominated this narrative, and were much of the inspiration that set the project going. When Mark Twain lifted *Those Extraordinary Twins* from *Pudd'nhead Wilson,* the two texts were published in the same covers; and, since readers can see the crude surgery that parted the tales, questions linger as to whether the right "text" to read is both together, or each as something distinct. My premise is this: that within the "tragedy" of David Wilson are several histories, small narratives that taken together make a kind of thematic sense, about consolations and torments of merely having a personal history, and of letting life become a tragic narrative. In that way, the implications of these tales conjoin with larger catastrophes in the novel's foreground, and even with the short farce that Mark Twain wrenched out of his novel and published as an afterpiece.

Pudd'nhead Wilson opens not with Roxy or Tom or Chambers or David Wilson, but rather with a jog-trot tour through the small town of Dawson's Landing, and with microsketches of the Driscolls, a Mrs. Rachel Pratt, and a Colonel Cecil Burleigh Essex — Virginians all, aristocrats with pedigrees supposedly running back to the First Families of Virginia. To this group there is only one living heir. Percy Driscoll and his nameless wife have Tom as the sole survivor of at least four children; Rachel Pratt is introduced as "childless — childless, and sorrowful for that reason";[12] York Driscoll, the "chief citizen," and his wife (again nameless) are likewise defined by Virginia blood and the woeful lack of "the blessing" of a child; Pembroke Howard, an aging bachelor, is presented briefly as a propagator of the Virginia "code" of gentlemanly conduct. These characters are named and pigeonholed in a few pages in the opening chapter. And so Dawson's Landing is introduced as a place of exile, animated, more or less, by people who are living static lives a thousand miles away in the western wilderness from where they were bred, and who are apparently fated to vanish without planting a family on the new soil. Ultimately this is how things turn out, for the one assumed heir to the collective FFV legacy, unmasked as a slave, changeling, and murderer, is sold down the river, while a suddenly discovered genuine heir faces life as a psychologically ruined man, exiled not just from Old Virginia but also from his own childhood and any sort of racial identity, advantaged or otherwise.

If we allow these opening pages to echo in the mind, the theme of disconnection and alienation only compounds. Percy, Essex, Burleigh, York, Cecil are all names on cenotaphs in Westminster Abbey, names reminiscent not of Jamestown and Williamsburg but of Tudor England, and their use here suggests more than just a streak of pretentiousness in how these displaced folk have been baptized. If these are Virginians, then Virginia itself, only invoked in this novel and never seen, is also invoked as a place of exile, a place whose First Families were in a sense Lost Families, strayed far from home, and perhaps never reconciled to a new land calling for new names and new ways of being. The patricians of Dawson's Landing are a people *burdened* by history, never strengthened or empowered by it, never freed of it to become something different, something more than a name.

In none of the Tom Sawyer and Huck Finn narratives is St. Petersburg, Missouri, imagined as such a place, where everyone of consequence stays unfulfilled and disconnected. And since Hadleyburg is presented as a town whose inhabitants evidently and damnably *do* belong there, one can wonder why this theme of exile warrants such play at the opening of *Pudd'nhead Wilson*. Mark Twain reinforces this theme in Wilson's arrival in town a page or so after, from "the interior of the State of New York" (the exile-home where Mark Twain was writing the novel), and by Wilson's twenty-three-year limbo thereafter, exiled not just from his upstate woods or ancestral Scotland but from Dawson's Landing itself, denied as a certified fool, unworthy of respect as a lawyer or citizen.

That David Wilson stays here to endure ostracism, and that he has come in the first place, may validate local opinion of him as a dunce. But no one of putatively honored "name" in this novel belongs in this town, or holds the right social status, the right cradle or bedroom, the right spot on earth that Tom Sawyer's beloved Providence would seem to decree. Dawson's Landing brims with such stereotypes, with out-of-place and dubious aristocracy, based on family histories that unfolded someplace else, on conduct and values ingrained far away, and on mutual agreement to accept these delusions. Such shorthand and repeated characterization can trouble a reading of the novel as tragedy (Wilson's, Roxy's, Tom's, the town's, or the nation's), and promote an impression of it as bitter farce. For what is more typical in farce, bitter or mild, than people in conflict because their pedigrees, moral codes, and affectations are out of place, people who have no sensible reason to be where they are, and people whose professed high-mindedness cannot keep them out of extraordinary mischief?

For a reading of *Pudd'nhead Wilson* as such a farce, or as a narrative whose essence is black comedy and irony, there can be many illustrations: Judge Driscoll's Tidewater chivalry and his "highest duty in life," to keep the family name "unbesmirched," do not stop him from using bribes to "persuade voters" in local elections or from slandering one of the Twins viciously on the say-so of his own notoriously unreliable nephew. Moving to Mississippi shores from exotic places for no apparent cause, fighting duels and running for the aldermanic board, the Twins — Italian counts, no less — may be relics of the protracted sit-com that Mark Twain carved out of the manuscript of *Pudd'nhead Wilson;* yet Angelo and Luigi do fit reasonably well in a town where no one seems to belong, and where nearly everyone goes wrong by staying. Rowena Cooper, "romantic, amiable, and very pretty," sits in her mother's cottage waiting for a lover and rescuer — and Providence brings her the worthless Tom Driscoll. Tom's putative father has "worn himself out with trying to save his great speculative landed estate" (65) a Virginia plantation dream he has failed to transplant to Arkansas; Roxy's free return after a free life on the *Grand Mogul* gets her reenslaved and sold down the river, and her escape from Cotton South bondage is a journey home to open-court humiliation and a grief that forever quenches "the spirit in her eye." Meanwhile, one of the Italian Twins is falsely accused of murder and almost hanged; Judge Driscoll is slain by his own nephew and ward; and finally Tom, unmasked as a murderer, "negro and slave," is himself sold down the river. A grim sequence: yet the narrative's quick telling of these disasters makes not for affecting drama but something like a frantic fable. As a rubric for *Pudd'nhead Wilson,* then, "fable" might serve as well as "farce" — provided there could be some agreement about what the moral is.[13]

But in keeping with the contorted and changeful way in which the book was written, evasion, and not merely irony, proves the hallmark of *Pudd'nhead Wilson.* Just as Tom and Roxy evade guilt, debt, direct questions, recognition, confrontation and capture, just as Wilson, the Driscolls, the Twins, and other whites never countenance the social hypocrisies that bear them up or the aimlessness of their own lives, the narrative itself twists free of moral burdens that threaten to define it, encumber it with consistency in mood or theme, or with characters caught too soon in webs of identity.

Too soon, because the fate of becoming, of being hideously coalesced and psychologically and socially defined, seems once again the fate to be most feared. The evasion of that nightmare is a wish-dream and an anxiety impelling this novel. The three central characters, Roxy, Tom, and Wilson himself, stand out because these three are each exploded or buried alive, and then reborn, two of them repeatedly. Thus they evade, at least for a while, the doom of everyone else in Dawson's Landing, everyone who has acquiesced to being what they were, or what others before them once were in a far-off someplace else.

As one of Mark Twain's most despicable villains — no other character in his fiction sells a mother into slavery or murders a guardian and benefactor — Tom Driscoll nonetheless remains plasmic as a psychological construct, and as a moral, social, and racial identity. Tom's unsettledness builds no suspense about his villainy, but rather assures that the moment of his unmasking in open court, as "Valet de Chambre, negro and slave!" will also be the moment when Tom Driscoll is "finished" in several dimensions: completed and fixed as a self, ended as a malefactor, done for as a free human being and perhaps also as a psyche: What mind could survive such a fall from white aristocracy straight into slavery? Yet even as a white man, Tom's family identity has never been solid: he has never had grounds to be absolutely sure who or what he was, or what to feel a bond with. White or black, he has been raised by proxy, by a slave nursemaid; in chapter 10, as he wanders the countryside, shaken by Roxy's revelations about his birth and skulking because he thinks he now feels "nigger" blood in his veins, Tom has already been passed through three sets of parents. First there were the York-Driscolls, both of whom have died; then the Percy Driscolls, one of whom has died before Tom was a week old; and finally (or firstly, depending on how you look at it) Roxy the slave and an unseen white patrician named Cecil Burleigh Essex, the latter dead, and the former a mother who has not mothered, and whom Tom cannot accept or love. And now Tom has discovered not merely that he has traces of African blood, but also that he is really someone else and has been living with the wrong name, wrong social station, and wrong mentality, as well as another man's fortune. Yet soon after Tom undergoes his "great mental and moral upheaval," he slides back into being "the weak and careless Tom of other days" (126), and his mordant questions to himself about race and social justice leave nothing but a lingering odor of self-pity.

For the creature that thought of himself as Tom Driscoll is not imaginatively conceived, or *self*-conceived, as either black or white. Tom Driscoll's nature stays infantile, his life a twenty-year variation on the " 'Awnt It! 'Awnt it!" bellowed from his crib; and his bouts of remorse and self-reformation show, or merely announce, how little he has moved beyond that first psychological state. A cold determinist theme here, then, about character as forged in the blood or in the nursery? These 1890s-turmoils overshadow *Pudd'nhead Wilson:* a seductive, frightening idea that human nature is decided long before the self grows self-aware, and that such awareness, feeble and sporadic as that condition can be, can make no difference. Nonetheless, given Tom's succession of births, demises, and shape-shifts, an opposite prospect seems likely here too: that Tom's protracted infancy is a damning, conserving prelude, a too-long sojourn in uncreatedness, without either the benefit or the catastrophe of self-definition. On the night he murders either his second or his third father (depending on how we figure), Tom assumes not one disguise but three or four; again, the tally stays unsure. In blackface when he stabs Judge Driscoll with a jeweled Indian knife belonging to Luigi, who is thus framed for the murder, Tom escapes dressed as a woman. A few minutes after, at the same "haunted house" where Tom has learned from Roxy who he really is—or rather what his name and biological parentage really are—Tom burns "his male and female attire to ashes," and dons "a disguise proper for a tramp" (254). Blurriness in the narration here only compounds the puzzle about Tom, about what he is doing, and has been doing, and what if anything he *is*. If Tom has done with "male and female" attire, then what sex is this tramp disguise? Does "a disguise proper for a tramp" mean what it seems to mean literally—what a real tramp might put on to disguise himself? Or is meaning more plausibly yet more loosely this: a disguise that allows a nontramp to look the part?

Perhaps the prose here is only sloppier than usual, but the interpretive problem is thus converged on or blundered into again. What sex, what race, what identity has Tom Driscoll, this perpetual infant who robs, lies, betrays, and kills in the shape of a grown man, or perhaps as a white-black man-woman patrician-tramp-slave? Is the "bad baby" of chapter 4 an essential self, finally revealed by Pudd'nhead Wilson in the town courthouse twenty-odd years on? Or is it *Tom's* tragedy that he has no self to be revealed, that the incriminating fingerprints are those of an infant that never became a full human being? Even Tom's name pulls speculation in opposite directions. For Tom's full name, or rather the name that, for most of his life, he equates with himself, is

Thomas à Becket Driscoll. He is thus absurdly named for the martyred English saint, while from another perspective he is also named for Mark Twain's most famous Tom, a Tom-child of blissful incompleteness, an unfinished, untempered, untraumatized, perfectly unstable Tom whom Mark Twain wrote about again and again and never allowed to grow up. Tom Driscoll doesn't plan to murder his uncle, just as he doesn't plan to sell his own mother, or to live by burglary and theft. His adult crimes he commits out of fear, because he feels himself cornered by circumstances. Although that exonerates Tom from nothing, it does reinforce a perception that Tom's depravity comes of his perpetual infancy, an unfinished self with no ethics, no social inhibitions, or to borrow a Freudian term, no superego. Couch the problem in any language and the same question comes up: Is identity, as investigated through Tom Driscoll, only an infant howl demanding the world? Or might it be those codes and controls by which social life modulates that howl — codes that are themselves satirized in the pompous FFV types who orate and duel their way through the narrative, these too-complete Driscolls and their pedigreed, useless cohorts? With no code of his own, Tom grows up depraved; his uncle, code to the bone, lives and dies hypocritical and absurd.

Tom Driscoll is not Tom Sawyer grown large; only true Tom Sawyer haters could support such a case. He cannot be in any dimension Thomas à Becket either, a martyr true above all to himself, and finished off by his king for becoming a wonderfully finished man. The compounded ironies of Tom Driscoll's name have to do with dilemmas about who or what is named and condemned in the criminal court: a human being born bad and complete at the start, thanks to blood and providence; or a disinherited changeling, motherless, fatherless, soulless, and never made whole. On the first-edition page upon which Tom is removed from the court (and the penultimate time he appears in the marginal illustrations) Tom is drawn by C. H. Warren as a white gentleman in handcuffs; three pages on, the erstwhile Tom Driscoll sold downriver has transmogrified into Sambo, his hair now kinked, his face coal-black, his back stooped, his mouth slack in the old caricature of the African slave. This preposterous shift in the illustrating does reflect the spirit of Mark Twain's narrative, this drama-comedy mélange about a species of confusion that lives deeper than trouble about social mores or about race and what it signifies. For although the novel's ironies about identity would seem to counter

each other, there is consistent irony about the compulsive act of interpretation, of *saying* what the self is, of defining oneself and others in
words, and of putting faith in such definitions. When Roxy offers her
notorious judgment of Tom's character she speaks truth and talks
nonsense; when Pudd'nhead Wilson ultimately reveals the "nigger" in
Tom Driscoll he also deals in fact and foolishness. The essence of the
novel's farce, insofar as it is farce, has to do with name-calling, and
name-believing, as an ingrained cultural deception and self-deception
about the possibilities of identity.

Even so, Roxy, and not Tom Driscoll, emerges as the most interesting character in *Pudd'nhead Wilson,* because she turns out to be the
novel's showiest whirligig of identities, a human being out of place in
several worlds at once. There are so many ways in which Roxy is *not*
herself, and not knowable *as* a self. Though she masquerades cleverly
enough to fool her own son, and can fool him for twenty years about
who his real parents are, she also tangles herself naively in Tom's
malignant deceptions. She deceives herself about who and what she is;
she lives and suffers as a showpiece of a vast cultural put-on, as enig-
matic as any such dismal joke ever could be.

The blood of one great-great-grandparent supposedly assigns her
racial identity, and Roxy and her world affirm such madness. Because
the same drop of blood mandates her to life as a chattel, she and her
culture accept that too; and living a lie as a faithful servant and nanny
in the Percy Driscoll household, Roxy accepts as "her place" twenty
years of abuse from the oblivious child of her womb. Her two most
dramatic acts in the novel rebel against race identity and the institution of slavery, yet also affirm them outrageously. For the same Roxy
who switches the infants and condemns an all-white child to live as
property also conspires to sell herself, as a free woman, back into
servitude, and as a fraud she is brutally defrauded and sold down the
river by the child of her loins. Like the Driscolls, Pembroke Howard,
and Colonel Cecil Burleigh Essex (the FFV of "formidable calibre"
who proves to be Roxy's secret seducer and Tom Driscoll's actual father), Roxy struts briefly as Old Virginny stock, a Smith–Pocahontas,
the tall-tale first of all Virginia First Families:

> "What ever has come o' yo' Essex blood? Dat's what I can't under-
> stan'. En it ain't on'y jist Essex blood dat's in you, not by a long
> sight — 'deed it ain't! My great-great-great-gran'father en yo' great-

great-great-great-gran'father was Ole Cap'n John Smith, de highest blood dat Ole Virginny ever turned out, en *his* great-great gran'mother or somers along back dah, was Pocahontas de Injun queen, en her husbun' was a nigger king outen Africa—en yit here you is, a slinkin' outen a duel en disgracin' our whole line like a ornery low-down hound! Yes, it's de nigger in you!" (189)

This speech smacks of minstrel show, and it culminates in the most difficult line in the novel. Portentous themes have been heard in Roxy's declaration: blackness as genetic curse, as biological dram of evil, or perhaps as an evil idea from a warped civilization that wills race and color to be the determinants of character. But perhaps the line has to do with racial self-hatred as a root-cause of depravity. Possibilities collide, as they do so often in Mark Twain's work, and any try at lifting out some tidy reading could founder on the evidence of *Pudd'nhead Wilson*'s exceedingly messy origins. Yet this inkling does shine through, that one intention of such humor as this, sloppy, brilliant, or possibly both at once, might be escape *from* intention, from all seriousness pertaining to pedigrees, identities, and novels about them both—and the confounding of interpretation in a another mirror-maze.

In other words, if interpretive strategy does not get us through the confusion, then the value and possible meaning of the confusion itself need to be reckoned. Exchanging the white baby for her own and setting disaster in motion, Roxy is a white woman who thinks herself black because her race-obsessed world thinks her so—which means that in at least two respects she *is* black. In this, her most famous speech, Roxy scorns her own even-whiter son for black-race depravity. So what does blackness mean here? Is Tom Driscoll's newfound self-hatred making him worse than he was, pushing him into grosser cowardice and eventually into murder? Is blackness, as Roxy invokes it, a destruction inflicted by the culture itself on human dignity? Or does the novel insinuate that some indwelling, unsuspected "nigger" within this almost-white man has in fact emerged and taken its course? Or is it rather that Tom's *whiteness*, his Virginia patrician slave-holder airs and his Yale half-education, ultimately bring on the grief? In other words, Roxy's "nigger" theory may be dead wrong, or absolutely right for the wrong reasons, and an outrageous joke on any readerly thought about what an utterance like this means or why it seems true or false: not because having "nigger" blood or Old Virginia Smith–Pocahontas blood or Driscoll blood does or does not matter, but because at this point in the novel we have no Tom Driscoll for blackness or whiteness to define. Accepting not just slavery but blackness, and accepting blackness as a way of life and a key to identity, Roxy is either a perfect expert on race and selfhood or a perfect fool about such things. Yet if she proves a fool, then so does everyone else of note in Dawson's Landing, including the supposedly tragic genius David Wilson. For in Dawson's Landing, blood lines and lineages — black, white Virginian, Irish, Scot, high-born Italian, whatever — do not merely influence conduct and the psyche. They dominate and even supplant the individual self.

We can speculate about whether David Wilson's resolve to stay so long in Dawson's Landing shows self-sacrifice, cynicism or stoic courage, passivity or cowardice (if in fact he is capable of deciding anything of consequence). But the question cannot be answered: there is too little of Wilson in the novel that bears his name, and his scarceness is both a virtue and a fault in the tale. Wilson's nonbeing has to be what interests, not if or how he has decided not to be. He may have resisted the danger of public identity, dodged entrapment in both the political and the psychological dimension; or, like Tom Driscoll, he may have failed to become, and is therefore by default the pudd'nhead that people call him, a man evidently shapeless, in a town where every self must have a shape.

And "pudd'nheadedness," in the sense of stupidity, can be seen rolling through Wilson's appearances in the novel, right to the end, when the town decides that he is a genius in their midst. In a multi-edged joke that unfolds much earlier, Judge Driscoll's local Free-thinker Society conducts formal meetings and business with a membership of two, the rank-and-file being only Wilson. If Judge Driscoll is pompous and ridiculous as such a president, then Wilson seems as big a fool for accepting the judge's dominion, accepting an idea that two people who think freely and heretically need to bang gavels and conduct formal business. A palm-reader as well as a fingerprinter, Wilson probes indiscreetly, and in Tom's presence, into Luigi's private history, and thereby starts a sequence of events leading to the judge's murder and Luigi's wrongful indictment. Later, stumped by the failure of his reward scheme to turn up either the stolen dagger or the thief, Wilson never suspects that the notorious Tom, in whom he has confided, might be the culprit. And Wilson's discovery that Tom is Chambers and that Chambers is Tom—on one level at least—happens entirely by accident, when Tom visits Wilson's office and plants his incriminating fingerprints virtually under the lawyer's nose. Even so, convincing evidence that Wilson is one more local fool may lie in the trial scene itself, because it is not Luigi's innocence or his lawyer's cleverness that wins the case, but only another stroke of luck. Wilson proves hard to accept as a man with talents that lie fallow for two decades, or as a voice of science, or fate, or any other great force. He seems nothing of the sort. Moreover, to *be* nothing is what he has chosen—or perhaps *not* chosen, as we never know whether he wants his long limbo of noncitizenship, with no profession, no aspirations, and no love.

We never know, because even a will *not* to be is a fingerprint, a mark of an identity. It is fitting that Wilson's big discovery is not who or what people really are, but who they are not. "Valet de Chambre, negro and slave!" is what Wilson calls Tom, or the man who has been Tom or somebody called Tom for all of his life, and Tom faints dead away for an answer, which is *not* an answer, but a passage out of consciousness, out of the wakeful self, which is precisely what Tom is about to lose. The Tom who swoons is not white any more, not yet a Negro and not yet anybody's slave. And Chambers, who is now Tom Driscoll in name only, is not white, and not a master, and can never become either one.

These are not merely cute identity puzzles worked up for reading a flawed text. In this same instant, Tom's murder of Judge Driscoll is revealed as absurd, the killing of a nonuncle by a "black" slave in blackface; Judge Driscoll's duel for the false Tom's honor glows with absurdity, as does Tom's life, and Chambers's, and Roxy's. Wilson has broken all delusions and pretenses with one blow, and has left nothing in their place: a nothing that is perhaps the truest truth of Dawson's Landing. For to name and limit or delimit such "nothing" could be to claim some impossible dominion over the mysteries of the self. And Wilson, who has been the town's nothing since the year of his absurd arrival, is now evidently something, a fate he did not want—or perhaps did, because discernible motives for staying, for collecting fingerprints, for seconding Driscoll, for being his patsy in the Freethinker Club, for letting Tom know Luigi's secret, or for anything else he does, would mean existence.

No, to be an instrument of truth in the novel that enigmatically bears his name, David Wilson remains a name, an array of cynical

"Calendar" wisecracks, and little more, a voice of outrageous false-hoods who also deals in all-disrupting truth. In an oft-quoted note to Olivia, Mark Twain called David Wilson "a piece of machinery—a button or a crank or a lever . . . with no dignity above that,"[14] and critics have taken Mark Twain's cue that the interest of the novel must lie elsewhere. But Pudd'nhead himself proves a menace, as well as a vessel of truth. He is every bit the machine, wobbly or not, that Mark Twain said he was, and another of this novel's doubly incomplete people, fetal selves as well as thin literary characters realized in haste. There is nothing wrong with seeing Wilson as all these things; like Wallace Stevens's snow man, David Wilson, as nothing himself, sees, reveals, and embodies the nothing that is not there and the nothing that is.

But what this novel is, or rather is not, and what this culture chooses to make of it, or needs to, might be very different things. If *Pudd'nhead Wilson* is shadowed with possibilities of a void where a self ought to dwell, and concerns deceptions and self-deceptions that allow such a vacuum to persist, then those deceptions are legion, and involve race, pedigree, and social habit as well as civil law, class, and gender. But what then of these accumulated tracks and traces of human selfhood, these prints and pocket-items as proofs of identity, or even as creators of it? When a self-aware and self-besotted American writer, at the top of his powers, wonders where one can find the "microscopic atom that is me," as opposed to the social encumbrances and the mass delusions, then a fingerprint on a slide can be both consoling and frightening. It reassures that something unique about the self can be found and conserved, if not by the heavens then at least on a greasy glass. But it also signifies that this array of whorls and curves may be all there really is, that Hank Morgan's microscopic atom has finally been found — and that what has been found is not nearly enough.

The companion story, published with *Pudd'nhead Wilson* from the first edition onward, functions as part of the same reading experience; Mark Twain's preface to *Those Extraordinary Twins* endorses it as coming from the same creative turmoil. As a dadaist conundrum about the Western cult of individuality, about distinctions we make not merely between one young man and the next, but between ourselves and others of our race, social rank, and time, *Those Extraordinary Twins* offers a giddy look into the same shadows that form *Pudd'nhead Wilson*. This farce is also suffused with the absurdity of nothing contemplating nothing, of the illusory self pondering its own illusion. Joined at the waist this time, the Twins are indistinguishable in ways so gross that distinctions in identity, as this culture belabors them, become ludicrous. Luigi smokes, drinks coffee, reads heresy and votes Democrat, boozes heavily and brawls; Angelo stays a pious, peaceful, nonsmoking, teetotaling Whig. Satiric fire rains upon such vices, virtues, and political inclinations, not in themselves but as preposterous indicators and measures of identity, as plausible definitions of human difference. Thus a deep-running theme of this sketch: that every Tweedledum or Tweedledee, with alterations in a few trivial habits, could really be anybody else, and that possibly everybody is fundamentally and inescapably just that: Tweedledum or Tweedledee.

The running gag of *Those Extraordinary Twins* involves telling them apart, and the long joke stings in this way: that you *can* tell them apart, but that there is really no reason to bother, that for all the tallyable differences, these two supposedly opposite people are one and the same creature in all respects that really matter, and that those respects involve action and biological mortality. If one of the Twins kicks somebody else, then they both do the kicking. If one drinks, then both get drunk; if one is hanged, then the world is rid of both of them, as a two-headed affront to the American sacrament of individuality. What the Extraordinary Twins joke assaults, in other words, is the idiocy of American cults of individual difference, the consensus that through a handful of either-or decisions about politics and personal conduct, middle-class people can distinguish themselves from one another in significant ways, or become unique and interesting. To be a doctor or lawyer, to smoke or not to smoke, to vote Democrat or Republican, to take one's opinions from the *Nation* or the *National Review*—in such culturally sanctioned definitions of self, can anything of consequence be going on? Has a human being taken shape and begun to matter? The real Siamese twins Chang and Eng obsessed Mark Twain because for all his outward fun with the idea of them, they were troubling. Their very existence subverted a hope that Mark Twain intermittently cherished and ridiculed, that at least one atom of the self exists as unique, transcendent, and worth the trouble to find and name. The *Twins* comedy casts a shadow over the ungainly novel it is bound with, for *Twins* completes a pair of extraordinary twins, two different faces and heads on the same creature. The reader turns from puzzled dialogue with one face to dialogue with the other, from somber *Pudd'nhead Wilson* to this burlesque following it. And the possibility speaks, stronger than a whisper, that after all the reading and the interpreting, these far-fetched yarns we dignify as novels may be only yarns after all. Their claim to moral authority or even distinction in the mind might possibly be as far-fetched as the ordeal that one dreamed-up, two-headed extraordinary stranger inflicts on one made-up, stereotypical, crazy American town.

holiness and identity

Though *Pudd'nhead Wilson* and *Following the Equator* were not the last long works that Mark Twain published in his lifetime, they are the last book-length narratives that his admirers have found worthy of praise or even much attention. Two other texts from after 1895 are orphans in the canon, rarely figuring in discussions of the shape and cultural importance of Mark Twain's career. One of these books, *Personal Recollections of Joan of Arc,* was published with a pseudonym on the title page in 1896. According to Paine and other biographers, Mark Twain (now and then, at least) thought it the very best long story he had ever written, a high-minded holiday from being always Mark Twain. The other volume, which he worked up in bursts over a period of nine years, is the rambling 1907 book called *Christian Science.* Out of print for decades, both of these texts have returned in small-press editions, perhaps because everything with Mark Twain's name on it can now find a public.

Commentary about *Joan of Arc* usually focuses on Mark Twain's fascination with the French saint's life, which seems a polite way of asking what mental lapse caused him to write these pietistic, rangeless tomes and drop abjectly into sentimentalism.[15] His spell of illness, if that is what it was, has been diagnosed as a recurring yen for respectability, an overflow of nostalgia for lost innocence, homage to the joys that his family of women (especially the lost Susy) had brought him; and perhaps an aging man's penchant for lively adolescent girls.[16] Although such evaluations cannot make *Joan of Arc* more interesting, none of them blocks a possibility that these "Personal Recollections" show the imprint of Mark Twain as the sort of literary artist I have been describing, an artist chancing both the limits of narrative and cultural consensus about the nature and possibilities of identity. What makes Joan herself seem weak, as a protagonist for the two-volume tale that Mark Twain constructed around her, might be precisely what made her so appealing to him as an historical and mythic self: her spectacular escape *from* selfhood.

In Mark Twain's hands, Joan of Arc becomes a shirttail relative of David Wilson. As serene nonpeople at the center of their respective novels, each of them operates as a stranger and an inexplicable presence, arriving on the scene apparently free of childhood trauma and defilement, untouched by love and its pains, and free of complicity in the social and psychological life of other human beings. Living with neither sin nor guilt, and even dying without passage into maturity, Saint Joan, as Twain re-creates her, signifies transcendence into sheer "selflessness," in both meanings of the word. Certainly she embodies dedication to the highest values; she also, however, represents a kind of nonexistence, a supposedly alive creature with no discernable psyche. What Saint Joan becomes at the start of the account, and stays relentlessly, is a beatific void. She seems quite the archetypal figure of the saint at the center of a *rétable,* one of those elaborately wrought martyrdom-scenes favored in Saint Joan's own century: on a broad panel, placid, beyond agony or understanding, the Christian martyr endures, suffering and yet dominating a merely human expanse of cruelty, stupidity, and chaos. The tableau scenes in Mark Twain's narrative unfold like this, with his heroine always playing the imperturbable center amid all the trouble. And the *literary* trouble amounts to this: that the human trouble around Joan grows more interesting than she does herself. One of the many *rétable* passages:

> For that sum Joan of Arc, the Savior of France, was sold; sold to her enemies; to the enemies of her country; enemies who had lashed and thrashed and thumped and trounced France for a century and made holiday sport of it; enemies who had forgotten, years and years ago, what a Frenchman's face was like, so used were they to seeing nothing but his back; enemies whom she had whipped, whom she had cowed, whom she had taught to respect French valor, new-born in her nation by the breath of her spirit; enemies who hungered for her life as being the only puissance able to stand between English triumph and French degradation. Sold to a French priest by a French prince, with the French King and the French nation standing thankless by and saying nothing. And she—what did she say? Nothing. Not a reproach passed her lips. She was too great for that—she was Joan of Arc; and when that is said, all is said.[17]

Thus the aesthetic conflict in *Joan of Arc*. Really the battle lost: this fantasy of absolute self-transcendence breaks against an imperative of modern Western storytelling, that a protagonist be psychologically in and of the world, and have a self—or as is the case with Tom Driscoll and Roxy, have some psychological crisis under way where another sort of self ought to be. Noble, inscrutable silence may be an asset in hagiography, but it can play havoc in a novel, even a novel flaunting its own fidelity to the historical record. Denied insight into the psychological turmoil of these ungrateful French who adore and sell their hero, or into the consciousness of the noble girl, Mark Twain's narrative seems stymied. Joan fails as a character in either a romantic or a realistic narrative *not* because she is too innocent and too pious—to modern ears such descriptions will probably ring flat anyway—but because she stays incomprehensible, even to the Sieur Louis de Conte, who supposedly tells this story as her companion and personal secretary. "A stupefying marvel," Sieur Louis calls her military campaign, and this proves a characteristic exclamation from him, for in a work supposedly about the life of a human being, Joan herself remains as much a stupefying marvel as her feats on the battlefield. Mark Twain allows her no id, no fear, no element of the irrational, none of the human traits that he could be so skillful at catching, yet also at times so desirous of confounding and escaping, as social habits and worldly frailties that can suffocate a true self. Confined by the ceremonial pageant of Joan's history, the novel locks into tighter configurations than even history seems to require, with scene after scene of an unimaginably wise, faithful, stoic Joan rising above foolishness and cowardice, above the banality and ordinary human life around her. Seen entirely from without, Joan shows only the face on the statues of her all over France: eyes elevated above the earth and humanity, and fixed on something wonderful that only she can comprehend.

Grumbling about *Personal Recollections of Joan of Arc* is easy, and one obvious target is Mark Twain's prose, which rattles back and forth here between pseudo-Scott fruitiness and lively but incongruous Missouri vernacular. These language troubles may connect to the excitement that caused Mark Twain to take up the subject in the first place, and to manage it badly. The end of Mark Twain's novel reads as panegyric, yet also perhaps as an expression of writerly desperation. How does a storyteller whose great strength is human nature write about a magnificent Nobody? As he dishes out superlatives and grand phrases that seem to belong on a post office pediment, an undertone of frustration can also be felt:

> She was the Genius of Patriotism — she was Patriotism embodied, concreted, made flesh, and palpable to the touch and visible to the eye.
>
> Love, Mercy, Charity, Fortitude, War, Peace, Poetry, Music — these may be symbolized as any shall prefer: by figures of either sex and of any age; but a slender girl in her first young bloom, with the martyr's crown upon her head, and in her hand the sword that severed her country's bonds — shall not this, and no other, stand for PATRIOTISM through all the ages until time shall end? (2:287–88)

As a protagonist for any breed of modern fiction, Joan of Arc seems as perfect and deadly as Rappaccini's daughter, and perhaps that danger causes Mark Twain to flinch from his own heroine behind not one mask but two. He dons the mask of the high-born secretary supposedly penning this account in "Ancient French" as the title page calls it, and the mask of a translator named Jean François Alden, who in his preface and an occasional footnote editorializes sourly about medieval politics and the ironies of worldly life. Jean François Alden: John "France" or Francis Alden? The name might be a joke, nudging at a historical and mythic figure not from French history but from American colonial times, and more directly from that earnest Yankee eminence Longfellow, who made of John Alden the consummate honor-bound and language-bound suitor who could not speak for himself. There perhaps lurks the barb of the joke. A modern worshiper of Joan of Arc, Jean François Alden speaks his devotion in another man's words, supposedly the words of a nobleman dead for four hundred years. "Jean Alden": is Mark Twain here stuck with being a modern sort of John Alden, who for this once cannot speak for himself? As a lover of unworldly perfection, perhaps he can come no closer imaginatively to that which he imagines and loves, precisely because doing so would break the spell, violate the selflessness that made Joan of Arc the sacred *non*identity he so much revered.

Or maybe not: we can look at this double-persona contrivance much more simply, as Mark Twain keeping a safe distance from his own poisonously static and gorgeous subject. But the narrative should also be read, I suggest, as an unlucky adventure far out from Mark Twain's own writerly selves: not just the literary personae by which he was known everywhere, but also from a public and even perhaps a family self, the man of political bon mots, ceremonial speeches, photo-opportunities and the occasional pithy heresy that his public translated and diluted into humor, and also the man of predictable irreverence at home. No matter what else it is, *Joan of Arc* may show us Mark Twain on the run from all such presuppositions about who he was and what he could say and do. A Mark Twain novel without Mark Twain's name in it, and two Frenchmen, one supposedly long dead, taking credit and blame on the title page. A marketing stunt? Perhaps, but also another way of breaking out, as it were, from life as a ponderous construct, just as the narrative itself tries to evade the practice of both realism and romance, and escape the required engagement with people psychologically and culturally *engaged,* as human beings in compelling novels and ordinary life usually are. *Joan of Arc* isn't a cramp of Christian piety. Joan fascinates Mark Twain not because she is morally perfect, but because she lives and dies above the political and moral messes that not only vex everyone else but make them who and what they are. *Joan of Arc* turns out to be not so much a religious work as an escapist work, tripped up by something it finally cannot escape: this need for a tale to immerse in conflicts related to human identity.

If *Joan of Arc* seems deadened by unity, then *Christian Science* looks to be an opposite sort of mess, an assemblage of contradictory musings about Mary Baker Eddy and her rapidly growing religious empire. Nonetheless, this book moves raggedly forward, from its obvious opening gags about the limits of faith-healing, through its critique — tinged with professional envy — of Eddy as a bad writer but skillful hustler in the P. T. Barnum mode, an author who generals capably in the creation of a literary self. A recurring pattern in the book is a movement from sarcastic respect toward something more like the real thing. The tonal change often happens quickly, sometimes in the space of a single heated paragraph:

> Each in his turn those little supernaturals of our by-gone ages and aeons joined the monster procession of his predecessors and marched horizonward, disappeared, and was forgotten. They changed nothing, they built nothing, they left nothing behind them to remember them by, nothing to hold their disciples to-

gether, nothing to solidify their work and enable it to defy the assaults of time and the weather. . . . They made one fatal mistake; . . . they failed to *organize* their forces, they failed to *centralize* their strength, they failed to provide a fresh Bible and a sure and perpetual cash income for business, and often they failed to provide a new and accepted Divine Personage to worship.

Mrs. Eddy is not of that small fry. The materials that go to the making of the rest of her portrait will prove it.[18]

A page or so later in the same chapter comes an unsettled panegyric, revealing the same tonal change that happens so frequently in the latter half of *Christian Science*. At times a ruthless professional himself, Mark Twain seems liable to these moments of seduction by Eddy's displays of ruthless professionalism. Here is one free-ranging rumination, triggered by The Founder's decision to recast her Christian Science Association into a full-blown church:

She must have made this intrepid venture on her own motion. She could have had no important advisers at that early day. If we accept it as her own idea and her own act — and I think we *must* — we have one key to her character. And it will explain subsequent acts of hers that would merely stun us and stupefy us without it. Shall we call it courage? Or shall we call it recklessness? Courage observes; reflects; calculates; surveys the whole situation; counts the cost, estimates the odds, makes up its mind; then goes at the enterprise resolute to win or perish. Recklessness does not reflect, it plunges fearlessly in with a hurrah, and takes the risks, whatever they may be, regardless of expense. Recklessness often fails, Mrs. Eddy has never failed — from the point of view of her followers. The point of view of other people is naturally not a matter of weighty importance to her. (154–55)

Although Mark Twain roasts Eddy for inconsistency as a theologian, this background noise of admiration continues in the book, mingled with Twain's potshots, yet never quite drowned out. Eddy's pursuit of wealth, power, and fame seem to evolve in Mark Twain's thinking, from a shameless dollar-grab into a species of transcendent capitalism, a capitalism made both spiritual and deathless. What Eddy comes to represent — again, late in this slapdash, self-subverting book — is an achievement of immortality through guileless, unhypocritical, spir-

itualized ambition, and a resolution of dichotomies between the religion and the American corporate mind:

> She could build a mighty and far-shining brass-mounted palace if
> she wanted to, but she does not do it. She would have had that
> kind of an ambition in the early scrabbling times. She could go to
> England to-day and be worshipped by earls, and get a comet's
> attention from the million, if she cared for such things. She would
> have gone in the early scrabbling days for much less than an earl,
> and been vain of it, and glad to show off before the remains of the
> Scotch kin. But those things are very small to her now — next to
> invisible, observed through the cloud-rack from the dizzy sum-
> mit where she perches in these great days. She does not want
> that church property for herself. It is worth but a quarter of a
> million — a sum she could call in from her far-spread flocks to-
> morrow with a lift of her hand. Not a squeeze of it, just a lift. It
> would come without a murmur; come gratefully, come gladly.
> And if her glory stood in more need of the money in Boston than
> it does where her flocks are propagating it, she would lift the
> hand, I think.
>
> She is still reaching for the Dollar, she will continue to reach for
> it; but not that she may spend it upon herself; not that she may
> spend it upon charities; not that she may indemnify an early dep-
> rivation and clothe herself in a blaze of North Adams gauds; not
> that she may have nine breeds of pie for breakfast . . . but that she
> may apply that Dollar to statelier uses, and place it where it may
> cast the metallic sheen of her glory farthest across the receding
> expanses of the globe. (202–3)

It seems hard to say whether Mark Twain made up his mind about
this new faith that interested Susy and eventually recruited Clara, or
that he ever believed he had to decide. As early as *Roughing It* and *The
Innocents Abroad,* Mark Twain knew that sniping at minority creeds, and
beliefs exotic from the perspective of mainstream Protestant American
readers, was safe entertainment to sell, and that failures in his own
argument made little difference so long as a target was amusingly
bloodied. But what does Mark Twain think of Eddy in the concluding
pages of *Christian Science?* What manner of human being does he imagine her to be, finally in the book if not finally in his mind? A recurring
concern of the late chapters (insofar as they *are* chapters) is whether

the self is essentially a thing created, sustained, and overthrown by what it does or by what it writes. Chapters 10 and 12 in particular seem to poke through this thicket of possibilities. Uneasy that Mary Baker Eddy has evaded him because her words are "incurably inconsistent; what she says to-day she contradicts tomorrow" (261), Mark Twain tries to nail down who she is by suddenly espousing a mongrelized theory of identity, part Paulist, but also part determinist:

> But her *acts* are consistent. They are always faithful to her, they never misrepresent her, they are a mirror which always reflects her exactly, precisely, minutely, unerringly, and always the same, to date, with only those progressive little natural changes in stature, dress, complexion, mood, and carriage that mark — exteriorly — the march of the years and record the accumulations of experience, while — interiorly — through all this steady drift of evolution the one essential detail, the commanding detail, the master detail of the make-up remains as it was in the beginning, suffers no change and *can* suffer none; the *basis* of the character; the temperament, the disposition, that indestructible iron framework upon which the character is *built*, and whose shape it must take, and keep, throughout life. We call it a person's *nature*. (261–62)

This is Mark Twain hurling language at a mystery that his Eddy-contemplations have led back to. The passionate, repetitive vagueness of these declarations may be sign enough that after a career of wrestling with this trouble, he has not broken free. But Mark Twain in this book stays as incurably inconsistent about such ideas of identity as he says Eddy is about her theology. Earlier, while fleshing out an outrageous speculation that Eddy did not and could not write *Science and Health*, Mark Twain tries to hedge his position by positing absolute, inherent relationships between a human being's "nature" (a word he belabors in this book) and her writing style:

> I leave the riddle with the reader. Perhaps he can explain how it is that a person — trained or untrained — who on the one day can write nothing better than Plague-Spot-Bacilli and feeble and stumbling and wandering personal history littered with false figures and obscurities and technical blunders, can on the next day sit down and write fluently, smoothly, compactly, capably, and

confidently on a great big thundering subject, and do it as easily and comfortably as a whale paddles around the globe.

As for me, I have scribbled so much in fifty years that I have become saturated with convictions of one sort and another concerning a scribbler's limitations; and these are so strong that when I am familiar with a literary person's work I feel perfectly sure that I know enough about his limitations to know what he can *not* do. If Mr. Howells should pretend to me that he wrote the Plague-Spot-Bacilli rhapsody, I should receive the statement courteously, but I should know it for a—well, for a perversion. If the late Josh Billings should rise up and tell me that he wrote Herbert Spencer's philosophies, I should answer and say that the spelling casts a doubt upon his claim. If the late Jonathan Edwards should rise up and tell me he wrote Mr. Dooley's books, I should answer and say that the marked difference between his style and Dooley's is argument against the soundness of his statement. You see how much I think of *circumstantial evidence.* In literary matters—in my belief—it is often better than any person's word, better than any shady character's oath. It is difficult for me to believe that the same hand that wrote the Plague-Spot-Bacilli and the first third of the little Eddy biography wrote also *Science and Health.* Indeed, it is more than difficult, it is impossible. (128–30)

For better or worse then, we are what we write? And *as* we write? Since *Christian Science* exudes a distinct whiff of idle thoughts pasted together, it seems foolish to try to pin down what Mark Twain means here, or to pin Mark Twain to what he says. It can be ventured, however, that in this book Mark Twain bumps repeatedly into prospects that steal his attention from the initial subject, which was the apparent nonsense of Eddy's religious convictions and the enviable worldly success of her church. But this other theme takes over: writing as power, writing as self-creation, self-liberation—and writing as self-definition and ultimately self-confinement, another fingerprint telling that a self was here, and that this self, like all unsaintly human beings, was insufficient and sadly bounded. *Christian Science* drifts far from the intentions it began with, and what it seems to drift toward is this vast, familiar dilemma about the possibilities and consequences for identity, of words and the act of writing.

Two failures, then, interesting perhaps as object lessons about the perils of going too far into fantasias about escape from earth-bound identity, and even from the natural laws and consequences of putting words on a page. Follow a line of thinking that such thinking as this must end tragically, that Mark Twain in his last fifteen years was wrung out by hopeless dreams of escape from psychological, cultural, and writerly confinement, and many texts from that time can bolster the case. It seems possible that in the much-discussed gloom of some of these late works, especially in the collections that Frederick Anderson, Janet Smith, and John Tuckey have expertly brought together, something reassures: a sign to us that at some point the anarchic practice of our most famous canonical writer found its catastrophe, or that fortune and fame do not really bring happiness, or that life without stable faith means a journey into grief. There are reasons, and perhaps imperatives, for looking to these narratives for pessimism, for existential vertigo, for resonance with the nightmares of Kierkegaard, William James, and other Mark Twain contemporaries affrighted by modernity and a waning of Christian faith. As late moderns, perhaps we need to imagine how we got here; if Mark Twain was fully attuned to spiritual crises of his time, then it seems consoling to have him play a part in this bigger drama.

brass-farthing opinions

Especially in the case of the Mysterious Stranger tales, which are still the most famous Mark Twain works after 1895, we can read for his personal struggle with fin de siècle nihilism, his disorderly old-age quest to *not* go gentle into his own or his culture's good night. But one can get lost in Mark Twain's tangles with theology and metaphysics, and to little purpose. If he had religious convictions, Mark Twain's cosmology remained changeful, at times naive, and dubious in its consequentiality to his art. For as unpublished and perhaps private utterance, these texts can seem from some uncertain realm of discourse among catharsis, foolery, and composed, fervent soliloquy. It goes without saying that talk of God's absence and the general nastiness of the human condition can be serious business. But it also can be a way of blowing off steam about things solidly mundane: family trouble, business downturns, old age and failing health.

What these fantasies and fragmentary tales signify together, as a jigsaw-puzzle of Mark Twain's metaphysics, is a problem I cannot fathom. I am more interested here in how Mark Twain's *characters* respond to the epistemological nightmares he drops them into. Their reactions lead to the important issue: not Mark Twain's unsteady and amateurish thoughts about what the universe is or isn't, but his thoughts about what to be and do in an endlessly uncertain condition. In some of Mark Twain's bleakest late stories — "Which Was the Dream?" and "The Great Dark" are prime examples — his adults, especially the white males, suffer terrible psychological pain, unable as they are to handle deracination and personal bereavement. However, children swept up in these same catastrophes adapt breezily well, and one of the comforting motifs of these nightmare tales is how often these youngsters stroll through valleys of death psychologically unscathed and fearing no evil. It takes more to prop up the spirits of young August Feldner, the narrator of "Number 44, the Mysterious Stranger": Forty-Four, himself an irrepressible boy-god from some other reality, has to infect his friend with a feeling that no matter what happens, a good time can be had by them both. The continued resilience of Mark Twain's young psyches, cheerful and Tom Sawyer–like as the universe goes to pot, could matter to understanding intention in these works: a common theme (whether or not children figure in a given story) is the inadequacy of human reason as penetration to truth. The imaginative constructs an individual mind might conjure up, or borrow from a culture's accumulated philosophy and dream-archive, prove incomplete, confining, and absurd.

Christian Science nearly derails at the start when Mark Twain lets fly with an idea that all human ideas are suspect, or as he puts it, that in all matters political or religious, "one man's opinion is worth no more than his peer's, and hence it follows that no man's opinion possesses any real value. It is a humbling thought, but there is no way to get around it; *all* opinions upon these great subjects are brass-farthing opinions" (43). In nightmarish fantasies, Mark Twain kept steadier faith with this anti-opinion of his than he could in his nonfiction polemics about politics, white imperialism, organized religion, and human nature. In the late stories that involve dreams or voyages to heaven or hell or some inescapable outer darkness, the effect of these excursions is generally the same, in how they oppress the individual consciousness of adult males: loneliness, vertigo, boredom, anomie, despair at a loss of possibilities. Heaven looks as bad as hell. The harp-playing and the puffy-cloud choruses that Satan ridicules in his first Letter from the Earth seem as grim, as a steady state, as the endless drift of the Edwardses in "The Great Dark," or the nameless crew of the *Mabel Thorpe* in "The Enchanted Sea-Wilderness," as they drift in boundless uncharted waters. Human prospects look terrible because we ourselves, as adults who have been truncated by our own cultural values, are compelled to see them so. Although certain images of natural and human brutality seem to obsess Mark Twain in some of these narratives, the solace and the scare usually have to do with our brutally narrow and dubious mortal understanding.

Because they recur, certain scenes and images from the unpublished manuscripts do seem to be private fixations: the seasonal horror of the spider paralyzed and slowly eaten alive; a recollection or fantasy of a heroic dog left to die on the deck of a burning ship. As I shall suggest in a moment, the repetition itself may indicate a process through which private terrors can be made privately tolerable. Out of the big, grim dislocations, however, Mark Twain often lets children lead the way, not to consolation, but rather to a possibility that any mind-made reality, horrible or not, can be lived with, if the mind is not yet irretrievably made. Divine or otherwise, Mark Twain's children in his writings after 1895 are his most buoyant explainers, investigators, and acceptors of the human condition. Their involvement in these narratives rarely makes the tales grimmer, or injects into them the "infinitely gentle, infinitely suffering thing" that T. S. Eliot torments himself with in "Preludes," his own obsessive dream of entrapment written less than ten years after Mark Twain finished "Number 44, The Mysterious Stranger." Mark Twain's children tell horrible truths and remain impervious to them, accept more terrible realities than parents or cultures can countenance, and yet remain full of inexplicable energy and hope. What they may intend is the limited reach of darkness, its limited hold on human beings who have *not* been diminished by overdoses of logic, or personal misery, or cultural habit, or chronological years. In "Which Was The Dream?" a disoriented father, awakening (or so he thinks) from a culturally grounded fantasy of modern Yankee success as a soldier and businessman, becomes a figure of agony and not a little self-pity. But his daughters, reduced to poverty after affluence, brought low entirely by his own delusions and disgrace, are incurably content in the supposed reality they are plunged into, provided they have their father, ruined or not, back after long absence.

From the last year of Mark Twain's life, "Little Bessie" is a tale of an intellectually relentless three-year-old who with the help of a local

cynic named Hollister, demolishes Judeo-Christian mythologies as well
as her mother's composure, but who is not in the least frightened by
what she thinks she has learned about this Darwinian universe. Recalling Philip Traum — the too-talky visitor in the abandoned first version
of "The Mysterious Stranger" — Bessie is cool in the face of disillusionment, because small as she is, she is psychologically free of illusions,
having never put faith in faith, nor in science, nor in other totalizing
constructs that seduce and betray her elders. The opinions and discourse of grown-ups is still not worth the brass farthing: not discourse about heaven and a merciful God; not logical formulations
about houseflies and their gratuitous torment of other creatures. The
drama in Little Bessie's mind is *not* of scientific truth against religious
doctrine, but of fallible human formulations against one another. This
is the psychological and epistemological escape-mechanism of the
story: that no escape is possible from the narrow trap of our own
thinking, except of course into some other narrow trap, concocted by
the same or another human mind. The closing exchange between
mother and daughter has an interesting twist:

> Mary Ann, come and get this child! There, now, go along with
> you, and don't come near me again until you can interest yourself
> in some subject of a lower grade and less awful than theology.
> *Bessie,* (disappearing.) Mr. Hollister says there *ain't* any.[19]

The stage-direction in the final line seems odd, as is the child's
rejoinder. In the instant of disappearance, Little Bessie, or the unseen
Hollister, or in any case some voice now coming out of the thin air or
the dark rather than from a human presence, overturns the hierarchies of abstract thought. Bessie vanishes, free not only from the
ways of the Western mind, but from physical being. In fact she never
does seem to have a corporeal existence, for throughout the sketch
she has popped up in her mother's presence, and in ours, like a grem-
lin. With no stage entrances, no context established, no indication of
what (if anything) she looks like, Bessie asks her disruptive questions,
and each scene likewise ends with no exits, no resolutions, no indications of where she is or where she goes. With no magic other than this
and her precociousness, Bessie seems only a distant cousin of the
supernatural Number 44; yet she does share that nonhuman, or at
least nonadult power that Mark Twain associated with children in his
late writings, the power to be free of both conventional doctrine — and
of conventional ways of being, thinking, and saying something *else.*

In shorter works from these last years of Mark Twain's life, the banality of the mind itself is a center of Mark Twain's interest, and also a favored mode of last-second escape from the fin de siècle wilderness of ideas, closing in on the artist and the individual self. The admixture of comedy and terror, the mélange of teleological nonsense with thoughts that might be called profound, can make better sense, as an artistic act, if we can describe the artistic and psychological catharsis of some of the more complex tales like "The Great Dark," "Which Was It?" and all three versions of "The Mysterious Stranger." None of these tales is a philosophical or theological tract. They represent not only human experience as pain, but also pathologies of a mind in search of liberation from pain — a search that is itself paradoxical, especially when it involves the construction of fiction, and doubly so in decades when "the novel of ideas" was coming into its own.

In the years after 1895, Mark Twain's literary plunges into despair are usually attempts to come out on the other side. No interpretive cleverness is required to see this pattern, nor appreciation of some unnoticed genius in Mark Twain's artistic intentions. What is shown here, rather, is a basic tactic of a mind in crisis. In telling the story of her own life, Mary McCarthy describes her way of living with inventories of terrible memory: not by suppressing them, but by indulging them to a point of exhaustion. That strategy is commonplace enough, but she limns it well. The trick for surviving the horror, she says, is to "*make* yourself relive it, confront it repeatedly over and over; till finally you will discover, through sheer repetition, it loses its power to pain you."[20] Mark Twain's "trick" with his own gruesome imaginings, his determinist and nihilist nightmares, often seems much like this, to escape from the grip of a paralyzing idea or mental image by letting go, going abjectly into horrible fantasies, biological facts, and natural possibilities — not as a masochistic binge, but as a way of exhausting the grip of the horror, or of accommodating the self to psychological survival under the pressure of some merciless idea-system. In every tale I have mentioned, Mark Twain seems out to get rid of something, not peddle it to the world or even himself in imaginative discourse.

fearless wanderers

No matter where precisely one starts counting, these "Great Dark Writings" can be seen as an intensely private yet shared monologue, much as Conrad's great narrator Charlie Marlow once talked to himself, and to a few friends, on a ship called the *Nellie* moored at Gravesend, to drain his own memories, his own dreams, and his own words of their power to give pain. One of Mark Twain's longest tales of complete disconnection, "The Great Dark," is a tale that exhilarated Mark Twain as he worked on it, just as he apparently enjoyed writing the scary, nihilistic comedy "3,000 Years Among the Microbes."[21] Though these tales are both variations on Mark Twain's nightmare of life as a voyage in unknown seas, replete with microbe-monsters, "The Great Dark" is also a dream that about halfway through slips over an epistemological cliff-edge, into a lost place between dreams and reality, between narrative fiction and whatever it is we choose to call truth. The apparently wholesome American father who tells most of the tale, Henry Edwards is being set straight by Alice, the loving wife he trusts completely, about what has "really" happened as opposed to what Henry has hallucinated—when suddenly Alice, collected and cheerful all the while, begins to describe her own reality as a mirror-house of compounding and interconnecting dreams. The conversation itself resembles domestic comedy, a sketch of tactful, well-meaning people trying to work out a misunderstanding, which in this case happens to be the biggest misunderstanding imaginable, because it concerns imagination itself and their mutual loss of any frame of reference:

> "It seems almost as if it couldn't have been a dream, Alice; it seems as if you ought to remember it."
>
> "Wait! It begins to come back to me." She sat thinking a while, nodding her head with satisfaction from time to time. At last she said, joyfully, "I remember almost the whole of it, now."
>
> "Good!"
>
> "I am glad to get it back. Ordinarily I remember my dreams very well; but for some reason this one — "
>
> "*This* one, Alice? Do you really consider it a dream, yet?"
>
> "I don't consider anything about it, Henry, I know it; I know it positively."
>
> The conviction stole through me that she must be right, since she felt so sure. Indeed I almost knew she was. I was privately becoming ashamed of myself now, for mistaking a clever illusion for a fact. So I gave it up, then, and said I would let it stand as a dream. Then I added —
>
> "It puzzles me; even now it seems almost as distinct as the microscope."

"Which microscope?"

"Well, Alice, there's only the one."

"Very well, which one is *that?*"

"Bother it all, the one we examined this ocean in, the other day."

"Where?"

"Why, at home — of course."

"What home?"

"Alice, it's provoking — why, *our* home. In Springport."

"Dreaming again. I've never heard of it."[22]

This dialogue grows stranger as other points of certainty are lost, subverting any provisional theory that the lost ship is "reality" and that the former life in the town of Springport is only a dream of middle-class contentment. The strangeness lies as much in Alice's composure as in the antiepistemology she seems to accept:

"Alice, what do you call the life we are leading in this ship? Isn't it a dream?"

She looked at me in a puzzled way and said —

"A dream, Henry? Why should I think that?"

"Oh, dear me, *I* don't know! I thought I did, but I don't. Alice, haven't we ever had a home? Don't you remember one?"

"Why yes — three. That is, dream-homes, not real ones. I have never regarded them as realities."

"Describe them."

She did it, and in detail; also our life in them. Pleasant enough homes, and easily recognizable by me. I could also recognize an average of 2 out of 7 of the episodes and incidents which she threw in. (130)

It was in revision that Mark Twain added these layers of disorientation to "The Great Dark": not merely loss of distinction between dream-experience and waking reality, but loss of a psychological imperative to enforce such distinctions.[23] When such walls are down, and when Henry, Alice, and the children have all given up worrying about where epistemologically they are, keeping only the hope named in the story's last line, to ultimately "fetch up somewhere," then other barriers fall as well. Those barriers have to do with stories and readers, and with fiction as a realm distinct somehow from real life. Henry Edwards discovers and apparently accepts a premise that his dear wife is a fiction, accepting *life* as a fiction, and that this monster-ridden sea on which they drift is and is not the drop of water he either saw or dreamed he saw in a microscope he either has or has not acquired for his daughter Jessie. The supposedly nondream world where the story begins involves a house in a town called Springport, which will not be found on any map; the Edwardses who live there do not exist, not as real folk nor even in some respects as characters, for they are all presented as middle-class American everybodies and nobodies, distinguished only for their bad luck in losing track of who and where they are, or of the delusions that had kept their own dream, or someone else's dream of *them,* stable and plausible.

In other words, this is a story in which nonpeople from nowhere get lost between realities — their own realities, anyway — in an endless nowhere, a nonworld where Pirandello and Stoppard might feel right at home. A short "Statement by Mrs. Edwards" introduces the "Statement by Mr. Edwards" that constitutes the story, and so Mrs. Edwards, attesting to nothing as true or real, creates a kind of frame tale for her husband's narrative. Which means (perhaps) that a dreamed-up woman who accepts dreams as both real and unreal offers a reference point for comprehending the report by her husband, who imagines that his wife lives happily without epistemological footing — unless her own "Statement" and her Springport life are only more fictions that Mr. Edwards has dreamed up, or which both of them have dreamed together. There is no sorting this out, and no need to, for the meaning of "The Great Dark" is that perhaps there is no meaning, or rather that any meaning sweated out by human logic is only another floating monster in a trivial raindrop or an infinite sea of possibilities. The fun and the scare in "The Great Dark" have to do with Mark Twain's apparently willful surrender of control over his own narrative, his misplacing of who knows what or has undergone which joy or calamity with whom. There is a parallel loss of control over time — if "parallel" isn't the wrong word, suggestive of orderings that in "The Great Dark" all prove deeply suspect.

Loss of narrative control is paradoxically a special strength of "The Great Dark," and perhaps also a clue about the dynamics of other works after "Hadleyburg" and *Pudd'nhead Wilson,* including *Extract from Captain Stormfield's Visit to Heaven* and the sequence of manuscripts commonly grouped as "The Mysterious Stranger." In "The Great Dark," as in "Little Bessie" and "Which Was It?" and even theological invective like *Letters From the Earth,* all-encompassing suspicion is potentially a way out of the predicament. Doubtful of doubt itself, nihilistic even about nihilism, a mind might possibly liberate itself from the clutch of its own reason, its own fantasies. Mark Twain's carefully wrought better-heavens and part-hells are frequently part funhouse; and the fun, though it involves questioning the truth of each wish and nightmare, has to do with how the human mind compulsively works, and these world-conserving, mind-saving delusions that are ridiculed, shuddered at, and affirmed all in the same narrative.

Elsewhere I have described how in several tries at writing the Mysterious Stranger tale, Mark Twain eventually broke free of psychological confinements imposed on his narrative by the sort of Stranger he had first contrived, a Stranger who in the first two versions was not sufficiently strange, not temperamentally free enough for the task of ultimate escape, from death, mutability, nature, cultural oppression, human stupidity — *and* from confinements of an individual self trying to figure all this out.[24] Philip Traum and the first Number 44 (in the "Schoolhouse Hill" fragment), are simply not crazy enough. And craziness is vital, not to make these tales into "fables" that the gods themselves are crazy and kill us for their sport, but to represent both a mad world and a way of living more or less happily within it, and even *beyond* it, as an artist and a free mind, dreaming of divine malevolence and caprice, and dreaming as well that all such dreams are insane.

We have a solid tradition, however, of reading the Mysterious Stranger manuscripts as a tragic culmination of Mark Twain's literary career, and as a point of connection between Mark Twain and modernity.[25] It is tempting to use "The Mysterious Stranger" in a story, as it were, of Mark Twain's storytelling, a black-hole narrative into which fictions of his late life, and perhaps all the imaginative writings of his last two decades, can be seen to converge. To bolster such a reading, one important study of Mark Twain's work determines, on uncertain evidence, that the first or "Eseldorf" manuscript, where Philip Traum is introduced, best indicates Mark Twain's intentions, just as Paine cobbled it together; and that "Number 44, The Mysterious Stranger" — longer, livelier, and apparently completed — was a mistake of later times.[26] Though "Eseldorf" would certainly work better for final-exam questions about Alienation and the Twentieth-Century Mind, the more outlandish story that Mark Twain did complete cannot be ignored. Nor should another tale that he finished, or at least brought to publishable shape, in those last years of his life, and that unlike most of the others, was serialized in *Harper's* not long before he died. *Extract from Captain Stormfield's Visit to Heaven* is a story about an incurably fun-loving, fearless wayfarer among the lonely eternities, a creature whose good humor about nearly everything he comes to, even the prospect of going to hell. Stormfield therefore shares bloodlines with Mark Twain's last Number 44, the boy-god who goes manic in the completed version of the tale, another compulsive game-player and traveler who can make himself incongruously happy wherever and whenever in the universe he "fetches up."

Captain Stormfield's Visit turns out to be not essentially about heaven or God any more than "Number 44" is about divine will or medieval Austria. The broader theme of both narratives involves how to think, and feel, and sustain an identity in a universe whose size and intentions cannot possibly be comprehended. Mark Twain had thought about his friend Ned Wakeman, the original for Stormfield, on and off for more than thirty years, and in various forms he turns up in Mark Twain tales from *Roughing It* onward. The long story that Mark Twain finally developed around Wakeman celebrates the temperament he attributed to this Pacific sailor in 1866: guilelessness, lively talk without pretension, courage without bravado, wisdom in his dangerous trade, and good-humored readiness for anything. On his visit to heaven, Stormfield faces enough disorientations, humblings, and overthrows of his own cosmology and sense of self-worth to cause plagues of nervous breakdowns to poor Edwards and most of Mark Twain's other human exiles. Stormfield not only hears but sees how big the universe is, and how inconsequential is the ordinary human life. He learns that harp-playing and angelic winging are not preferred sports in paradise, and that nothing else he expected goes on there either: not even escape from human loneliness, or loving reunion with family and old friends. "*What a man mostly misses in heaven, is company*—company of his own sort and color and language,"[27] says a stranger he meets, an "old bald-headed angel" named Sandy, from "somewhere in New Jersey" who offers Stormfield what companionship he finds (and the italics are in the text). Sandy's skein of advice seems to expand on the cryptic last words of "Number 44," when August Feldner, the narrator of that tale, finally recognizes that Number 44 and the whole experience are only a dream of his own. Heaven, as Sandy describes it, is what you make of it, where you wish yourself to be and what you decide to do when you get there. And the satire of the Sunday school model of paradise, the satire that Mark Twain had developed in what became *Letters from the Earth,* gives way here to contemplation of limitless options, to solitude and an understanding of one's absolute inconsequence. Sandy does not stint on the distressing details:

> You can't expect us to amount to anything in heaven, and we *don't*—now that is the simple fact, and we have got to do the best we can with it. The learned men from other planets and other systems come here and hang around a while, when they are touring around the Kingdom, and then go back to their own section of heaven and write a book of travels, and they give America about five lines in it. . . . It's a mighty sour pill for us all, my friend— even the modestest of us, let alone the other kind, that think they are going to be received like a long-lost government bond, and hug Abraham into the bargain. I haven't asked you any of the particulars, Captain, but I judge it goes without saying—if my experience is worth anything—that there wasn't much of a hooraw made over you when you arrived—now was there? (103–5)

Yet Captain Stormfield, from a planet the heavenly bureaucrats dismiss as The Wart, never seems fazed for more than a moment. Fainting at the sight of "gates, miles high and made all of flashy jewels," and "billions" of people at heaven's border after his thirty-year solitary ride through black interplanetary space, he bounces back ready for new adventures, and stays that way to the last page of the *Extract.* Every expectation of his can be dashed or stood on its head, and the captain shines through, eager for the next show.

Beginning with the scene in which he hangs upside down from a rafter and plays a Jew's harp in the face of a death sentence, the supernatural boy who calls himself Number 44 embodies some of the same virtues as old, human Stormfield. They share unflappable curiosity and adaptability, rejection of despair as a waste of time, and the consolation of *not* being stuck in a mentality or a cultural framework, of not mattering as an individual self. Even so, constructing such parallels between narratives may only amount to building more of the cultural limits and barriers these two tales seem to despise: this human compulsion to formulate false universes and ride into them on a gossamer of intellectualized connections. A fundamental theme, in other words, might be that these tales should *not* add up thematically, or reconcile ingeniously with themes in other works from the last years of Mark Twain's life. If changefulness and absolute liberty were central to Mark Twain's personal and artistic quest, then perhaps nothing good can be gained by affirming that he ever settled down to be optimistic, nihilistic, or anything else as a literary artist. And if his imaginative writings about God, heaven, science, nature, politics, or human worth can be seen as contradictory, then in contradiction may lie a clue for "reading" the life-drama and this last literary phase of it, and for understanding what processes might have been under way as he wrote on to his final year.

The published criticism shows that an accepted way to read the Stranger manuscripts and the Great Dark Writings is as a story of Mark Twain struggling to tell stories, to get them created as the sort of language artifact that modern critics can admire: shapely, polished, and if not consistent of theme, then at least consistently portentous. It is possible, however, that in works of these last years we see Mark Twain working to liberate the act of writing, and to redefine, or rather *de*-define, relationships among teller, tale, and reader. There is much harmony between a personal or psychological process of the sort Mary McCarthy valued, of reimagining a disturbing dream to the point of its exhaustion, and Mark Twain's artistic rebellion, stretching back to the first years of his career, against cultural and rationalist expectations governing narrative and the written word. Mark Twain had bad dreams in abundance to get rid of, and in his life as a writer he had often attacked incompatibility between cultural rules for imagining and our unimaginable human condition. The disrupted nature of these fragmentary last fictions, and even their status as fragments, may mark an evolution in the relationship Mark Twain affirmed or conceded between a story and its writer, a contemplation of the possibility that literary meanings and even endings are at odds with telling truth or making sense.

Even *Captain Stormfield's Visit,* which looks structurally and thematically tame next to "Number 44, the Mysterious Stranger," "Which Was It," and something as out of control as "The Refuge of the Derelicts," has anti-story configurations. Though Mark Twain thought it finished enough to send to press, *Extract* does not end. It merely stops, and it stops in the midst of as vast a nowhere as closes "Number 44":

> And he said *we* were in luck, too; said we might attend receptions for forty thousand years to come, and not have a chance

to see a brace of such grand moguls as Moses and Esau. We found afterwards that we had come near seeing another patriarch, and likewise a genuine prophet besides, but at the last moment they sent regrets. Sandy said there would be a monument put up there, where Moses and Esau had stood, with the date and circumstances, and all about the whole business, and travellers would come for thousands of years and gawk at it, and climb over it, and scribble their names on it. (121)

At this nonending, who or what is Stormfield? Is he, for instance, dead or alive? This heaven "visit" has been reported to somebody named Peters, who evidently knows nothing of the place, which seems to mean that Stormfield has found his way back to the land of the living. But how, and as what? As a visiting angel? Has he been reincarnated, or come home somehow as his old self, though his star-flight to Heaven has by his reckoning taken thirty earth-years? Stormfield has apparently escaped from the world, and escaped also from heaven and the laws of mortality and angelhood. That is all we know, or perhaps need to know. For this triumph over fears and metaphysical dislocations is what matters most in his *Extract,* not how to classify the Captain epistemologically as the tale leaves off. Mark Twain's earliest sketches seemed to pour all-dissolving acid upon thematic and imaginative boundaries of sketches; stories that brought him fame made war on storyness and the cultural requirement that fiction mean something stable and keep separate from nonstory truth. If there was darkening in Mark Twain's mood in his final years, if the assault of idea-systems at the century's end caused tremors in his view of his race and his universe, then those catastrophes brought only more urgency to the literary revolution he had been involved with since the 1860s, and unprecedented reconciliation between psychological and artistic imperatives. The telling of the story indeed becomes the story. A fundamental motion of these tales is difficult passage *through* fantasy or nightmare, and onward to larger, indefinite contemplations, conditions lonely, free, and unvexed by illusions, not even by illusory unity in the tale that provides the passage.

Such an approach to these late narratives, if it has value, only confirms Mark Twain's place in the best of literary company at the century's turn, and makes for better connections between modernity and his final writings than talk of his personal alienation and the modernist collapse of faith. Written in the same year as "The Great Dark," Joseph Conrad's "Heart of Darkness" makes in some ways a handsome opposite to Mark Twain's ventures in nightmare and disillusionment. For Conrad's, or rather Marlow's, ultimate if cynical affirmation of duty, of Redcoat cultural habit and the self pressing on in full awareness of its own contingency, seems a consummate late Victorian or early modernist address to such vast trouble: not "determinism" per se or the death of old Western values, but rather how to live with all that, how to respond to pressure from terrible, seductive formulations. Yet as he himself assures us, Marlow has not gone ashore for the howl and the dance, not embraced life without meaning. And though his narrative in several places risks disruption or breakdown, Conrad, like his distressed captain, carries on to a shapely end, never scuttling the form of his tale. There are important parallels between "Heart of Darkness" and several of Mark Twain's late tales of deep disorientation: "Which Was It?" "Indiantown," "The Great Dark," "The Enchanted Sea-Wilderness," and the Mysterious Stranger narratives. The relationship becomes clear if, in the case of "Heart of Darkness," we think of the story also as the story of its telling, by an apparently recovered Charlie Marlow, back home in safe harbor outside London, among professional colleagues if not true friends, and telling of dead Kurtz and the Congo wilderness, nightmares that happened years before. Marlow has been at least as far into the abyss of self-doubt and cultural disillusionment as Mark Twain's personae ever go; Marlow has felt his terror more acutely than Mark Twain's voyagers or puzzled, misplaced boys and men, and Marlow describes that late-century misplacement with unnerving eloquence:

> Droll thing life is — that mysterious arrangement of merciless logic for a futile purpose. The most you can hope from it is some knowledge of yourself — that comes too late — a crop of unextinguishable regrets. I have wrestled with death. It is the most unexciting contest you can imagine. It takes place in an impalpable greyness, with nothing underfoot, with nothing around, without spectators, without clamour, without glory, without the great desire of victory, without the great fear of defeat, in a sickly atmosphere of tepid skepticism, without much belief in your own right, and still less in that of your adversary.[28]

An idea here about selfhood and darkness, however, holds Marlow together even in this supreme doubt. That idea is of the self as conserved, and perhaps even created, in and by the act of resistance. Struggling this way when belief is gone makes Marlow Marlow—at least for Marlow. Nonetheless, when his Congo story is told, Marlow and the others rise from the deck of the *Nellie* and go back to the business and their (contingent) identity as salt-water sailors. Marlow has had his world tipped over, seen it drained of surety and absolute value. Up close he has witnessed the worst possibilities of the human spirit. Yet he has not gone mad, at least not permanently, nor lost his ability to function; and judging by the language he summons, he has not lost his creativity and verve. The telling of his story has been his story. What this means is that struggling for words to express personal and cultural nightmare can be part of a process of healing, a process that must stay incomplete, yet nonetheless fosters a kind of dominion over imagination, over experience, over the world-wrecking, identity-destroying idea. Though Marlow assures his listeners that he has not gone ashore for that dance of self-obliteration, in a sense he has done just that: in reimagining the journey and giving the experience voice, he has gone into his abyss and come out again, with linguistic, imaginative, and psychological respite from, if not actual control over, the nightmare that obsesses him.

There may be differences, however, between the drama that American culture, or at least an academic component of it, requires of an artist-hero of Mark Twain's dimensions, and what Mark Twain in his last years might have sought from and for himself in the continuing process of writing. It is not that such motives are at odds. It is merely that they may differ, or even reside in separate realms. I have suggested throughout this book that Mark Twain was spirited in rebellion against Western conventions of selfhood, that he questioned unspoken assumptions about psychological consistency, cultural assimilation, the primacy of reason, the resolution of internal conflict, of paradox, of uncertainty. But what must be said about Mark Twain as a modern cultural presence is perhaps part of a different conversation. Reading his late work as struggling toward final serenity, some tragic recognition, or toward an all-reconciling "form," amounts to reading "Mark Twain" as a text, interpreting life and career according to our own cultural imperatives to map and explain great careers.[29] Explaining ourselves satisfactorily may require us to find or contrive dramatic form in lives of such dimensions, and do the job over and over, to provide analogues or object-lessons we may continue to need. But the amazing miscellaneousness of Mark Twain's late work, and the insurgencies within that work, tell a story of an artist who may not have required such a story of himself, because at the center of such stories is a hero coalesced, stable, and made: an identity of just the sort he had never accepted.

For Mark Twain the ultimate trap of the self, the ultimate limitation upon being, was the banality of the imagination. Originality, genius, insight — these were all relative. In its earthly and cultural form, loaded near to collapse by conventions, clichés, and mind-habits of whatever human group and time it happens to belong to, the self can never break free to apprehend truth, except perhaps the hopeless incompleteness of what it thinks, dreams, or accepts as true. That is a recurring theme in most of the difficult late writings. The tales of theological angst, the disheveled political satires, the stories that get lost, by intention or default, between dream and "real life" — these are fundamentally about the hopelessness of seeing face to face, as common citizen, parishioner, prophet, elder statesman of the literary world, or even as dreamer, supposedly unrestrained by the civilities, excuses, and inhibitions of the wakeful self. For even dreamers and dreamselves seem to get no closer to truth than fleeting recognitions of their own banality. As an alternative to the waking state, they cast suspicion on reason and the habits of wakefulness, yet they cannot supplant the conscious mind or recognition with more. The trap is what Marlow called it on that one evening of absolute candor: a choice of nightmares. And it is the essence of nightmare that it cannot overmaster or remake truth.

I have been making a case that a drive for absolute liberation, from a host of social, psychological, artistic, and even biological confinements, energizes and informs Mark Twain's work, fosters his continuing triumph with a vast public, and strengthens him as one of the true American cultural icons. I have also suggested that Mark Twain's penchant for anarchic humor and *détournement* for the hell of it have been generally downplayed by Mark Twain's critics, who for many good reasons have preferred to discuss boundedness, domesticity, and affirmations in the prose he published. Mark Twain commentary is not marked by obtuseness or lack of nerve, and his thorough acceptance as an academic subject comes of seven decades of hard scholarly work and intellectual courage. Even so, the habit of insisting on Mark Twain's moral steadiness and artistic shapeliness is an interesting cultural phenomenon in itself, a long-term and many-handed project to tame a cultural hero and a body of work that from some perspectives stays inherently wild, and hinting perhaps of an unshapely side to American cultural life: something that we are, perhaps, rather than something we feel we ought to be.

But to read Mark Twain's work in this way is not to knock down one mythic Mark Twain and propose another in its place. One understanding has endured in discussions of American literature, a value that shows up as readily among our late-century, theory-based formulations as it does in the now-not-so-New Criticism, and in those unregenerate historicist readings that held sway earlier. That understanding is this: that a truly interesting text will ultimately escape methodologies of reading, evade the reach of commentary that intends to get it all down pat: the meanings, the inferences, the inherent paradoxes, the embedded irrationalities, everything that might steal our attention. To sketch Mark Twain as potentially more reflexive, more paradoxical, and more absolute in his refusals is only to broaden a sense of why he has been the best escape artist in the American canon, as hard to catch and domesticate as Captain Stormfield or Number 44, or those two orphan boys from the Missouri shore who will not stay put, not even among the living or the dead.

An American hunger for the unnameable is a century-old subject in cultural studies, and perhaps partly to blame for the amazing vitality and infectiousness of our way of life. Even in morose times, America satellite-bounces its own turbulence everywhere on the planet, overwhelming young people and muddling traditional practices in a hundred other nations. No amount of published and broadcast handwringing about this tide has made a difference in its effect, its power to saturate the world. We broadcast litanies of outrage about American outrageousness; our own pop-cultural critique of American culture is part of the package.

By consensus the American circus is loud, crude, violent, chaotic, greedy, tormented — a string of adjectives that could be applied, with a qualification here and there, to aspects of this ungainly and compelling presence referred to as Mark Twain; and that sound uncannily like the word-strings that John Ruskin, soberest of Victorians, once spun to catch the essence of what he regarded as a true golden age: "Savageness, Changefulness, Naturalism, Grotesqueness, Redundance. . . ." If it seems odd that traits Ruskin extolled in the High Gothic — every element except "Rigidity" — could also apply to this modern Yankee madness that the world queues up for, then connections might extend beyond the fog-bank of the terms themselves. The twelfth century was a great age of faith; our own is supposedly an age of great confusion. Yet if Ruskin were even half-right about the mind of the High Middle Ages, then this much at least might link that distant time to our own: an aspiration for undefinable wonder, for transcendence, for escape not just from the confinement and squalor of our own social institutions, from worldly ugliness and human depravity, but also from mortality itself and the limits that come with being civilized and human. In spiritual crisis, we seem to aim as high, in a sense, as the nave-builders at Chartres. For by the evidence we are a culture out to beat everything: age, want, silence, the limits of noise, of fashion, of death; the burden of the private psyche and the accumulated intellectual heritage, the limits of joy, the limits of culture itself. Crazy or not, and fatal perhaps, this seems at least a fragment of what is going on out there, and no small part of the image we export, as America's worshipers and consumers in far-off markets will vigorously attest. Exuberant uncertainty, all-encompassing impatience, and what Nick Carraway seventy years ago called "an extraordinary gift for hope" — if you cannot hear such chords in the music, in the avalanche of fads, in the exhibitionist quarrels among ourselves, in the festivals of sheer motion, and in our collective plaint that bigger, louder, faster, and closer to God might all someday come to a stop, then you may have stayed away too long. At the opening of Stormfield's *Extract,* published only a year before Mark Twain's death, the old captain, only "a little anxious" after thirty years in the black infinite, has been sailing through interplanetary space, speeding along at a million miles a minute, racing comets bound for hell when they come near him, and never knowing whether he himself is on a course for heaven, or "the wrong place," or nowhere at all. As prophetic a metaphor, this, as Mark Twain ever coined for his own artistic quest, or for the destiny of the nation he wrote for. Like August Feldner or whoever it is that ultimately does the dreaming in "Number 44, The Mysterious Stranger," Stormfield is indeed a lonely thought wandering among the empty eternities, learning about his own immense inconsequence.

Yet Stormfield all the while has *fun,* delights in the perfect, terrifying freedom of virtual nonexistence, of dominion over everything and absolutely nothing, of being the master of a star and helpless in the infinite. Can such a spirit make sense? Of course not. The moment, the canon, the legend of Mark Twain's life speak to America in a language transcending reason, whispering of undiscovered country beyond the national dream of expansion and liberation. The eighty years since Stormfield's voyage have seen Henry Adams's law of acceleration take hold and carry this culture into hyperspeed, not just in technology and fad, but also in intellectual life, where meticulously constructed and totalizing idea-systems now seem to devalue toward nothing just as quickly as last year's software. If our canonical writers have spent much of this century mourning the death of old values and absolutes, then the culture at large seems to have been euphorically busy with other adventures, incessantly reinventing itself, and trusting in headlong, vibrant improvisation to keep the darkness away.

Friends assure me that at the end of a simple book on a single writer, social prophecy is an unpardonable mannerism of style, and that no one will be convinced by such capework if they do not already believe what I am trying to suggest. Fair enough: if a mound of authorities can document such generalizations, other heaps can surely be built to refute them; after that, personal experience and intuitions will decide the matter for most sane readers. One point, however, may stand up in all the speculation. Regardless of what model one builds or refers to, concerning who or what we are as a culture, and what elements of the irrational might define us best, Mark Twain, as text, myth, and courageous artist, will figure in that narrative. Though his name, life, and words have been invoked to sanction many social prophecies and ideas that have had their hour in the unending debate about American identity, Mark Twain's continuing transformation, in the minds of strong readers, makes a kind of sense, and assures that no matter what turns that conversation takes next, Mark Twain will be in the thick of it. Change never ceased to be a center of Mark Twain's own attention, the heart of his long troubles over the enigma of personal identity, and the wellspring of his terror and his hope.

Notes ＼

I Mark Twain and the Escape from Sense

1   Louis J. Budd's *Our Mark Twain: The Making of His Public Personality* (Philadelphia:
     University of Pennsylvania Press, 1983), chronicles how this reputation and mythic
     presence was achieved, through self-marketing by Mark Twain, commercialization
     after his death, and luck in his biographers and critics. Guy Cardwell's recent *The
     Man Who Was Mark Twain* (New Haven: Yale University Press, 1991) may please few
     Mark Twain admirers, arguing as it does that Clemens was susceptible to the worst
     in the ideology of the late nineteenth-century American bourgeoisie. Cardwell
     offers insight, however, into how Mark Twain has been sustained as an "American
     eidolon" (225), essentially because the debate begun decades ago by Brooks and
     DeVoto was not about Mark Twain's stature as a cultural hero. The issue now,
     Cardwell holds, is whether Mark Twain was heroic in his torment and alienation, or
     instead one with the culture and the mentality of common people. Cardwell faults
     standard readings of the canon as perpetrating a "myth of national character, . . . a
     great hairy mammoth that never existed except as a projected image" (228).

2   I thank Taylor Roberts, a doctoral candidate at MIT and a learned Mark Twain
     enthusiast, for sharing this tally of the Twain citations in the current *OED*.

3   Though I am indebted to landmark works that have tried to define where, at
     various stages of Samuel Clemens's life, Clemens leaves off and Mark Twain begins,
     this book avoids such speculations. Because "identity" itself is the enigma I am
     examining in the texts, and because Mark Twain's unregulated exploration of that
     enigma leads to refusal of one narrative convention after another, and ultimately to
     subversions of the idea of literary meaning, "Mark Twain" has to be allowed the
     undefined condition that seems yearned for. Enforcement of a Twain–Clemens
     distinction would seem to violate that freedom. It is axiomatic that a biographical
     work, and especially a work that intends a distinction between private and public
     selves, must be founded in assumptions about the nature of the self: Mark Twain
     readers are lucky that the best biographical works are both supple and self-aware
     regarding their own investigative processes. Justin Kaplan's *Mr. Clemens and Mark*

Twain (New York: Simon and Schuster, 1966) is Freudian in its assumptions yet not dogmatically so; Hamlin Hill's account of Mark Twain's last years in *Mark Twain: God's Fool* (New York: Harper and Row, 1973), posits "Mark Twain" as essentially Clemens's "comic mask" (xxiii) and regards Clemens as psychoanalytic himself in his inclinations. Yet Hill's narrative of the life seems to follow the structure of tragic drama, especially the drama of Wagner and Sophocles: Clemens as Wotan bereft; Clemens as Oedipus after the blinding.

Also seeking "the shape of Clemens's life" (xiii), Everett Emerson in *The Authentic Mark Twain* (Philadelphia: University of Pennsylvania Press, 1984) reads the major published works and private papers as recording a long literary apprenticeship, progressing from Southwest humor to accommodation to genteel literary tastes and a role as "a serious social critic" (111). Observing that in works such as *The Prince and the Pauper* "an important theme is the mystery of identity" (110), Emerson sees the issue as closed by Mark Twain's gravitation to determinist doctrines. Readers of Mark Twain should value Emerson's integration of public, professional, and personal life into one narrative. James M. Cox's *Mark Twain: The Fate of Humor* (Princeton: Princeton University Press, 1966) made humor, in and of itself, a more consequential subject than it had been before in Mark Twain studies, and the book complements Pascal Covici's volume on the question, *Mark Twain's Humor: The Image of a World* (Dallas: Southern Methodist University Press, 1962), which treats humor as a craft that Mark Twain elevated into social commentary. Cox holds that the consequences of humor were for Mark Twain unexpected and even disastrous: that the public identity that humor imposed spurred his attempts to overthrow the imposed self, and that a move into satire led Mark Twain into pessimism and unmanageable narrative structures. Cox's exposition of humor as a problem, with potential for crisis within self and text, has been central to thinking thereafter about Mark Twain's humor.

4   With regard to Mark Twain studies, the stabilizing effect of strong New Critical readings such as Gladys Bellamy's *Mark Twain as a Literary Artist* (Norman: University of Oklahoma Press, 1950) and Philip Foner's *Mark Twain: Social Critic* (New York: International Publishers, 1958) is self-evident. At the other end of the spectrum, however, Maria Orella Marotti, in *The Duplicating Imagination: Twain and the Twain Papers,* (University Park: Pennsylvania State University Press, 1990), invokes Bakhtin, Greimas, Genette, Barthes, and Lacan frequently in presenting Mark Twain's pioneering refusal of Western conventions of utterance and signification. However, Marotti cannot avoid describing this radical refusal in a vocabulary of parallels, binaries, and geometrical oppositions.

Among social constructionist readings of Mark Twain, the most provocative are Forrest Robinson's *In Bad Faith: The Dynamics of Deception in Mark Twain's America* (Cambridge: Harvard University Press, 1986) and Susan Gillman's *Dark Twins: Imposture and Identity in Mark Twain's America* (Chicago: University of Chicago Press, 1989). Robinson argues that a culture based on the institutionalized sin of race slavery not only figures as a theme in *Tom Sawyer* and *Huckleberry Finn* but also inflects the telling of these stories and their popular reception. The structures he locates are again geometric: *Tom Sawyer* reveals "concentric circles of unwitting complicity in bad faith" that offer "a strongly implied and quite plausible hint as to a continuity between the book's 'parts' " (79). Gillman's interest is in "identity," but her definition is materialist: she addresses what she calls "questions of identity, framed in terms of their economic, legal, social, psychological, and metaphysical dimensions" (5). But like Cardwell, Gillman sees Mark Twain as essentially a culturally confined bourgeois writer; and neither Cardwell nor Gillman seem to allow that self-awareness and even self-hatred might themselves be significant attributes of the American bourgeois mind, Mark Twain's included.

5   There are lasting values in several other narratives of Mark Twain's career and major writings, none of which seems fundamentally incompatible with reading for Mark Twain's subversive and anarchist dimensions. Henry Nash Smith's *Mark Twain: The Development of a Writer* (Cambridge: The Belknap Press of Harvard University Press, 1962), accepted an opposed-forces model of Mark Twain's career, but led a break from the East-West conflict favored by both Brooks and DeVoto. For Smith, "The conflict was rather between the conventional assumptions [Mark Twain] shared with most of his countrymen and an impulse to reject these assumptions, also widely shared, that found expression in humor" (3). Avoiding a definition of humor, Smith finds in Mark Twain's brand of it "a point of view hostile to values ostensibly dominant in American culture" (4)—a hostility shared, paradoxically, by the America he wrote to and about. More recently, Susan K. Harris's *Mark Twain's Escape From Time* (Columbia: University of Missouri Press, 1982) draws upon formulations of Georges Poulet and Gaston Bachelard to argue that major works, especially *Connecticut Yankee* and *Huckleberry Finn*, are fantasies of evasion at least as much as they are engagements with social and moral issues. Harris offers a more complex Mark Twain to read, and I have valued her perspectives. William M. Gibson's *The Art of Mark Twain* (New York: Oxford University Press, 1976) emphasizes strains of violence and far-fetched adventure in Mark Twain's imaginings, strains often downplayed in readings that have sought to establish Mark Twain's dignity as an American writer.

James L. Johnson's *Mark Twain and the Limits of Power* (Knoxville: University of Tennessee Press, 1982), focuses on Tom Sawyer, Hank Morgan, and Huckleberry Finn as wish-dreams of personal dominion over worldly experience. Though I argue here that the wish-dream was more ubiquitous and wilder than Johnson finds it, and that the impact on these and other narratives is more profound, Johnson's book is valuable for recognizing the strength of this yearning in Mark Twain's work, and the "lapse of moral imagination" (118) it could lead to: incompatibility, in other words, with conventions of nineteenth-century fiction.

6   Virtually all of Mark Twain's professional incarnations—journalist, traveler, lecturer, cultural pundit, and artist—have been written about in detail. After an era in which phases of the life were investigated (Arthur Scott and Dewey Ganzel on the travel writer, Fred W. Lorch, Ivan Benson, and Edgar M. Branch on the frontier journalist and platform speaker, Kenneth Andrews on the more-or-less domesticated and settled East Coast author), attention has shifted to transitions in the life. Jeffrey Steinbrink's *Getting to be Mark Twain* (Berkeley and Los Angeles: University of California Press, 1991) deals with the period between Mark Twain's return from the *Quaker City* excursion and his settlement in Buffalo as a married man, part-owner of a daily newspaper, accommodating to his public image and the literary

persona that was making his fortune. Steinbrink holds that love and some sobering personal experience made a great difference in just a few months' time. More conventional in its outlook, John Lauber's *The Making of Mark Twain* (New York: Noonday, 1988), follows the DeVoto approach to Mark Twain as a consummate salt-of-the-earth American, nurtured rather than traumatized by his growing up in the Mississippi River valley and the Wild West.

7   Commentary about the relationship between Mark Twain's narratives and bourgeois American values has proven durably useful. See, for example, Louis J. Budd, *Mark Twain: Social Philosopher* (Bloomington: Indiana University Press, 1962), Philip Foner, *Mark Twain: Social Critic,* and Thomas Blues, *Mark Twain and the Community* (Lexington: University of Kentucky Press, 1970). David E. E. Sloane's *Mark Twain as a Literary Comedian* (Baton Rouge: Louisiana State University Press, 1979) builds a case for Mark Twain as a humorist whose comedy, like that of his contemporaries and predecessors, finally affirms middle-class social ethics; see especially 58–80. On Sloane, see also note 15.

8   Lively discussion of *détournement,* as insurrection against all social institutions and practices, including sanity and meaning, is to be found in Greil Marcus's *Lipstick Traces: A Secret History of the Twentieth Century* (Cambridge: Harvard University Press, 1989), which follows this fiercely antisocial, antisense impulse back to the Middle Ages, with a heyday in Western Europe during Mark Twain's major phase as a writer. *Détournement,* as used by the situationists of the late 1960s, means the sudden overthrow of all expectations, even of the expectation that reasons will be furnished for that overthrow. The most eloquent situationist manifesto, indicating the breadth of its comic-furious refusal of Western habits of mind, is Guy Debord's *Society of the Spectacle* (Detroit: Black and Red, 1977). The "put-on," which will be addressed in a moment, seems similar as an act of large-scale refusal, but in a milder-mannered form, better suited to the etiquette of the sociable and even organizational revolutionary-artist, the figure of the SoHo art gallery rather than the *rive gauche* barricade.

9   The phrase comes from Richard Wilbur's "Year's End," first published in 1949.

10 I take encouragement from the fact that the best discussions to date of the problem of "self" and "identity" in Mark Twain's works avoid restrictive definitions of the term. Written in different critical eras, Smith's *Mark Twain* and Robinson's *In Bad Faith* both address identity as an enigma that Mark Twain spent a lifetime struggling with; though the perspectives of Kaplan and Hill are psychoanalytic, neither of these studies presumes to locate the self in the libido, childhood experience, economic circumstance, class socialization, or any amalgam of such influences. But see also Kaplan, *Mr. Clemens and Mark Twain,* 377–78, for descriptions of how Twain could use provisional models of truth and bouts of self-accusations as "bulwarks against chaos," with no sure connection to doctrines he might have espoused.

11 Interestingly, one of the key theorists of New Historicism, Stephen Greenblatt, does not seem insistent on materialist definitions of selfhood. See, for example, Greenblatt's *Learning to Curse: Essays in Early Modern Culture* (New York: Routledge, 1990), in which he affirms, among other things, that the essential and useful purpose of the contemporary critic is "making strange what has become famil-

iar, . . . demonstrating that what seems an untroubling and untroubled part of ourselves . . . is actually part of something else, something different" (8). For comparison, Cardwell's exposé of Samuel Clemens's moral failings and period-piece values leads to diminution: "What we shall no longer be comfortable believing is that [Mark Twain] was uniquely, wholesomely heroic, the marvelous child of American Nature in its tamed grandeur and, . . . the author of a nearly flawless novel" (228). It is hard to think of a competent critic in the past fifty years who has believed any such thing.

12   Michael Davitt Bell, *The Problem of American Realism: Studies in the Cultural History of a Literary Idea* (Chicago: University of Chicago Press, 1993), especially 44 and 57.

13   Sydney J. Krause's *Mark Twain as Critic* (Baltimore: Johns Hopkins University Press, 1967), makes a convincing argument for the wit and wisdom of Mark Twain's critical writings, and like Bell, rightly avoids reading them, or any substantial fragment of them, as constituting a defense of realist formulations. In Mark Twain's famous diatribe on "Fenimore Cooper's Literary Offenses," Krause finds that Cooper's romanticism and violation of realist principles is a secondary complaint: what Mark Twain was really after, says Krause, was America's self-deception about "their own traditions and about a native approach to literature" (135), and failure to recognize that Cooper's American epic was only Walter Scott imported and rebottled.

14   Krause seems to concur, finding in Mark Twain's published criticism an array of judgments having to do with specific writers and works, rather than an explicit or implicit general definition of his own artistic practice. See also Bell, *Problem*, 41–43.

15   Sloane reads Mark Twain's literary comedy as moral and essentially bourgeois, applying "the American egalitarian viewpoint in the comic mode" (*Mark Twain as a Literary Comedian*, 192). Twenty years before Sloane, Pascal Covici contended that Mark Twain was out to "perform a multiple function through his humor" (*Mark Twain's Humor*, ix), encompassing realist values, "laying bare the human heart" (19), and jolting the reader's literary expectations by means of the occasional hoax (143–56). Frank Baldanza reads Mark Twain's humor as a variation on the appearance versus reality dilemma that literature of the West has been fixated on for six hundred years: the discrepancy between socially accepted illusions and the truth, and the "difference between what was actually said and what was meant" (*Mark Twain: An Introduction and Interpretation* [New York: Holt, Rinehart, and Winston, 1961], 23). Some of the best resistance to reading Mark Twain's humor as ultimately serious, and charged with idealism, political message, and lessons in literary conduct, is in Franklin R. Rogers's *Mark Twain's Burlesque Patterns* (Dallas: Southern Methodist University Press, 1960). Focusing on burlesques before 1885, Rogers holds that much of what Mark Twain was up to was "merely a humorous imitation and exaggeration of the conventions in plot, characterization, or style peculiar to a literary type, or a particular book, play, short story, or poem" (10) and that "aversion to the target work is not a necessary adjunct to the burlesque spirit" (10–11). Retelling Mark Twain's career in the American West, and closing with the return of *The Quaker City*, Nigey Lennon's *The Sagebrush Bohemian* (New York: Paragon House, 1990) concludes: "Instinctively, as a man and as a writer, Samuel Clemens was imbued with an anarchistic spirit," and that "such a volatile, independent talent could only have been nurtured on the Western frontier" (197).

I see no reason why such views of Mark Twain's humor have to be reconciled, or why one reading should be privileged over others. There is no reason why the comic outbreak must have a single or consistent effect upon an individual mind, or upon a given culture. Patterns, idealism, realist values, Jacksonian politics — all of these and more may reveal themselves in Mark Twain's comedy, when it becomes, as it must, a subject of contemplation. In the instant when it catches us, it can be nothing or everything, including denial of the sanity of contemplating anything.

16   After seventy years of psychological and literary theorizing about humor, Bergson's *Laughter*, trans. Cloudesley Bereton and Fred Rothwell (New York: Macmillan, 1914) remains the touchstone work. Though Bergson's categories of the comic are well known (rigidity, repetition, the mechanical encrusted on the living, inversion, the release of the repressed feeling, etc.), often forgotten is Bergson's opening disclaimer, that humor is something unpredictable, and ultimately resistant to logic and philosophy (1–2). One key Bergsonian premise about "The Comic in General" is that it aims at "a certain rigidity of body, mind, and character that society would still like to get rid of in order to obtain from its members the greatest possible degree of elasticity and sociability" (21). Later, in his discussion of wit, Bergson seems to devalue sociability as an intention, in favor of freedom from every constraint:

> So any poet may reveal himself as a wit when he pleases. To do this there will be no need for him to acquire anything; it seems rather as though he would have to give up something. He would simply have to let his ideas hold converse with one another "for nothing, for the mere joy of the thing!" He would only have to unfasten the double bond which keeps his ideas in touch with his feelings and his soul in touch with life. (106)

Consistent or not in his pursuit of humor's raids on consistency, Bergson's thinking was something of a modernist liberation from Victorian prescriptions like Edwin Paxton Hood's in *The Mental and Moral Philosophy of Laughter* (London: Partridge and Oakey, 1852):

> The two great causes for laughter everywhere, are wit and humor, or the ludicrous expressed, and the ludicrous exhibited; but the *chief* cause of laughter is our love of order, and beauty, and consistency. We seem to be constituted thus for laughter, as a natural consequence of our perception of the most decorous and beautiful things in nature, and viewed in this light, the ludicrous becomes the safeguard of society, a great teacher of every kind of truth. (10)

Even so, in Bergson, in the commentaries he superseded, and in the commentaries that came after, one unfortunate pattern remains: the categorical descriptions of a human power that may intend the disruption of all categories. Bergson had powerful formalist instincts; so did Bakhtin. In a few pages in his "Epic and Novel" essay, however, Bakhtin comes closer than most other modern theorists to cutting the comic moment loose from responsibilities; see M. M. Bakhtin, *The Dialogic Imagination*, ed. Michael Holquist, trans. Caryl Emerson and Michael Holquist (Austin: University of Texas Press, 1981), 3–40. He celebrates laughter for demolishing "fear and piety before an object, before a world, making of it an object of familiar contact and thus clearing the ground for an absolutely free investigation of it" (23). But then Bakhtin prescribes a sober and stable purpose for such moments of liberation: "Laughter is a vital factor in laying down that prerequisite for fearlessness without which it would be impossible to approach the world realistically" (23). This habit of seeing the comic outbreak as a *preliminary* experience, as a limited or self-limiting prelude to earnest contemplations, characterizes twentieth-century discussion of the comic.

There are a few interesting exceptions. Finding Bergson confining, V. K. Krishna Menon, in *A Theory of Laughter* (London: Allen and Unwin, 1931), suggested a theory of humor as "mental hopping," the power of a mind to "go round and round an object . . . in an inconsecutive manner" (43), and undergo great "storms and tempests, but . . . bearing [itself] through this in the grand manner of the Pacific waters when the skies are clear and everything is bright" (47). More recently, T. G. A. Nelson's *Comedy* (New York: Oxford, 1990) reproblematizes literary comedy, arguing for opposed and perhaps unreconcilable forces within it: laughter, which is potentially disruptive, disharmonious, even malicious; and comedy, which aspires to harmony:

> To make this separation in the early stages is necessarily to postpone detailed discussion of the relationship between those two contradictory, yet equally fundamental, tendencies of comedy, the impulse to laughter and the movement towards harmony. . . . But it is important for us to bear in mind . . . that any discussion of laughter in isolation from comic form, and any discussion of comic form in isolation from laughter, will be incomplete as a discussion of comedy. Bergson's *Laughter* (1900) and Freud's *Jokes and Their Relation to the Unconscious* (1905) are both important contributions to their subjects, but they fail to deal adequately with comedy because they consider only one of its main features. (2)

For a useful review of conceptions of humor developed by major thinkers between Aristotle and the moderns (Hobbes, Addison, Lamb, Hazlitt, Dumont, Hegel, Spencer), see also Ralph Piddington, *The Psychology of Laughter* (New York: Gamut, 1963), 13–33.

For a useful review of contemporary theorizing and research regarding laughter, humor, and the comic, see Paul Lewis, *Comic Effects: Interdisciplinary Approaches to Humor in Literature* (Albany: State University of New York Press, 1989), especially 3–26. Though Lewis is insistent that distinctions be heeded between laughter and humor, puts considerable faith in social-science formulations, and offers a set of potentially constrictive "established points" about how literary humor works and what it intends, Lewis seems quite right to observe that "humor criticism, especially in the area of comic theory, has suffered far too much already from overgeneralization: attempts to argue that humor can be easily explained or subsumed under a catchy formula or definition" and that "existing studies of literary humor, from Henri Bergson through Harry Levin, often create an unearned sense of unity by way of Procrustean adjustments: by choosing examples that happen to fit their theses or by stretching and shrinking examples that will not quite fit. To avoid this, humor criticism must become as pluralistic as ongoing humor research" (x).

17   Marcus, *Lipstick Traces* (124–47, 187–244) is especially good on anticulture uprisings on the Continent from 1871 through to the dadaist movement of the 1920s. Though many late-century American artists and writers, including Mark Twain,

were roving in Europe as these anticulture movements took shape, Marcus and other cultural historians have said little about their impact on art and literature in the United States before 1914.

18   A good retrospective on situationism, its antecedents, and its legacy is *on the passage of a few people through a rather brief moment in time,* ed. Elizabeth Sussman (Cambridge: MIT Press, 1991). For an account of Debord's warfare against not only contemporary cinema but also against conventional semiotics, see especially 73–109.

19   Summarizing many theories of humor and laughter from Hobbes through Bergson, Grieg, Siddis, and Kallen, and noting enormous differences among these theories, Piddington offers a simple biological explanation for smiles and laughter, having to do with the satisfaction of an animal need, and the achievement of "a pleasant stimulus of sufficient intensity to hold the attention, but which nevertheless does not stimulate the organism to any specific bodily response" (*Psychology of Laughter,* 74).

20   Cox, *Mark Twain: The Fate of Humor,* 14–16.

21   Cox summarizes Mark Twain's last twenty years as a "long aftermath of failures, fragments, and disillusion" (*Mark Twain: The Fate of Humor,* 222), a period in which he was professionally and psychologically "threatened by the repression implicit in the dominant figure of the ironic stranger" (247). Hill describes the final decades as Mark Twain's struggle "to retain control over his universe, over his despair, pessimism, frustration, and insensitivity, by his artistic capacities." But Hill finds that eventually Twain's fiction and his personal life collapsed because "he outdistanced in tragedy his own ability to transmute fact into literature. . . . Something occurred which made the adversity and the conflicts no longer convertible into finished art" (*Mark Twain: God's Fool,* 272–73).

22   Covici, Rogers, Sloane, and Smith make no mention of the piece in their books on Mark Twain as a humorist and literary artist. The "map" is odd enough that there is uncertainty about which rendition to look at. Louis J. Budd's invaluable *Mark Twain: Collected Tales, Sketches, Speeches, and Essays, 1852–1890* (New York: Library of America, 1992), opts for the version that appeared in the *Galaxy* about two months after it appeared in the Buffalo *Express.* The *Galaxy* version has yet another layer of put-on, indicating that Twain was "obliged to reproduce" the map because of "the extraordinary demand for it which has arisen in military circles throughout the country" (471). The *Express* version, simply labeled "Fortifications of Paris," now became "Mark Twain's Map of Paris" — the author's name running across the top of the woodcut. The insertion has obvious impact on the joke, its dislocations, and reverberations. Mark Twain left the map out of his 1875 edition of *Sketches New and Old* (Hartford, Conn.: American Publishing); when it appeared in other volumes later in his lifetime, and much further from the year of the Franco-Prussian war, there was no title on the map itself.

23   Kaplan, *Mr. Clemens and Mark Twain,* 123–24, recounts the map's creation, noting its republication in the *Galaxy,* and Mark Twain's decision to send a copy to the "geographical treasures" of the Library of Congress.

24   For a reliable edition of "The Petrified Man," see *Early Tales and Sketches,* vol. 1, *1851–1864,* ed. Edgar M. Branch and Robert H. Hirst (Berkeley and Los Angeles:

University of California Press, 1979), 159. The editors' introduction to the piece (157–58) notes its wide reprinting by newspapers whose editors apparently accepted it as truth, though the San Francisco papers thought otherwise. In his Library of America edition of the early sketches, Budd reviews newspaper appearances of the piece, and notes that the established text is a "reconstruction based on . . . four independently derived texts" (1001) — in other words, versions appearing in western journals in October 1862, as no copy survives of the *Enterprise* issue that first carried "Petrified Man."

25 Bergson, *Laughter,* 8–22. Piddington faults Bergson for asserting that rigidity is something that society finds objectionable, rather than something individual and possibly antisocial in the amused witness. Piddington observes that "society very frequently demands unquestioning conformity to a rigidly fixed pattern of behaviour" (*Psychology of Laughter,* 36).

26 Jacob Brackman, *The Put-On: Modern Foolery and Modern Mistrust* (Chicago: Henry Regnery, 1971), 62–65.

27 A year after "Petrified Man," Mark Twain published a hoax that went further in war against what Harold Bloom calls "facticity," the establishment of cultural absolutes by means of newspapers and other authoritative media. Variously called "The Dutch Nick's Massacre," "A Bloody Massacre near Carson," and simply "My Bloody Massacre," the counterfeit news item is about a madman butchering his wife and seven of his nine children. For obvious reasons, Mark Twain's public did not find the story funny. Years after he wrote the piece, Mark Twain called it a satire on shady financial dealings in the goldfields; what is interesting in retrospect is how far he was willing to go, beyond taste and the standards of professional journalism, to explode the credibility of the newspapers he was writing for, and the credulousness of the people who read them; see Branch and Hirst, *Works of Mark Twain,* 320–26.

28 In his thorough account of the Whittier Birthday dinner (*Mark Twain: The Development of a Writer,* 94–104), Henry Nash Smith reviews the speech itself, accounts of audience reaction, and newspaper reports, and concludes that the humiliations were essentially in Mark Twain's conscience, in Howells's prudery, and in the sensationalism and moral pomposity of the press. Smith suggests that "Mark Twain's unconscious antagonism toward the literary Titans caused him to feel uneasy while he was delivering his speech" (97). Everett Emerson offers a concise account of the Whittier Birthday evening, concluding that the speech "must have been a delight," and that "most of the audience was entertained," though the trusted Howells was mortified by what he heard (*Authentic Mark Twain,* 97–98), and local papers printed harsh reviews. Kaplan notes that "in actuality, the speech had been greeted with a fair amount of laughter" (*Mr. Clemens and Mark Twain,* 211), but that in the recollection of Clemens himself, the night was a disaster which he spent months agonizing over.

29 Smith (*Mark Twain: The Development of a Writer,* 99–100) quotes Mark Twain's fulsome letter of apology. For Howells's comment, see William Dean Howells, *My Mark Twain,* ed. Marilyn Austin Baldwin (Baton Rouge: Louisiana State University Press, 1967), 50–51. For Mark Twain in defense of his own intentions, see *Mark Twain to Mrs. Fairbanks,* ed. Dixon Wecter (San Marino, Calif.: Huntington Library, 1949), 217.

30   *Mark Twain's Autobiography,* 2 vols. (New York: Harper and Brothers, 1926), 2:5.

31   *Mark Twain: Collected Tales, Sketches, Speeches, and Essays, 1852–1890,* 698.

32   Ibid., 781.

33   *Humor of the Old Southwest,* ed. Hennig Cohen and William B. Dillingham (Athens: University of Georgia Press, 1975), offers this overview of the Southwestern humorist, an overview bearing down on solidarity and social high-seriousness:

> Often a devoted Whig, he was convinced that if the nation was to be saved from chaos and degradation, only the honor, reasonableness, and sense of responsibility of gentlemen — Whig gentlemen — could save it. Usually he was a lawyer and often also a judge, a state legislator, a congressman, or even a governor. . . . Frequently he was also a newspaper editor. For the South he felt a protective and defensive love, though he might have been born elsewhere. He was keenly angered by the North, which seemed to show little understanding of the South and its institutions. He defended slavery and, when the time came, secession, with passion. . . . This is a rigid mold, perhaps, but the Southwestern writers who do not fit into it are few. Seldom has a literary movement or school of writers of any time or place reflected more unanimity in background, temperament, literary productions, aims, and beliefs. (xv–xvi)

34   Kenneth S. Lynn, *Mark Twain and Southwestern Humor* (Westport, Conn.: Greenwood, 1959), 23–31, 55–61.

35   *Mark Twain: Collected Tales, Sketches, Speeches, and Essays, 1852–1890,* 339. Budd establishes the title as "An Awful ---- Terrible Medieval Romance," though it appeared under the shortened title in the 1875 edition of *Sketches New and Old.*

36   *Mark Twain: Collected Tales, Sketches, Speeches, and Essays, 1852–1890,* 171.

37   Stephen W. Hawking, *A Brief History of Time* (New York: Bantam, 1988), 1.

38   *The Crack Up,* ed. Edmund Wilson (New York: New Directions, 1945), 69.

39   Alexis de Tocqueville in 1835: "In Europe we were wont to look upon a restless disposition, an unbounded desire of riches, and an excessive love of independence as propensities very dangerous to society. Yet these are the very elements that ensure a long and peaceful future to the republics of America. Without these unquiet passions the population would collect in certain spots and would soon experience wants like those of the old world, which it is difficult to satisfy. . . . What we should call cupidity, the Americans frequently term a laudable industry; and they blame as faint-heartedness what we consider to be the virtue of moderate desires" (*Democracy in America,* ed. Phillips Bradley [New York: Knopf, 1945], 1:296).

And D. H. Lawrence in 1923: "Liberty in America has meant so far the breaking away from *all* dominion. The true liberty will only begin when Americans discover IT, and proceed possibly to fulfil IT. IT being the deepest *whole* self of man, a self in its wholeness, not idealistic halfness" (*Studies in Classic American Literature* [New York: Viking, 1961], 7).

2 *Fool's Paradise*

1   In his Library of America edition of *The Innocents Abroad* and *Roughing It* (New York: Library of America, 1984), Guy Cardwell reviews the disheveled history of re-editings and publishing-house alterations that affected *The Innocents Abroad,* at

home and overseas, in Mark Twain's lifetime. Cardwell observes that in the 400-odd changes for the first authorized British edition (there was a pirate version in 1870), Mark Twain restyled his narrative voice to be "less materialistic and chauvinistic, less given to vulgar jokes, and less enthusiastic" (997). Cardwell guesses that the intention was to comply with what Mark Twain thought of as "the sophisticated and conservative taste of the English" (998). Cardwell also notes that the first authorized British edition, from Routledge and Sons, became the source of several American reprintings.

2   *The Innocents Abroad, or the New Pilgrims' Progress* (London: Routledge and Sons, 1872), 113–14. For a careful tour of the Routledge version, see Arthur L. Scott, "Mark Twain's Revisions of *The Innocents Abroad* for the British Edition of 1872," *American Literature* 25 (March 1953): 43–61. Tony Tanner discusses the unintentional banality of such passages in Twain's works in *The Reign of Wonder: Naivety and Reality in American Literature* (Cambridge: Cambridge University Press, 1965).

3   For example, a Chatto and Windus edition (London, 1901) includes the panegyric in full, with the dignified portraits of both Napoleon III and Abdul Aziz, as they appeared in the first American edition; see the 1872 Routledge and Sons edition, 103–6. When the American Publishing Company failed in the late 1890s, Harper and Brothers took over the republishing of *The Innocents Abroad,* and their London and New York editions of the book became nearly identical.

4   *The Innocents Abroad,* 3. This and all subsequent citations of *The Innocents Abroad* refer to the 1984 Library of America Edition, ed. Guy Cardwell.

5   Everett Emerson describes the narrative strategy this way: "He is the honest innocent who is ready to become the skeptic; the iconoclastic democrat; and, at worst, the ignorant philistine. Usually his good nature and sense of humor permit him to maintain and even enhance the reader's acceptance of him, so that his report remains good fun. But sometimes his skepticism is not so much a weapon as a limitation; his constant shifts from present to past, from the serious to the humorous, from topic to topic, and from places to person, both keep the book alive and keep it superficial" (*The Authentic Mark Twain,* 52).

  Arthur L. Scott's *Mark Twain at Large* (Chicago: Henry Regnery, 1969), still the most thorough and comprehensive study of Mark Twain's travel narratives, sees *The Innocents Abroad* as ordered by contrasts of sentimental idealism with messy truth, appearances from a distance undone by appearances up close: "Although Mark Twain read the guidebooks which his companions read, he refused to see with another man's eyes or speak with his tongue. It did puzzle him, however, when his own eyes received different images of one scene, and that happened with a frequency that surprised him. He should have realized that it was simply a matter of distance or clarity. His long or hazy view was frequently like that of the romantic guidebooks, whereas his close-up was often realistic, harsh, and discrediting" (42–43).

  A short, bracingly heterodox book on Mark Twain's travel writings is Richard Bridgman's *Traveling in Mark Twain* (Berkeley and Los Angeles: University of California Press, 1987). Breaking with the practice of finding consistent themes in the travel texts and reconciling those themes with crises in the fiction, Bridgman reads *The Innocents Abroad* and other travel accounts as holidays from consistency:

Travel itself had powerful attractions for a skeptical intelligence like Twain's. Its formal displacements generated the very situations that produce humor: values clashed, perspectives underwent abrupt shifts, and around the next corner, surprise. . . . Like most humorists, who by definition have a professional interest in disparities, Twain was a deeply serious person faced with a world whose ostensible order remained tantalizingly elusive for him. In his travel books one can often listen to him thinking out loud about problems . . . then abruptly "solving" them by an explosive joke. If at times his thoughts turned opaque or confused, that was the price of independent reflection. (3–4)

6   Bridgman's assertion that travel narratives allowed Mark Twain a way of exploring problems and perceptions that "his conscious mind had not yet mastered" (4) seems in harmony with Forrest Robinson's "Patterns of Consciousness in *The Innocents Abroad*," *American Literature* 58, no. 1 (March 1986): 46–53. Robinson holds that the text is distinguished, if not actually unified, by the unstable narrative consciousness, but that this instability is intentional. Robinson sees an oscillation between themes of loss and themes of salvation, and thus remains in the neighborhood of older assertions that the book has patterns and forms that somehow keep it whole. Other interesting commentary on *The Innocents Abroad* turns up in book-length studies of Mark Twain's achievement. Cox, in *Mark Twain: The Fate of Humor*, 39–43, faults the practice of reading the text on a matrix of contrasts between appearance and reality, between light-hearted comedy and earnestness, or between other contradictory attitudes. The intention, he finds, is that "as long as the narrator is honest, there is no real distinction between narrator and reader. The narrator's feelings and vision stand for the reader's own" (41). Smith, in *Mark Twain: The Development of a Writer*, sees the structure of the text as reflecting Mark Twain's need "to demonstrate his command of a serious style to himself as well as to others" (35), and therefore resembling a sequence of serious "plugs jammed into regularly spaced holes" (35). In *Mark Twain and the Art of the Tall Tale* (New York: Oxford University Press, 1993), Henry B. Wonham finds that "The tall tale did not resolve the contradictions [in] the narrator's game of exaggerated contrasts, but it gave his many poses a coherent dramatic principle, a way of connecting with one another. The narrative consciousness of *The Innocents Abroad* is indeed divided, as the book's readers have always understood, but the tall tale's interpretive game allowed Mark Twain to enact those divisions, enabling him to convert them into a form of play" (88).

7   For a review of American romantic and anti-romantic narratives of European travel in the nineteenth century, see Scott, Mark Twain at Large, 1–13, 28–31.

8   *The Collected Works of Ralph Waldo Emerson*, vol. 2, *Essays: First Series*. With an introduction and notes by Joseph Slater; text established by Alfred R. Ferguson and Jean Ferguson Carr (Cambridge: The Belknap Press of Harvard University Press, 1979), 46.

9   The illustration by Dan Beard appears as a frontispiece for the second volume of *Following the Equator* in the American Publishing Company's 1899 Autograph Edition of *The Writings of Mark Twain*. In volume 2 of the Hillcrest Edition from Harper and Brothers (1904), the Author's National Edition from Collier (1920), and the Stormfield Edition (Harper and Brothers, 1929), it appears facing pages 26, 28, and 16 respectively.

10 Robinson helpfully breaks the old critical pattern of looking at this narrative as an arrangement of opposed coherent states of mind. "The verbal record," says Robinson, " . . . reveals a consciousness irremediably at odds with itself, moving at great speed between mental states, struggling quite in vain to find a comfortable point of vantage on a deeply unsettling experience" ("Patterns of Consciousness in *The Innocents Abroad*," 51). He finds in the book a "frantic rhythm" and a "painful frustration not in experience but in consciousness itself" (51). A few years before, Philip Beidler, in "Realistic Style and the Problem of Context in *The Innocents Abroad*," *American Literature* 52, no. 1 (March 1980), 33–49, argued usefully that at famous comic moments in the text, "Twain [was] at his most subversive, and hence, at his most creative, and their continuing vitality is largely a function of a calculated adventurousness, a fracturing of the boundaries of expression on various time-honored topics coupled with at least some success in rearranging them on new grounds of vision" (39).

11 *Roughing It,* ed. Franklin R. Rogers and Paul Baender (Berkeley and Los Angeles: University of California Press, 1972), 47. Subsequent references to *Roughing It* are to this widely available edition.

12 In "The Monomythic Structure of *Roughing It*," *American Literature* 61, no. 4 (December 1989): 563–85, Drewey Wayne Gunn holds a customary position that "rites of passage provide the structure of the book" (564), but adds that by playing out an archetypal hero-adventure faithful to Joseph Campbell's prescriptions, "Twain transcended the genre of the travel journal" (584), and achieved "a remarkably unified structure. Of his contemporaries, only Melville wrought anything with the raw materials of life that was comparable in nature and greatness" (584). Closer to my own thinking about *Roughing It* is Lee Clark Mitchell, "Verbally *Roughing It*: The West of Words," *Nineteenth Century Literature* 44, no. 1 (1989): 67–92. Mitchell reads the text as "attending more fully to language than to landscapes, attesting repeatedly to the premise that words create worlds fully as much as they appear to represent them. The tenderfoot narrator learns in his seven-year sojourn that nothing is ever quite what it seems, in part because words seem to enact such a robust life of their own" (80). Though I argue here for a more absolute rebellion against language and cultural constructions of sanity and identity than Mitchell seems to find, we apparently agree that the dictionary episode, the abandonment of the mail, and the tale of the word-choked camel are important indications of what this narrative is about.

13 See Smith, *Mark Twain, The Development of a Writer,* 40–42. For Clemens's long uncertainty and periodic agonizings over what to call the book, see also Kaplan, *Mr. Clemens and Mark Twain,* 63–68.

14 See Wonham, *Mark Twain and the Art of the Tall Tale,* 82–84. See also Bruce Michelson, "Mark Twain the Tourist: The Form of *The Innocents Abroad*," *American Literature* 49, no. 3 (1977): 385–98.

15 The *Alta California* letters that Mark Twain reworked for *The Innocents Abroad* are collected in *Mark Twain's Travels With Mr. Brown,* ed. Franklin Walker and G. Ezra Dane (New York: Knopf, 1940). For discussion of how the *Alta* letters were modified, see Smith, *Mark Twain: The Development of a Writer,* 46–49.

16 See for example the way Mark Twain is accosted by the Australian "larrikins," in *Following the Equator, The Writings of Mark Twain* Stormfield Edition (New York:

Harper and Brothers, 1929), 20:147. All subsequent references, in this chapter, to *The Writings of Mark Twain,* refer to this widely available 1929 imprint of texts that are not yet available in definitive editions.

17   For all his vaunted Victorian earnestness, Ruskin could be funny and poignant on the subject of his own enormous influence, which spread far out beyond his intentions. He wrote to the *Pall Mall Gazette* in 1872 about his impact on his own neighborhood: "I have had indirect influence on nearly every cheap villa-builder between this and Bromley; and there is scarcely a public-house near the Crystal Palace but sells its gin and bitters under pseudo-Venetian capitals copied from the Church of the Madonna of Health or of Miracles. And one of my principal notions for leaving my present home is that it is surrounded everywhere by the accursed Frankenstein monsters of, *in*directly, my own making" (quoted in Quentin Bell, *Ruskin* [London: Oliver and Boyd, 1963], 30).

Still an excellent summary, not only of Ruskin's influence on the culture of the United States, but also of his presence throughout the nineteenth-century Western world, is Roger B. Stein's *John Ruskin and Aesthetic Thought in America, 1840–1900* (Cambridge: Harvard University Press, 1967); see especially 78–100 and, for brief remarks on Twain as an anti-Ruskinian, 217–19.

18   Pater's *The Renaissance* was published in New York by the Modern Library of the World's Best Books in 1873, the same year it appeared in London as *Studies in the History of the Renaissance* (Macmillan).

19   *Tent Life in the Holy Land* (New York: Harper and Brothers, 1857), 2.

20   See, for example, the Reverend D. A. Randall's popular account, *The Handwriting of God in Egypt, Sinai, and the Holy Land,* 2 vols. in 1 (Philadelphia: John E. Potter, 1862), regarding his own visit to the Holy Sepulchre:

My visit was brief. A throng of pilgrims was coming and going, crowding the little sanctuary, and jostling against me. But I heeded them not. How much of the past — of the future — was crowded into the reflections of that short season of communion with the Son of God, as I bowed my head upon his [*sic*] tomb! I saw his mangled, bleeding form taken from the cross on yonder hill-side, and borne by his afflicted disciples to this lone receptacle of the dead. I saw the ponderous stone rolled to the door. . . . But while night lay upon Olivet and Gethsemane, and sleep had hushed to silence the tumultuous city, this lone sepulchre of the dead was the last great battle-field of the conquering Son of God. Here he grappled with death, the last enemy of man, in his own dark dominions. The last stern contest was over; the victory was won; death was vanquished, and the prey wrested from his grasp. The victorious conqueror came thundering at the door of the tomb. An angel from the courses of glory answered the summons. A greater than Pilate broke the seal, and rolled back the massive stone. . . . The great question has been settled; life and immortality brought to light! A great highway has been opened from the portals of the grave beneath, to the everlasting gates of glory on high. . . .

My visit to the Holy Sepulchre was ended. I arose from my knees, and leaving the marks of my tears upon the marble slab, I slowly and reluctantly turned away, but not as the bereft and sorrowing one, who leaves behind the moldering dust of beloved kindred or friend. I left behind me, O rapturous thought! an empty tomb. I heard the soft rustle of an angel's wing, and a voice of unearthly sweetness whispered in my ear: "He is not here; he has risen;" and I turned and looked upward and fancied, like Stephen of old, I saw heaven opened, and this same Jesus arrayed in the glory of Paradise, sitting at the right hand of God. (2:123–24)

21 *Roughing It,* with an introduction by Rodman W. Paul (New York: Rinehart, 1953), eliminates the Sandwich Islands material, doing so "in order to limit itself to the organic western whole." For decades a widely available paperback, this edition also eliminates the three appendixes that appeared in American Publishing imprints of the text.

22 See for example Cox, *Mark Twain: The Fate of Humor,* 94–97. See also Gibson, *The Art of Mark Twain,* 42–44. Bridgman sees the moment not as a climax, but rather as an epitome of the character Mark Twain's predicament, "adrift in this book, trying out the terms the world has presented him," and possessed by an imagination whose hallmark is "unfocused restlessness" (36).

23 Beverly David has determined that seven illustrations from the 1880 edition of *A Tramp Abroad* were borrowed (to put it mildly) from Edward Whymper's 1871 volume *Scrambles Amongst the Alps,* and that another illustration in Mark Twain's text is pirated from a lithograph by Gustave Doré; see her "Tragedy and Travesty: Edward Whymper's *Scrambles Amongst the Alps* and Mark Twain's *A Tramp Abroad, Mark Twain Journal* 27, no. 1 (1989): 2–8.

24 For the figures on *A Tramp Abroad*'s extraordinary success with the British public, see Dennis Welland's handsomely researched *Mark Twain in England* (Atlantic Highlands, N.J.: Humanities Press, 1978), 235.

25 *The Writings of Mark Twain* (New York: Harper and Brothers, 1929), 10:145. This Stormfield Edition of *A Tramp Abroad* (volumes 9 and 10 of the set) has not yet been superseded by a more reliable text.

26 *Following the Equator, The Writings of Mark Twain,* Stormfield Edition (New York: Harper and Brothers, 1929), 20:25–26.

27 Except for discussions of historical background, places mentioned, and censorship of the manuscript, commentary on *Following the Equator* has been sparse. William Gibson, for example, calls the text a "decidedly better book than all but a few critics have said in print, and the chapters devoted to India have never been surpassed" (*The Art of Mark Twain,* 158–59); he does not elaborate however. Louis J. Budd, in *Our Mark Twain,* is also brief about the book, but sharp and provocative, observing that "because the text itself presented him as planning on a book all along, its author-traveler came much closer to what the real-life Twain was thought to be," but also that "*Following the Equator* presented, once more, a mélange held together by a uniqueness each reader defined by his own lights" (142).

   Among the few recent lengthy discussions, Peter Massent's "Racial and Colonial Discourse in Mark Twain's *Following the Equator,*" *Essays in Arts and Sciences* 22 (October 1993): 67–84, offers a political reading of the book, and not surprisingly discovers that Twain's "challenge to racial oppression, and even to the validity of racial categorizations . . . is not sustained throughout the text" (72).

28 At once a genetic study and a detailed commentary on *Life* as a literary work, Horst H. Kruse's *Mark Twain and "Life on the Mississippi"* (Amherst: University of

Massachusetts Press, 1981), is an invaluable resource on the book, reviewing how Mark Twain wrote it, what sources he consulted and borrowed from, and his collaborations on the text with friends and editors. Also important are Stanley Brodwin, "The Useful and Useless River: *Life on the Mississippi* Revisited," *Studies in American Humor* 2 (1976): 196–208; and Dewey Ganzel, "Twain, Travel Books, and *Life on the Mississippi*," *American Literature* 34, no. 1 (1962): 40–55.

29   Mark Twain, *Mississippi Writings,* ed. Guy Cardwell (New York: Library of America, 1982), 360. Until a definitive Iowa–California edition is available, this well-produced volume will probably be the standard, though it lacks useful documents and apparatus available in John Seelye's Penguin paperback edition of *Life* (see note 32). With the exception of the material cited in that note, all references to *Life on the Mississippi* refer to the Library of America edition.

30   See Kruse, *Mark Twain and "Life on the Mississippi,"* 5–15, 23–26.

31   More than sixty years ago, Bernard DeVoto's *Mark Twain's America* (Boston: Little, Brown, 1932; repr. Boston: Houghton Mifflin, 1967) tried to set the record straight about the realities of the riverboat era, noting the ruthlessness and corruption of the business, and "the squalid venery of the steamboats, which were consistently a habitation for the loves of travelers, river rats, and frontiersmen" (110). But DeVoto's anti-romantic picture of the truth of river life picks up a romantic verve of its own: "Harlots of all degree, New Orleans courtesans in the grand manner as well as broken-down yaller gals no longer useful to riverside dives, were habituées of the boats. They and their pimps and all the machinery of bought protection, of display and sale, of robbery and murder were a constant in the trade. There is no mention of them [in *Life*]. . . . There is no mention, either, of the parasitism that was also constant in the trade. The skin games, the frauds, the robberies, the gambling, the cozenage, the systematic organization of the sucker trade are wholly absent from its pages" (110).

32   *Life on the Mississippi,* ed. John Seelye, with an introduction by James M. Cox (New York: Viking Penguin, 1984), 255–56. In this splendid edition, Seelye inserts Mr. Harvey's balloon nightmare immediately after chapter 34, with an indication that these pages were "originally intended as the next chapter" (253).

33   Kruse (*Mark Twain and "Life on the Mississippi,"* 24–26, 37–39) makes a convincing case for the Ritter story as planned from very early in the writing of *Life,* and observes the complexity of the author-narrator identification, but sees it as essentially "suited to the intended emphasis on factual reports and material about the Mississippi" (39).

3   The Quarrel with Romance

1   For the last twenty years, commentary on *Huckleberry Finn* has seen sporadic rebellions against exclusively formalist and moralist readings of the novel, though the fun-house dimensions of the text remain largely unaddressed. John Seelye's *The True Adventures of Huckleberry Finn* (Evanston: Northwestern University Press, 1970) is a comic time capsule, a parody on what Freudians like Leslie Fiedler and champions of form like Lionel Trilling and Leo Marx have wanted the novel to be: more unified, more shapely, more overtly symbolic, and more sexual.

Fiedler's own thinking, however, seems to have evolved to the point where he has made his break from Freudian and formalist prescriptions. In *"Huckleberry Finn: The Book We Love to Hate,"* *Proteus* 1, no. 2. (Spring 1984): 1–8, he reads the novel as a multilevel attack on serious issues, including personal duty, conscience, and morally engaged fiction. A recent, effective challenge to *Huckleberry Finn* as a plausible artifact of the American realist movement is Michael Davitt Bell's discussion of the novel in *The Problem of American Realism*, 47–58. In *Mark Twain as a Literary Comedian*, David Sloane explores the novel's indebtedness to political and literary burlesque, thus moving gently away from Trilling's assertion that the book's structure and greatness are lodged in the awakening moral sympathies of its protagonist. David Kaufmann's "Satiric Deceit in the Ending of *Adventures of Huckleberry Finn,*" *Studies in the Novel*, 19 (1987): 66–78, ingeniously attempts to explain the novel's formal breakdown as Mark Twain's strategy, to draw the reader's attention away from the psychological and moral unreliability of Huck himself. And Guy Cardwell's analysis of Jim as a racist stereotype challenges not only the conventional wisdom that he and Huck are triumphs of characterization, but also attacks the idea that *Huck* is an American masterpiece. See Cardwell, *The Man Who Was Mark Twain*, 183–200.

Yet with good reason, formalist and moralist readings of the novel continue to flourish, although methodologies have somewhat altered. Alan Trachtenberg's loosely Marxist return to the novel, "The Form of Freedom in *Adventures of Huckleberry Finn,*" *Southern Review*, n.s., 6 (October 1970): 954–71, finds certain James Dean qualities in Huck, as a young man unable to achieve freedom within any social context—"freedom" being defined essentially as escape from materialist and classist pressures. Similar is Bruce King's "*Huckleberry Finn,*" in *Ariel* 2:4 (1971): 69–77. In King's view, a boy who is true to his own nature cannot achieve cultural assimilation.

2 Trilling's "The Greatness of *Huckleberry Finn*" in his *The Liberal Imagination* (New York: Viking, 1950), 104–17, remains a keystone among the moralist readings that, having achieved wide acceptance, are now part of the cultural artifact that the novel remains in our time. In *The Machine in the Garden* (New York: Oxford University Press, 1967), Leo Marx explains Huck in terms of the nature-technology crisis that Marx finds fundamental to understanding the modern American mind. Reading the book as an important moment in America's quest to achieve a literary morality, Richard Chase, in *The American Novel and Its Tradition* (Garden City, N.Y.: Doubleday, 1957), argues that the book involves an "exorcism" (146) of European civilization and "false romance" (147) from the American scene.

3 Readings of *Huckleberry Finn* that see the book as organized by patterns and recurring motifs include some impressive criticism. See Daniel G. Hoffman, "Black Magic—and White—in *Huckleberry Finn,*" in his *Form and Fable in American Fiction* (New York: Oxford University Press, 1961), 315–50; Martha Banta, "Escape and Entry in *Huckleberry Finn,*" *Modern Fiction Studies* 14 (Spring 1968): 79–91, and Harold P. Simonson, "*Huckleberry Finn* as Tragedy," *Yale Review*, 59 (1970): 532–48. In "Remarks on the Sad Initiation of Huckleberry Finn," *Sewanee Review* 62 (Summer 1954): 389–405, James M. Cox established in the novel a pattern of symbolic death and rebirth that has been frequently reworked by critics since. Other read-

ings have drawn attention to large discontinuities in the novel, and these readings
have been hard to displace. In an early New Critical study of *Huck,* Frank Baldanza,
in "The Structure of *Huckleberry Finn,*" *American Literature* 27 (1950): 347–55,
observes that "if we try to see the book as a progression towards Jim's liberation, we
must ask why the Boggs episode, the Shepherdson–Grangerford feud, and the
Wilks interlude, which compose the bulk of the central portion, are so remarkably
irrelevant to the thesis" (347–48). More recently, Keith Opdahl has argued that
Mark Twain's shift of narrative focus, from personal perceptions toward objective,
dispassionate observation, is important in the novel's structural crisis ("The Rest is
Just Cheating: When Good Feelings Go Bad in *Adventures of Huckleberry Finn,*" *Texas
Studies in Literature and Language* 32 (1990): 277–93.

4   One such complaint against Tom as a thoughtless, domineering menace in Huck's
book can be found in Judith Fetterley's "Disenchantment: Tom Sawyer in *Huckleberry Finn,*" *PMLA* 87 (1972): 69–73. See also Cox, *Mark Twain: The Fate of Humor,*
140ff., and Simonson, "*Huckleberry Finn* as Tragedy," 534–536.

5   In addition to Trilling's "The Greatness of *Huckleberry Finn*" and T. S. Eliot's introduction to *Adventures of Huckleberry Finn* (London: Cresset Press, 1950), vii–xvi,
repr. as "Mark Twain's Masterpiece," in *Huck Among the Critics: A Centennial Selection,*
ed. M. Thomas Inge (Frederick, Md.: University Publications of America, 1985),
103–11, many other commentators have asserted the cultural centrality of this
text. The centennial of the novel saw the publication of three different collections
of critical essays, each with observations like this by Inge: "Huck himself has passed
into folk-knowledge and stands as a living literary legend alongside such universal
figures as Falstaff, Hamlet, and Don Quixote" (vii). Harold Bloom, arguably the
dean of American critical theorists, introduces his collection of essays on Mark
Twain with these meditations on the great work: "What is the secret of an appeal
that affected Eliot and Faulkner, Hemingway and Joyce, with almost equal intensity? Is it because the book tells the truth? . . . I am not moved to dismiss such a
judgment lightly. The book tells a story which most Americans need to believe is a
true representation of the way things are, and yet might be"; see Bloom, *Mark
Twain: Modern Critical Views* (New York: Chelsea House, 1986), 2.

6   Locating the novel "within the debates over racism after the end of Reconstruction" (108), Stephen Mailloux both continues the practice and challenges the
postwar tradition of reading *Huckleberry Finn* as an observation and ethical critique
of American cultural practice. "Reading Huck Finn," in *New Essays on Adventures of
Huckleberry Finn,* ed. Louis J. Budd (New York: Cambridge University Press, 1985),
107–33.

7   In *Mark Twain at Work* (Cambridge: Harvard University Press, 1942), DeVoto expressed high respect for *The Adventures of Tom Sawyer* (see 9–18), and in his edition
of *The Portable Mark Twain* (New York: Viking, 1946), he put up a spirited and
lonely defense for *Tom Sawyer Abroad* as an exploration of "three stages" of the
backwoods American mind, in Huck, Tom, and Jim (31–32), meaning that the
book, for all its faults as a structured narrative, penetrates and observes important
pathologies in the American psyche. Robinson's *In Bad Faith,* which includes one of
the most sustained critical studies of *Tom Sawyer* in recent years, addresses Tom as a
psychological victim of culturally based delusions that Robinson sees as also ensnar-

ing Mark Twain himself, delusions having to do with morals and proper social behavior in a world founded on race slavery (see especially 92–108). Robinson makes brief mention of "Tom Sawyer, Detective," and no mention at all of *Tom Sawyer Abroad* or "Tom Sawyer's Conspiracy." There is little commentary on "Tom Sawyer, Detective"; Frank Baldanza seems to express the consensus about *Tom Sawyer Abroad*, that it is "in many ways a tired book," and "lacks the verbal magic of *Huckleberry Finn*" (*Mark Twain: An Introduction and Interpretation*, 120–21).

8   *Huck Finn and Tom Sawyer Among the Indians and Other Unfinished Stories*, with a foreword and notes by Dahlia Armon and Walter Blair (Berkeley and Los Angeles: University of California Press, 1989). All citations of "Conspiracy" and *Among the Indians* are from this edition.

9   *Mark Twain: Mississippi Writings*, 187–89. All subsequent references to *The Adventures of Tom Sawyer* are to this Library of America edition.

10 The most recent such effort, Shelley Fisher Fishkin's *Was Huck Black?* (New York: Oxford University Press, 1993), traces Huck's speech patterns to an encounter between Mark Twain and an African American child, and from that premise builds a case that the novel is essentially antiracist.

11 Robinson offers a spirited refutation of anti-Tom accusations by Fetterley, Simonson, and others cited above; see *In Bad Faith*, 126–31.

12 Letter to Howells, 15 July 1875, *Mark Twain–Howells Letters*. ed. William M. Gibson and Henry Nash Smith (Cambridge: The Belknap Press of Harvard University Press, 1960), 1:91.

13 *The Adventures of Tom Sawyer; Tom Sawyer Abroad; Tom Sawyer, Detective*, ed. John C. Gerber, Paul Baender, and Terry Firkins (Berkeley and Los Angeles: University of California Press, 1980), 156–57. All subsequent citations of these three texts refer to this Iowa–California edition.

14 See introduction to *Tom Sawyer Abroad* in *The Adventures of Tom Sawyer; Tom Sawyer Abroad; Tom Sawyer, Detective*, ed. Gerber et al., 242–44. Everett Emerson (*The Authentic Mark Twain*, 178–81) observes, however, that Mark Twain began writing up the idea of the boys on a balloon trip before he saw Verne's novel.

15 See *Mark Twain's Letters to His Publishers*, ed. Hamlin Hill (Berkeley and Los Angeles: University of California Press, 1967), 314.

16 See note 7.

17 See Susan Gillman, *Dark Twins*, 86–88. See also Everett Emerson, *The Authentic Mark Twain*, 213–14, and Howard Baetzhold, *Mark Twain and John Bull: The British Connection* (Bloomington: Indiana University Press, 1970), 299–304.

18 F. Scott Fitzgerald, *The Last Tycoon* (New York: Scribner, 1941), 163.

19 See Everett Emerson, *The Authentic Mark Twain*, 148–49.

20 *Mississippi Writings*, 748. Subsequent citations of *Adventures of Huckleberry Finn* refer to this edition.

21 Although the missing manuscript chapters of *Huckleberry Finn*, together with some very interesting deleted passages, have only recently been discovered, the standard works on the novel's composition are Walter Blair, *Mark Twain and Huck Finn* (Berkeley and Los Angeles: University of California Press, 1960) and Victor Doyno, *Writing Huck Finn: Mark Twain's Creative Process* (Philadelphia: University of Pennsylvania Press, 1991).

22   Robinson's *In Bad Faith* (138–39) reads the Duke and the King as enforcing a "pattern of disenchantment" (138) in the novel, rather than dislocating its points of reference. "This general and persistent pattern recurs in the sequence of shows . . . all somehow compromised, and many linked in more or less obvious ways," developing a theme of "the failure of amusements to amuse in the larger action of the novel" (138). A more conventional view is offered by Baldanza's *Mark Twain: An Introduction and Interpretation* (115–16), which sees the con men as forcing Huck into self-confrontation and moral growth.

23   Robinson (*In Bad Faith,* 138–39) holds that Huck's complicity signifies his seduction by a society fabricated out of cruel and even murderous hypocrisy.

24   Doyno reads the Shepherdson–Grangerford episode as "a chance for both subtle and obvious satire on conventional religion" (143). See also Bruce Michelson, "Huck and the Games of the World," *American Literary Realism* 13, no. 1 (Spring 1980): 108–21.

25   One of the strongest claims for the novel's importance as American mythology is still DeVoto, "The Artist as American," in his *Mark Twain's America* (Boston: Little, Brown, 1932, repr. Boston: Houghton Mifflin, 1967), 299–321. See also Leo Marx, "The Pilot and the Passenger: Landscape Conventions and the Style of *Huckleberry Finn,*" *American Literature* 28 (May 1956): 129–46.

26   In Budd's *New Essays on Adventures of Huckleberry Finn,* Lee Clark Mitchell's essay ("Nobody but Our Gang Warn't Around: The Authority of Language in *Huckleberry Finn*") takes a mildly Lacanian approach to the novel, seeing Huck as caught by his "alleged faith in an integrated self that might stand somehow outside of society" (91), and the "self-encircling narrative within which Huck expresses his naive realism [revealing] instead a self created entirely through language" (97). Finding the ending of *Huckleberry Finn* darkly appropriate, as the triumph of language-based fictions and prescriptions and the end of Huck's naive quest to get away from them, Mitchell finds in the novel a "troubling resistance to fixed categories, whether moral, psychological, or linguistic" (84). In contrast, my own premise is that the novel's anarchic resistance to categories extends even to the categorical definition of the self as a linguistic construct, and that the hope and pleasure that readers find in the text indicates that its many-dimensioned resistance to words, logic, and culture, is neither encircled nor defeated.

27   Though recognized as a study of how the novel was written, Doyno's *Writing Huck Finn* recently and thoughtfully expanded the tradition of approaching the book as an account of Huck's psychological and moral growth: "Huck can adopt the guise and guile of an auto-autho-biographer, making up stories of his past, duplicating, at the same time, some activities of a novelist. Instead of being determined or defined by the past, as nobility is, the orphaned or abandoned child must, like the novelist, continually create a past and a self" (116). Doyno sees the essential moral conflicts in the novel as involving traditional ideas of nobility endangering the individual spirit (111–29), and conventional slave-culture Christianity obstructing "Huck's common sense and naive literalism" (137), that allow him to see social hypocrisies around him.

28   Challenging numerous readings that have equated the dark angel with Tom Sawyer, religious hypocrisy, the slave culture, social pressure, or Huck's deformed

conscience, David E. E. Sloane has reaffirmed a straightforward connection between the dark angel and Pap Finn; see his *Adventures of Huckleberry Finn: American Comic Vision* (Boston: Twayne, 1988), 41–42.

29 *Adventures of Huckleberry Finn*, ed. Bradley et al., 169.

30 See Smith, *Mark Twain: The Development of a Writer*, 116–18; See also Cox, *Mark Twain: The Fate of Humor*, 176–79.

31 The most thorough treatment of these issues in recent years, Susan Gillman's *Dark Twins* makes brief mention of *The Prince and the Pauper*, as an early and simple version of identity problems that compounded in Mark Twain's mind a few years later; see 5–6.

32 Moving beyond the familiar judgment that *The Prince and the Pauper* is a contrived potboiler, Tom H. Towers sees the novel as indicative of a strain of political conservatism in Mark Twain, in part an effect of the affluent and genteel life he was living at the time. "*The Prince and the Pauper:* Mark Twain's Once and Future King," *Studies in American Fiction* 6 (1978): 194.

33 Tom Stoppard, *Rosencrantz and Guildenstern are Dead:* (New York: Grove, 1967), 28.

34 See Albert Bigelow Paine, *Mark Twain: A Biography*, 3 vols. (New York: Harper and Brothers, 1912), 2:752–53.

35 *The Prince and the Pauper*, foreword and notes by Victor Fischer and Michael B. Frank (Berkeley and Los Angeles: University of California Press, 1983), 86–88. All subsequent citations refer to this Mark Twain Library edition.

36 Two readings of *The Prince and the Pauper* have made a strong case for the thematic importance of the father-son relationships in the novel. In *Unpromising Heroes: Mark Twain and His Characters* (Berkeley and Los Angeles: University of California Press, 1966), Robert Regan reads the novel as an instance of a mythic archetype, with an array of fathers and pseudofathers connecting the story's three heroes to one another (150–53). Reading the text as one in which "themes of Mark Twain's psychological obsessions and his quest for cultural identity meet" (205), John David Stahl also sees a myth unfolding, a quest to recover the lost father and true identity, with Mark Twain's own lost and distant father expanding here into a "mythic trinity of fathers" (215). "American Myth in European Disguise: Fathers and Sons in *The Prince and the Pauper*," *American Literature* 58 (1986): 203–16. In both of these studies, reconnection is the ultimate theme; my own reading holds that disconnection and liberation hold the foreground.

37 One of the most provocative essays yet written on the novel is Everett Carter's "The Meaning of *A Connecticut Yankee*," *American Literature* 50 (1978): 418–40. Working from Twain's notes on Malory, the lore of Camelot, modern England, and the formative stages of his Yankee hero, Carter counters the argument that Hank Morgan was designed as a moral monster, that the Battle of the Sand-Belt is a climax that Twain was forced to as a result of a moral awakening, that the slaughter is meant to cast blame on Hank, or that there is sustained variance between Hank's opinions on any subject and Mark Twain's own thinking at the time. The "fable of progress" reading of *A Connecticut Yankee*, that the book is a cautionary tale about technology and the justification of means with ends, seems therefore insufficiently borne out by the facts.

Henry Nash Smith argued that the novel is "urgently focused on the state of the nation and of the world at the moment of the writing. The burlesque tale expresses a philosophy of history and a theory of the capitalist system . . . and the story breaks under the pressure of the thought and emotion that the writer poured into it" (*Mark Twain's Fable of Progress: Political and Economic Ideas in "A Connecticut Yankee"* [New Brunswick: Rutgers University Press, 1964], 7). Similar treatments of the novel as a commentary on technology run wild and power's corruptions include Clark Griffith, "Merlin's Grin: From 'Tom' to 'Huck' in *A Connecticut Yankee*," *New England Quarterly* 48 (March 1975): 28–29, and James M. Cox, "*A Connecticut Yankee in King Arthur's Court*: The Machinery of Self-Preservation," *Yale Review*, 50 (Autumn 1960): 89–102. Commentaries by critics such as Louis J. Budd and Howard Baetzhold, who have read the novel as an indictment of romantic illusions about chivalry, England, and a pre-scientific past, are not injured by Carter's revelations about how the novel was written.

38   A number of critics make the case that Mark Twain's most interesting fiction grows somehow out of the personality of the author. The problem has been to say how form, language, theme, and consciousness relate to one another. Important work in this direction includes Edward Wagenknecht, *Mark Twain: The Man and His Work*, 3d ed., rev. (Norman: University of Oklahoma Press, 1967), and Robert Wiggins, *Mark Twain: Jackleg Novelist* (Seattle: University of Washington Press, 1964).

39   *Mark Twain's Notebook*, ed. Albert B. Paine (New York: Harper and Brothers, 1925), 28–29.

40   *A Connecticut Yankee in King Arthur's Court*, ed. Bernard L. Stein, with an introduction by Henry Nash Smith (Berkeley and Los Angeles: University of California Press, 1979), 141–42. All subsequent citations of the novel refer to this Iowa-California edition.

41   *Mark Twain to Mrs. Fairbanks*, 257–58: "I am only after the *life* of that day, that is all: to picture it; to try to get into it; to see how it feels and seems" (258).

4   The Wilderness of Ideas

1   See for example Henry Nash Smith's chapter, "The Pathetic Drift between the Eternities" in his *Mark Twain: The Development of a Writer*, 171–88. See also Everett Emerson's chapter, "Despair," in his *Authentic Mark Twain*, 204–32, which sees 1894 as a turning point in Mark Twain's fortunes, morale, and art. Kaplan (*Mr. Clemens and Mark Twain*, 339–48) takes a similar view of Mark Twain in the middle 1890s.

2   Susan Gillman's *Dark Twins*, which investigates *Pudd'nhead Wilson* and other late Mark Twain works as immersed in the politics and economics of the 1890s, offers this premise: "Among the changing nineteenth-century realities that induced the sensation of weightlessness in Mark Twain, the most important centered around man's often contradictory efforts to ground his environment through technological and corresponding social inventions: the creation of a culture industry . . . paralleled by increases in population and literacy; the twin movements of immigration and imperialism that, along with civilization's 'triple curse' of railroad, telegraph, and newspapers, made the world seem simultaneously smaller and more alien; and, finally, the curves of scientific thought, especially the proliferation of conceptual systems, such as Darwin's Marx's, and Freud's" (4–5).

Mark Twain's Pudd'nhead Wilson: Race, Conflict, and Culture, ed. Susan Gillman and Forrest Robinson (Durham: Duke University Press, 1990), includes New Historicist interpretations by Eric Sundquist, Michael Rogin, and John Carlos Rowe. Essays from this collection will be cited in subsequent notes.

3 In contrast to the findings of Brooks, Kaplan, Emerson, and Hill, William Macnaughton, in *Mark Twain's Last Years as a Writer* (Columbia: University of Missouri Press, 1979), expands the DeVoto premise that some important part of Mark Twain's psyche and artistic powers survived these late-century difficulties: "the words *despair* and *obsession* will be conscientiously avoided in this study, not only because they have serious theological and psychological implications, but also . . . because such abstractions are misleading when used to explain complex states of mind. . . . When Mark Twain's hiatuses, his changes in direction, and his stops are examined closely, one comes to realize the wisdom of specificity, of focusing on a particular decision at a particular time" (4–5).

4 For example, in *Mark Twain: The Fate of Humor,* Cox calls "The Man That Corrupted Hadleyburg" "the furthest extension of all the tendencies of *Pudd'nhead Wilson.* It is a story of total irony, total plot. The epigrams which stood above the fiction in *Pudd'nhead Wilson* have been assimilated into the . . . taut, arbitrary plot and the triumphant bitterness . . . which characterize the story" (265). Henry Nash Smith comments that "Hadleyburg is Dawson's Landing without either the intimations of evil radiating from the character of Tom Driscoll or the vivid thrust of Roxy's passion. It is not tragic, even potentially, but merely smug and hypocritical" (*Mark Twain: The Development of a Writer,* 184).

5 Alan Gribben's *Mark Twain's Library: A Reconstruction* (2 vols. Boston: G. K. Hall, 1980) demonstrates that many intellectually unsettling works of the later nineteenth century passed through Mark Twain's hands, and often bear the marks of his intensive reading and annotating. Gribben presents evidence that by 1900 Mark Twain owned and probably had read at least four works by Darwin, four by Ruskin, Thomas Huxley's *Evolution and Ethics,* two important books by Renan and several by Tolstoy. Mark Twain had evidently also read William James's *Principles of Psychology,* fiction by Sudermann, Zola, and a swarm of other writers involved in the cultural ferment of that time but largely forgotten now. Gribben also notes that by 1888, Mark Twain was reading Sergei Kravchinski's *Underground Russia: Revolutionary Profiles and Sketches,* and sympathizing with the nihilist cause against the czar. Though Mark Twain's familiarity with some of this material is an educated guess, the breadth and number of Mark Twain's literary encounters speaks for itself.

In *Mark Twain and Science* (Baton Rouge, Louisiana State University Press, 1988), Sherwood Cummings demonstrates the importance of Taine in Mark Twain's thinking, especially Taine's "brilliant attempt to apply the laws and methods of the physical sciences to the humanities and the social sciences" (68). Several essays in Gillman and Robinson, eds., *Mark Twain's Pudd'nhead Wilson* argue for Mark Twain's familiarity with the Plessy-Ferguson case, Galton's treatises of fingerprinting, and other political, scientific, and legal interests at century's end: see, for example, Michael Rogin, "Francis Galton and Mark Twain" (73–85); Eric Sundquist, "Mark Twain and Homer Plessy" (46–72), and Michael Cowan, " 'By Right of the White Election': Political Theology and Theological Politics in *Pudd'nhead Wilson*" (155–76).

6 Two useful chronicles of Mark Twain's social encounters with movers and shakers of the 1890s are Dennis Welland's *Mark Twain in England* and Carl Dolmetsch's *"Our Famous Guest": Mark Twain in Vienna* (Athens: University of Georgia Press, 1992). Vignettes of Mark Twain's social life in fin de siècle England are scattered through Welland's book, including encounters and correspondence with Kipling, Turgenev, Bram Stoker, Walter Besant, and other leaders in the arts; after 1899 the list included Shaw, Anthony Hope, Max Beerbohm, Conan Doyle, and Winston Churchill. Dolmetsch documents Mark Twain's social life in 1890s Vienna and Continental Europe more thoroughly, and finds Mark Twain in the company of Herzl, Mahler, Dvořák, and Freud. Dolmetsch believes it "safe to assume" that Mark Twain had "discussed and may even have read" work of Max Nordau while in Vienna (228), and notes Mark Twain's efforts at collaboration with Siegmund Schlesinger, a leader in the Austrian decadent movement, in a city where "aestheticism [was] carried to excess" (16). See also Stanley Weintraub's general but atmospheric account of Mark Twain's 1896–97 experiences around Tedworth Square in *The London Yankees* (New York: Harcourt Brace Jovanovich, 1979), 11–41.

7 One of the liveliest recent readings of "Hadleyburg" is Earl F. Briden, "Twainian Pedagogy and the No-Account Lessons of 'Hadleyburg,' " *Studies in Short Fiction* 28 (Spring 1991): 125–34. Briden reads the text as an attack on Christian conceptions of the Fortunate Fall, and argues that the town's final name change "suggests that the town is making no active, redemptive use of its history but, instead, is repudiating its past and, in a single stroke, fictionalizing itself" (133).

8 *Mark Twain: Collected Tales, Sketches, Speeches, and Essays, 1891–1910*, ed. Louis J. Budd (New York: Library of America, 1992), 421–22. Subsequent citations from "Hadleyburg" refer to this edition.

9 In addition to Gillman and Robinson, eds., *Mark Twain's Pudd'nhead Wilson*, see for example Brook Thomas, "Tragedies of Race, Training, Birth, and Communities of Competent Pudd'nheads," *American Literary History* 1 (Winter 1989): 754–85. Aiming to "situate the novel historically" (755), Thomas concludes that *Pudd'nhead Wilson* "is tragic, as it confirms the impotency of Roxy's 'rage against the fates' " (754).

10 In contrast to the general position of essayists in Gillman and Robinson, eds., *Mark Twain's Pudd'nhead Wilson*, Shelly Fisher Fishkin's "Race and Culture at the Century's End: A Social Context for *Pudd'nhead Wilson*," *Essays in Arts and Sciences* 19 (1990): 1–27, reads the novel as against racism and repression, rather than as ambivalent about these issues, or on the other side.

11 Hershel Parker, "*Pudd'nhead Wilson:* Jack-leg Author, Unreadable Text, and Sense-Making Critics," in his *Flawed Texts and Literary Icons: Literary Authority in American Fiction* (Evanston: Northwestern University Press, 1984), 147–80.

12 *Pudd'nhead Wilson and Those Extraordinary Twins*, a facsimile of the first edition, ed. and intro. by Frederick Anderson (San Francisco: Chandler, 1968), 21. Though the Library of America *Mississippi Writings* has an authoritative text, Anderson's facsimile preserves the illustrations by F. M. Senior and C. H. Warren, which seem important to the narrative. Subsequent citations refer to this facsimile.

13 See, for example, George M. Spangler, "*Pudd'nhead Wilson:* A Parable of Property," *American Literature* 42 (March 1970): 28–37.

14   *The Love Letters of Mark Twain,* ed. Dixon Wecter (New York: Harper and Brothers, 1949), 291. The letter is dated 12 January 1894.

15   See, for example, Everett Emerson, *The Authentic Mark Twain,* 195–201; Cox, *Mark Twain: The Fate of Humor,* 249–52.

16   Everett Emerson (*The Authentic Mark Twain,* 200) cites an unpublished manuscript indicating that Joan was based on Susy Clemens as she was at age seventeen. Concerning Clemens's late-life interest in adolescent and pre-adolescent girls, see Hill, *Mark Twain: God's Fool,* 127, 195.

17   *Personal Recollections of Joan of Arc,* by the Sieur Louis de Conte [pseud.] trans. Jean François Alden. 2 vols. (New York: Harper and Brothers, 1929), 2:106. Subsequent citations of *Joan of Arc* refer to these Stormfield Edition volumes, the text of which seems no better or worse than the original Harper and Brothers edition of 1896.

18   *Christian Science* (New York: Harper and Brothers, 1907), 152–53. Subsequent citations refer to this edition.

19   *Mark Twain's Fables of Man,* ed. with intro. by John S. Tuckey (Berkeley and Los Angeles: University of California Press, 1972), 44.

20   Mary McCarthy, *How I Grew* (San Diego: Harcourt Brace Jovanovich, 1987), 156.

21   In his collection of *Letters From the Earth,* with an introduction by Henry Nash Smith (New York: Harper and Row, 1962), Bernard DeVoto chronicles Mark Twain's emotional highs and lows in composing "The Great Dark"; see 292–302. In his introduction to *The Devil's Race-Track: Mark Twain's Great Dark Writings* (Berkeley and Los Angeles: University of California Press, 1980), John S. Tuckey finds Mark Twain "writing with great creative exuberance" (xvii) as he worked on "Microbes," and observes in "The Great Dark" a recovery of Mark Twain's "capacity for rebound and affirmation" (xiii–xiv).

22   "The Great Dark," in *Mark Twain's "Which Was the Dream?",* ed. and intro. by John S. Tuckey (Berkeley and Los Angeles: University of California Press, 1967), 129–30. Subsequent citations of "The Great Dark" refer to this edition.

23   See Tuckey's introduction to *Mark Twain's "Which Was the Dream?"* 18–20; see also Macnaughton, *Mark Twain's Last Years,* 95–100.

24   For speculations on Mark Twain's evolving strategy in the Mysterious Stranger manuscripts, see Bruce Michelson, "Deus Ludens: The Shaping of Mark Twain's Mysterious Stranger," *Novel* 14, no. 1 (Fall 1980): 44–56.

25   For example, Sholom Kahn concludes his study of the Mysterious Stranger tales and manuscripts by proposing "Mark Twain as a sort of archetypal modern American, exquisitely sensitive to many of the currents of religion, philosophy, science, society, and culture that made the nineteenth century so exciting and upsetting"; see his *Mark Twain's Mysterious Stranger: A Study of the Manuscript Texts* (Columbia: University of Missouri Press, 1978), 192.

26   See Cox, *Mark Twain: The Fate of Humor,* 266–72.

27   *Extract from Captain Stormfield's Visit to Heaven* (New York: Harper and Brothers, 1909), 106–7. Subsequent citations refer to this first edition.

28   *Joseph Conrad: Complete Works* (New York: Doubleday, page, 1924), 16:150.

29   For brilliant discussion of this issue, see Hayden White, *Metahistory: The Historical Imagination in Nineteenth-Century Europe* (Baltimore: Johns Hopkins University Press, 1974).

Works Cited

Andrews, Kenneth. *Nook Farm: Mark Twain's Hartford Circle*. Cambridge: Harvard University Press, 1950.

Baetzhold, Howard. *Mark Twain and John Bull: The British Connection*. Bloomington: Indiana University Press, 1970.

Bakhtin, Mikhail M. *The Dialogic Imagination*. Edited by Michael Holquist. Translated by Caryl Emerson and Michael Holquist. Austin: University of Texas Press, 1981.

Baldanza, Frank. *Mark Twain: An Introduction and Interpretation*. New York: Holt, Rinehart, and Winston, 1961.

———. "The Structure of *Huckleberry Finn*." *American Literature* 27 (1950): 347–55.

Banta, Martha. "Escape and Entry in *Huckleberry Finn*." *Modern Fiction Studies* 14 (Spring 1968): 79–91.

Beidler, Philip. "Realistic Style and the Problem of Context in *The Innocents Abroad*." *American Literature* 52, no. 1 (March 1980): 33–49.

Bell, Michael Davitt. *The Problem of American Realism: Studies in the Cultural History of a Literary Idea*. Chicago: University of Chicago Press, 1993.

Bell, Quentin. *Ruskin*. London: Oliver and Boyd, 1963.

Bellamy, Gladys. *Mark Twain as a Literary Artist*. Norman: University of Oklahoma Press, 1950.

Benson, Ivan. *Mark Twain's Western Years*. Stanford: Stanford University Press, 1958.

Bergson, Henri. *Laughter*. Translated by Cloudesley Bereton and Fred Rothwell. New York: Macmillan, 1914.

Blair, Walter. *Mark Twain and Huck Finn*. Berkeley and Los Angeles: University of California Press, 1960.

Bloom, Harold, ed. *Mark Twain: Modern Critical Views*. New York: Chelsea House, 1986.

Blues, Thomas. *Mark Twain and the Community*. Lexington: University of Kentucky Press, 1970.

Brackman, Jacob. *The Put-On: Modern Foolery and Modern Mistrust*. Chicago: Henry Regnery, 1971.

Branch, Edgar M., ed. *Clemens of the Call: Mark Twain in San Francisco*. Berkeley and Los Angeles: University of California Press, 1969.

Briden, Earl F. "Twainian Pedagogy and the No-Account Lessons of 'Hadleyburg.' " *Studies in Short Fiction* 28 (Spring 1991): 125–34.

Bridgman, Richard. *Traveling in Mark Twain.* Berkeley and Los Angeles: University of California Press, 1987.

Brodwin, Stanley. "The Useful and Useless River: *Life on the Mississippi* Revisited." *Studies in American Humor* 2 (1976): 196–208.

Budd, Louis J. *Mark Twain: Social Philosopher.* Bloomington: Indiana University Press, 1962.

———, ed. *New Essays on Adventures of Huckleberry Finn.* New York: Cambridge University Press, 1985.

———. *Our Mark Twain: The Making of His Public Personality.* Philadelphia: University of Pennsylvania Press, 1983.

Cardwell, Guy. *The Man Who Was Mark Twain.* New Haven: Yale University Press, 1991.

Carter, Everett. "The Meaning of *A Connecticut Yankee.*" *American Literature* 50 (1978): 418–40.

Chase, Richard. *The American Novel and Its Tradition.* Garden City, N.Y.: Doubleday, 1957.

Cohen, Henning, and William B. Dillingham, eds. *Humor of the Old Southwest.* Athens: University of Georgia Press, 1975.

Conrad, Joseph. *Joseph Conrad: Complete Works.* 24 vols. New York: Doubleday, Page, 1924.

Covici, Pascal. *Mark Twain's Humor: The Image of a World.* Dallas: Southern Methodist University Press, 1962.

Cowan, Michael. " 'By Right of the White Election': Political Theology and Theological Politics in *Pudd'nhead Wilson.*" In *Mark Twain's Pudd'nhead Wilson: Race, Conflict, and Culture,* edited by Susan Gillman and Forrest G. Robinson, 155–76. Durham: Duke University Press, 1990.

Cox, James M. "*A Connecticut Yankee in King Arthur's Court:* The Machinery of Self-Preservation." *Yale Review* 50 (Autumn 1960): 89–102.

———. *Mark Twain: The Fate of Humor.* Princeton: Princeton University Press, 1966.

———. "Remarks on the Sad Initiation of Huckleberry Finn." *Sewanee Review* 62 (Summer 1954): 389–405.

Cummings, Sherwood. *Mark Twain and Science.* Baton Rouge: Louisiana State University Press, 1988.

David, Beverly. "Tragedy and Travesty: Edward Whymper's *Scrambles Amongst the Alps* and Mark Twain's *A Tramp Abroad.*" *Mark Twain Journal* 27, no. 1 (1989): 2–8.

Debord, Guy. *Society of the Spectacle.* Detroit: Black and Red, 1977.

DeVoto, Bernard. *Mark Twain at Work.* Cambridge: Harvard University Press, 1942. Reprint, Boston: Houghton Mifflin, 1967.

———. *Mark Twain's America.* Boston: Little, Brown, 1932. Reprint, Boston: Houghton Mifflin, 1967.

Dolmetsch, Carl. *"Our Famous Guest": Mark Twain in Vienna.* Athens: University of Georgia Press, 1992.

Doyno, Victor A. *Writing Huck Finn: Mark Twain's Creative Process.* Philadelphia: University of Pennsylvania Press, 1991.

Eliot, T. S. Introduction to *Adventures of Huckleberry Finn,* vii–xvi. London: Cresset, 1950. Reprinted as "Mark Twain's Masterpiece," in *Huck Finn Among the Critics: A Centennial Selection,* edited by M. Thomas Inge, 103–11. Frederick, Md.: University Publications of America, 1985.

Emerson, Everett. *The Authentic Mark Twain.* Philadelphia: University of Pennsylvania Press, 1984.

Emerson, Ralph Waldo. *The Collected Works of Ralph Waldo Emerson,* vol. 2, *Essays: First Series.* With an introduction and notes by Joseph Slater. Text established by Alfred R. Ferguson and Jean Ferguson Carr. Cambridge: The Belknap Press of Harvard University Press, 1979.

Fetterley, Judith. "Disenchantment: Tom Sawyer in *Huckleberry Finn.*" *PMLA* 87 (1972): 69–73.

Fiedler, Leslie. "*Huckleberry Finn:* The Book We Love to Hate." *Proteus* 1, no. 2 (Spring 1984): 1–8.

Fishkin, Shelley Fisher. "Race and Culture at the Century's End: A Social Context for *Pudd'nhead Wilson.*" *Essays in Arts and Sciences* 19 (1990): 1–27.

———. *Was Huck Black?* New York: Oxford University Press, 1993.

Fitzgerald, F. Scott. *The Crack-up.* Edited by Edmund Wilson. New York: New Directions, 1945.

———. *The Last Tycoon.* New York: Scribner, 1941.

Foner, Philip. *Mark Twain: Social Critic.* New York: International Publishers, 1958.

Ganzel, Dewey. "Twain, Travel Books, and *Life on the Mississippi.*" *American Literature* 34 (1962): 40–55.

Gibson, William M. *The Art of Mark Twain.* New York: Oxford University Press, 1976.

Gillman, Susan. *Dark Twins: Imposture and Identity in Mark Twain's America.* Chicago: University of Chicago Press, 1989.

———, and Forrest G. Robinson, eds. *Mark Twain's Pudd'nhead Wilson: Race, Conflict, and Culture.* Durham: Duke University Press, 1990.

Greenblatt, Stephen. *Learning to Curse: Essays in Early Modern Culture.* New York: Routledge, 1990.

Gribben, Alan. *Mark Twain's Library: A Reconstruction.* 2 vols. Boston: G. K. Hall, 1980.

Griffith, Clark. "Merlin's Grin: From 'Tom' to 'Huck' in *A Connecticut Yankee.*" *New England Quarterly* 48 (March 1975): 27–38.

Gunn, Drewey Wayne. "The Monomythic Structure of *Roughing It.*" *American Literature* 61, no. 4 (December 1989): 563–85.

Harris, Susan K. *Mark Twain's Escape from Time.* Columbia: University of Missouri Press, 1982.

Hawking, Stephen. *A Brief History of Time.* New York: Bantam, 1988.

Hill, Hamlin. *Mark Twain: God's Fool.* New York: Harper and Row, 1973.

Hoffman, Daniel. *Form and Fable in American Fiction.* New York: Oxford University Press, 1961.

Hood, Edward Paxton. *The Mental and Moral Philosophy of Laughter.* London: Partridge and Oakey, 1852.

Howells, William Dean. *My Mark Twain.* Edited by Marilyn Austin Baldwin. Baton Rouge: Louisiana State University Press, 1967.

Inge, M. Thomas, ed. *Huck Finn Among the Critics: A Centennial Selection.* Frederick, Md.: University Publications of America, 1985.

Johnson, James L. *Mark Twain and the Limits of Power.* Knoxville: University of Tennessee Press, 1982.

Kahn, Sholom. *Mark Twain's Mysterious Stranger: A Study of the Manuscript Texts.* Columbia: University of Missouri Press, 1978.

Kaplan, Justin. *Mr. Clemens and Mark Twain*. New York: Simon and Schuster, 1966.

Kaufmann, David. "Satiric Deceit in the Ending of *Adventures of Huckleberry Finn*." *Studies in the Novel* 19 (1987): 66–78.

King, Bruce. "Huckleberry Finn." *Ariel* 2:4 (1971): 69–77.

Krause, Sydney J. *Mark Twain as Critic*. Baltimore: Johns Hopkins University Press, 1967.

Kruse, Horst H. *Mark Twain and "Life on the Mississippi."* Amherst: University of Massachusetts Press, 1981.

Lauber, John. *The Making of Mark Twain*. New York: Noonday, 1988.

Lawrence, D. H. *Studies in Classic American Literature*. New York: Viking, 1961.

Lennon, Nigey. *The Sagebrush Bohemian*. New York: Paragon House, 1990.

Lewis, Paul. *Comic Effects: Interdisciplinary Approaches to Humor in Literature* Albany: State University of New York Press, 1989.

Lorch, Fred W. *The Trouble Begins at Eight: Mark Twain's Lecture Tours*. Ames: Iowa State University Press, 1968.

Lynn, Kenneth S. *Mark Twain and Southwestern Humor*. Westport, Conn.: Greenwood, 1959.

Macnaughton, William. *Mark Twain's Last Years as a Writer*. Columbia: University of Missouri Press, 1979.

Mailloux, Stephen. "Reading Huck Finn." In *New Essays on Huckleberry Finn*, edited by Louis J. Budd, 107–133. New York: Cambridge University Press, 1985.

Marcus, Greil. *Lipstick Traces: A Secret History of the Twentieth Century*. Cambridge: Harvard University Press, 1989.

Marotti, Maria Orella. *The Duplicating Imagination: Twain and the Twain Papers*. University Park: Pennsylvania State University Press, 1990.

Marx, Leo. *The Machine in the Garden*. New York: Oxford University Press, 1967.

——. "The Pilot and the Passenger: Landscape Conventions and the Style of *Huckleberry Finn*." *American Literature* 27 (1956): 129–46.

Massent, Peter. "Racial and Colonial Discourse in Mark Twain's *Following the Equator*." *Essays in Arts and Sciences* 22 (October 1993): 67–84.

McCarthy, Mary. *How I Grew*. San Diego: Harcourt Brace Jovanovich, 1987.

Menon, V. K. Krishna. *A Theory of Laughter*. London: Allen and Unwin, 1931.

Michelson, Bruce. "Deus Ludens: The Shaping of Mark Twain's Mysterious Stranger." *Novel* 14, no. 1 (Fall 1980): 44–56.

——. "Huck and the Games of the World." *American Literary Realism* 13, no. 1 (Spring 1980): 108–21.

——. "Mark Twain the Tourist: The Form of *The Innocents Abroad*." *American Literature* 49, no. 3 (1977): 385–98.

Mitchell, Lee Clark. "Verbally *Roughing It*: The West of Words." *Nineteenth Century Literature* 44, no. 1 (1989): 67–92.

——. "Nobody but Our Gang Warn't Around: The Authority of Language in *Huckleberry Finn*." In *New Essays on Adventures of Huckleberry Finn*, edited by Louis J. Budd, 83–106. New York: Cambridge University Press, 1985.

Nelson, T. G. A. *Comedy*. New York: Oxford University Press, 1990.

Opdahl, Keith. "The Rest is Just Cheating: When Good Feelings Go Bad in *Adventures of Huckleberry Finn*." *Texas Studies in Literature and Language* 32 (1990): 277–93.

Paine, Albert Bigelow. *Mark Twain: A Biography: The Personal and Literary Life of Samuel Langhorne Clemens.* 3 vols. New York: Harper and Brothers, 1912.

Parker, Hershel. "*Pudd'nhead Wilson:* Jack-Leg Author, Unreadable Text and Sense-Making Critics." In his *Flawed Texts and Verbal Icons: Literary Authority in American Fiction,* 147–80. Evanston: Northwestern University Press, 1984.

Pater, Walter. *The Renaissance.* New York: Modern Library, 1873.

———. *Studies in the History of the Renaissance.* London: Macmillan, 1873.

Piddington, Ralph. *The Psychology of Laughter.* New York: Gamut, 1963.

Prime, William C. *Tent Life in the Holy Land.* New York: Harper and Brothers, 1857.

Randall, D. A. *The Handwriting of God in Egypt, Sinai and the Holy Land.* 2 vols. in 1. Philadelphia: John E. Potter, 1862.

Regan, Robert. *Unpromising Heroes: Mark Twain and His Characters.* Berkeley and Los Angeles: University of California Press, 1966.

Robinson, Forrest G. *In Bad Faith: The Dynamics of Deception in Mark Twain's America.* Cambridge: Harvard University Press, 1985.

———. "Patterns of Consciousness in *The Innocents Abroad.*" *American Literature* 58, no. 1 (1986): 46–53.

Rogers, Franklin R. *Mark Twain's Burlesque Patterns.* Dallas: Southern Methodist University Press, 1960.

Rogin, Michael. "Francis Galton and Mark Twain." In *Mark Twain's Pudd'nhead Wilson: Race, Conflict, and Culture,* edited by Susan Gillman and Forrest G. Robinson, 73–85. Durham: Duke University Press, 1990.

Scott, Arthur L. *Mark Twain at Large.* Chicago: Henry Regnery, 1969.

———. "Mark Twain's Revisions of *The Innocents Abroad* for the British Edition of 1872." *American Literature* 25 (1953): 43–61.

Seelye, John. *The True Adventures of Huckleberry Finn.* Evanston: Northwestern University Press, 1970.

Simonson, Harold P. "*Huckleberry Finn* as Tragedy." *Yale Review* 59 (1970): 532–48.

Sloane, David E. E. *The Adventures of Huckleberry Finn: American Comic Vision.* Boston: Twayne, 1988.

———. *Mark Twain as a Literary Comedian.* Baton Rouge: Louisiana State University Press, 1979.

Smith, Henry Nash. *Mark Twain's Fable of Progress: Political and Economic Ideas in "A Connecticut Yankee."* New Brunswick: Rutgers University Press, 1964.

———. *Mark Twain: The Development of a Writer.* Cambridge: The Belknap Press of Harvard University Press, 1962.

Spangler, George M. "*Pudd'nhead Wilson:* A Parable of Property." *American Literature* 42 (March 1970): 28–37.

Stahl, John David. "American Myth in European Disguise: Fathers and Sons in *The Prince and the Pauper.*" *American Literature* 58 (1986): 203–16.

Stein, Roger B. *John Ruskin and Aesthetic Thought in America, 1840–1900.* Cambridge: Harvard University Press, 1967.

Steinbrink, Jeffrey. *Getting to be Mark Twain.* Berkeley and Los Angeles: University of California Press, 1991.

Stoppard, Tom. *Rosencrantz and Guildenstern Are Dead.* New York: Grove, 1967.

Sundquist, Eric. "Mark Twain and Homer Plessy." In *Mark Twain's Pudd'nhead Wilson:*

Race, Conflict, and Culture, edited by Susan Gillman and Forrest G. Robinson, 46–72. Durham: Duke University Press, 1990.

Sussman, Elizabeth, ed. *on the passage of a few people through a rather brief moment in time.* Cambridge: MIT Press, 1991.

Tanner, Tony. *The Reign of Wonder: Naivety and Reality in American Literature.* Cambridge: Cambridge University Press, 1965.

Thomas, Brook. "Tragedies of Race, Training, Birth, and Communities of Competent Pudd'nheads." *American Literary History* 1 (Winter 1989): 754–85.

Tocqueville, Alexis de. *Democracy in America.* Edited by Phillips Bradley. New York: Knopf, 1945.

Towers, Tom H. "*The Prince and the Pauper:* Mark Twain's Once and Future King." *Studies in American Fiction* 6 (1978): 194–202.

Trachtenberg, Alan. "The Form of Freedom in *Adventures of Huckleberry Finn.*" *Southern Review,* n.s., 6 (October 1970): 954–71.

Trilling, Lionel. *The Liberal Imagination.* New York: Viking, 1950.

Twain, Mark. *Adventures of Huckleberry Finn.* Edited by Sculley Bradley, Richard Croom Beatty, E. Hudson Long, and Thomas Cooley. New York: Norton, 1977.

——. *The Adventures of Tom Sawyer, Tom Sawyer Abroad, Tom Sawyer, Detective.* Edited by John C. Gerber, Paul Baender, and Terry Firkins. Berkeley and Los Angeles: University of California Press, 1980.

——. *Christian Science.* New York: Harper and Brothers, 1907.

——. *A Connecticut Yankee in King Arthur's Court.* Edited by Bernard L. Stein. With an introduction by Henry Nash Smith. Berkeley and Los Angeles: University of California Press, 1979.

——. *The Devil's Race-Track: Mark Twain's Great Dark Writings.* With an introduction by John S. Tuckey. Berkeley and Los Angeles: University of California Press, 1980.

——. *Early Tales and Sketches,* vol. 1, *1851–1864.* Edited by Edgar M. Branch and Robert H. Hirst. Berkeley and Los Angeles: University of California Press, 1979.

——. *Extract from Captain Stormfield's Visit to Heaven.* New York: Harper and Brothers, 1909.

——. *Huck Finn and Tom Sawyer Among the Indians and Other Unfinished Stories.* With a foreword and notes by Dahlia Armon and Walter Blair. Berkeley and Los Angeles: University of California Press, 1989.

——. *The Innocents Abroad.* London: Routledge and Sons, 1872.

——. *The Innocents Abroad* and *Roughing It.* Edited by Guy Cardwell. New York: Library of America, 1984.

——. *Letters from the Earth.* Edited by Bernard DeVoto. With an introduction by Henry Nash Smith. New York: Harper and Row, 1962.

——. *Life on the Mississippi.* Edited by John Seelye. With an introduction by James M. Cox. New York: Viking Penguin, 1984.

——. *The Love Letters of Mark Twain.* Edited by Dixon Wecter. New York: Harper and Brothers, 1949.

——. *Mark Twain: Collected Tales, Sketches, Speeches and Essays, 1852–1890.* Edited by Louis J. Budd. New York: Library of America, 1992.

——. *Mark Twain: Collected Tales, Sketches, Speeches and Essays, 1891–1910.* Edited by Louis J. Budd. New York: Library of America, 1992.

——. *Mark Twain–Howells Letters*. Edited by William M. Gibson and Henry Nash Smith. Cambridge: The Belknap Press of Harvard University Press, 1960.

——. *Mark Twain's Autobiography*. 2 vols. New York: Harper and Brothers, 1926.

——. *Mark Twain's Fables of Man*. Edited and with an introduction by John S. Tuckey. Berkeley and Los Angeles: University of California Press, 1972.

——. *Mark Twain's Letters to His Publishers*. Edited by Hamlin Hill. Berkeley and Los Angeles: University of California Press, 1967.

——. *Mark Twain's Notebook*. Edited by Albert B. Paine. New York: Harper and Brothers, 1925.

——. *Mark Twain to Mrs. Fairbanks*. Edited by Dixon Wecter. San Marino, Calif.: Huntington Library, 1949.

——. *Mark Twain's Travels with Mr. Brown*. Edited by Franklin Walker and G. Ezra Dane. New York: Knopf, 1940.

——. *Mark Twain's "Which Was the Dream?"* Edited and with an introduction by John S. Tuckey. Berkeley and Los Angeles: University of California Press, 1967.

——. *Mississippi Writings*. Selected by Guy Cardwell. New York: Library of America, 1982.

——. *Personal Recollections of Joan of Arc*. By the Sieur Louis de Conte [pseud.]. Translated by Jean François Alden. 2 vols. New York: Harper and Brothers, 1929. (Original edition 1896).

——. *The Portable Mark Twain*. Edited by Bernard DeVoto. New York: Viking, 1946.

——. *The Prince and the Pauper*. With a foreword and notes by Victor Fischer and Michael B. Frank. Berkeley and Los Angeles: University of California Press, 1983.

——. *Pudd'nhead Wilson and Those Extraordinary Twins*. Facsimile of the First Edition. Edited and with an introduction by Frederick Anderson. San Francisco: Chandler, 1968.

——. *Roughing It*. Edited by Franklin R. Rogers and Paul Baender. Berkeley and Los Angeles: University of California Press, 1972.

——. *Roughing It*. With an introduction by Rodman W. Paul. New York: Rinehart, 1953.

——. *Sketches New and Old*. Hartford, Conn.: American Publishing, 1875.

——. *The Works of Mark Twain: Roughing It*. Edited by Franklin R. Rogers and Paul Baender. Berkeley and Los Angeles: University of California Press, 1972.

——. *The Writings of Mark Twain*. Autograph Edition. 22 vols. Hartford, Conn.: American Publishing, 1899.

——. *The Writings of Mark Twain*. Hillcrest Edition. 25 vols. New York: Collier, 1904.

——. *The Writings of Mark Twain*. Author's National Edition. 25 vols. New York: Harper and Brothers, 1920.

——. *The Writings of Mark Twain*. Stormfield Edition. 37 vols. New York: Harper and Brothers, 1929.

Wagenknecht, Edward. *Mark Twain: The Man and His Work*. 3d ed., rev. Norman: University of Oklahoma Press, 1967.

Weintraub, Stanley. *The London Yankees*. New York: Harcourt Brace Jovanovich, 1979.

Welland, Dennis. *Mark Twain in England*. Atlantic Highlands, N.J.: Humanities Press, 1978.

White, Hayden. *Metahistory: The Historical Imagination in Nineteenth-Century Europe*. Baltimore: John Hopkins University Press, 1974.

Wiggins, Robert. *Mark Twain: Jackleg Novelist.* Seattle: University of Washington Press, 1964.

Wilson, Edmund, ed. *The Crack Up.* New York: New Directions, 1945.

Wonham, Henry B. *Mark Twain and the Art of the Tall Tale.* New York: Oxford University Press, 1993.

Index